Fiction as Wisdom

Fiction as Wisdom

From Goethe to Bellow

Irvin Stock

The Pennsylvania State University Press
University Park and London

Library of Congress Cataloging in Publication Data

Stock, Irvin, 1920–
  Fiction as wisdom: from Goethe to Bellow.
  Includes bibliographical references and index.
  1. Fiction—History and criticism—Addresses, essays,
lectures. I. Title.
PN3491.S7   809.3'3   79-23684
ISBN 0-271-00253-0

This book is for my mother
and the memory of my father.

Contents

Acknowledgments

Thanks are due to the following, which first published my essays on the works named: *Accent* (Gide's *Theseus* and Mann's *The Holy Sinner*); Allen and Unwin and Columbia University Press (the novels of William Hale White, from my book *William Hale White (Mark Rutherford): A Critical Study); Commentary* (Bellow's *Mr. Sammler's Planet); Mosaic* (Goethe's *Elective Affinities); Novel* (Hawthorne's *The Blithedale Romance*); PMLA (Goethe's *Wilhelm Meister's Apprenticeship*); the *Southern Review* (Bellow's first six novels); the University of Minnesota Press (the novels of Mary McCarthy, from its American Writers Series); and *Yale French Studies* (Gide's *The Counterfeiters*).

For encouragement that was especially valuable because of my admiration for their own writing, I want to thank Professors Heinrich Henel, Henri Peyre, and George P. Elliott. To Professors Peyre and Elliott I am also grateful for their help in bringing these essays to book publication.

More immediately involved in turning my essays into a book were two Penn Staters: John M. Pickering, an Editorial Director whose championing of a collection of critical essays in the present time of commercial caution took a certain stubborn independence of mind; and Professor Michael Begnal, a university press reader who shares my view that pleasure and wisdom are legitimate interests of criticism. I'm grateful to both.

Finally, I want to express my gratitude to Professor Jack Davis of the University of Connecticut. All writers, even critics, should have at least one friend who is a friend of their writing too and who is there whenever he is needed—to give encouragement if faith totters, correction if it grows excessive, the essential first response that helps the piled-up fragments become a whole, and so on. Jack Davis has been such a friend to me, and for all that, as well as for intelligence and learning which are a constant source of stimulating intellectual news, I am glad to acknowledge my debt.

Introduction: "Affectionate Partiality"

This is a book about my experiences with some marvelous novels. As the Contents shows, my writer-subjects include the "unknown" (William Hale White), the unfashionable (Goethe and Gide), the celebrated, but represented by works I think undervalued (Eliot, Hawthorne, Mann), current writers with still fluctuating reputations (McCarthy and Bellow), and the universally admired (Dostoevsky). One aim of the book is to draw readers back to excellence in fiction which has been neglected or misjudged or is worth exploring again. But the book has another aim as well. It can be suggested by what Goethe wrote to Schiller on June 14, 1796: "Books as well as actions should be discussed with affectionate partiality. . . . Delight, joy, sympathy with things is the only genuine attitude which leads to a genuine result." These essays are all attempts to convey the experience of delight and joy and the understanding arrived at through sympathy. And the other aim of this book is to serve as a reminder of an old idea, that the chief object of literature is to give pleasure and wisdom, and that to share these is at least as legitimate an interest of criticism as to display expertise.

Of course, this idea sounds obvious when it is put into words. And yet we are all aware that with the rich development in our time of the literature *profession*, pleasure and wisdom have ceased to be respectable as guides and subjects of critical discourse. In fact, our own unaccredited responses have ceased to be respectable. Serious readers—teachers and students, certainly—have found it hard to avoid the feeling that before they choose or discuss a book they had better check it out with the proper authorities. I hope these essays will encourage some of them to forget about the authorities, and not only to explore novels that are not on the currently approved lists, but to read without forestalling their own responses by first acquiring the "right" ones.[1]

To be sure, with great books a little prior education will be helpful, and sometimes essential. But it is equally true that if a book is alive, it is "a man speaking to men," and appealing to our humanity and intelligence. And this being so, our humanity and intelligence may hear what

it is saying more accurately than expertise, which is so often busy veri-
fying its own preconceptions. It happens that I can give a small example of what I mean. Though myself an English teacher, I took the
risk of writing about Mann's *The Holy Sinner* because I love his work
and I thought people were getting the novel wrong. Sure enough,
when I sent my essay on it to the learned journal PMLA, the essay
came back with adverse comments signed by two well-known German-
ists that were frankly offered as specialists' judgments on an amateur. I
had tried to show (among other things) how the novel hinted at a
parallel between its sinful hero—husband and, as pope, "father" of his
own mother—and Christ, Who can also be considered, in His oneness
with God, His mother's husband and her father. Both scholars objected
as if this shocking idea were my own. One called my essay "methodi-
cally unsound because done without sufficient background," referred
me to his own study of the novel's sources, and later, when I ventured
to ask him why his examination of old sources didn't complement,
rather than compete with, my analysis of present meanings, confessed,
"I find the close parallelism that you attempt to draw between Grego-
rius and Christ wholly unconvincing: in fact, I do not see how a parallel
can exist between holiness arrived at by way of deepest involvement in
sin on the one hand and complete sinlessness on the other." The second expert was also "staggered" ("My pedantic mind is staggered,"
were his exact words) by a sacrilege his learning told him Mann could
never have intended. The point of this descent into literary gossip is in
what follows. When Mann's *Letters* were published here in 1970, it
turned out he had written to Professor Herman J. Weigand on April
29, 1952, that the gentleness of his comic monk-narrator to the hero's
sexual "sin" came from a "dim notion" that incest had always been a
privilege of kings and deities. "All mythology teems with marital unions
of brothers and sisters, sons and mothers," Mann went on. "And such
minglings extend from the Near East down to the Christian mystery of
the Mother of God. Not for nothing does Sibylla [the sinner's mother-
wife, addressing herself to Mary] pray: 'Thou of the Highest child,
mother and bride.'"

Of course, such confirmation by the author *proves* nothing. We
don't go to the poet for the meaning of the poem, as someone has said;
we go to the poem for the meaning of the poet. It is conceivable that
those specialists read the novel correctly after all, even if Mann himself
intended something else. And it hardly needs to be added that my
self-reliance (*ignorance* they might properly call it) can make its own
kind of mistakes. Still, there is at least a hint here—is there not?—that
what matters most when we look for the meaning of a novel, even a
novel made out of old materials, is what its materials are saying in their

new arrangement, that without alertness to the work before one's eyes the richest "background" will not be "sufficient." And though this was an anecdote about expertise in scholarship, its moral surely applies to the other kind as well, the critical expertise that examines particular works through the grid of theories about literature in general or about what approach is the right one. Affectionate partiality may be a sounder guide for the critical intelligence than the literature profession tends to allow. And it is so in literature for the same reason it is so elsewhere. Love discovers details, a maxim of my own I prefer to the old saw that love is blind. It is when we are led by a genuine attraction to *look* at a thing—and to look at it for its own sake, not to prove a theory or to place it in its "field"—that we are likely to see best what it is. And what it is will usually tell us how it is to be approached.[2]

A word about the wisdom my essays explore. As I say, in this matter too, that is, in discussing what my chosen novels teach us about human beings and how we go wrong and right, I run counter to certain elements in the literature profession. I don't agree with those who think that by cutting art loose from ideas we preserve its special qualities and its dignity, who say a poem—that is, art—should not mean but be, or speak of the heresy of paraphrase, or declare themselves boldly against interpretation, or, more recently, tell us a poem or novel has no meaning except what each reader puts into it. I won't argue the matter here; let my essays, in their practice, be my argument. I will only say that if "a poem must not mean but be," this is because a poem must be before its meaning can be of interest, not because it has no meaning. It seems to me that Frost's maxim does the issue more justice: "Poetry begins in pleasure and ends in wisdom," and that great fiction, whatever else it is, is great understanding. For that matter, we are not leaving aesthetic effects behind when we engage in interpretation. We are simply getting closer to the context, the web of relationships, which is the real source of those effects and which gives them their particular character. What we must try to avoid is not interpretation, but misinterpretation. To scorn interpretation is to trivialize criticism by separating aesthetic effects from their deepest roots and their widest significance.

Nor do I go along with those who, concerned indeed with the meaning of literary works, aspire not so much to grasp what they say as to *see through* them. Granted, such works, like any human utterance, may mean more or other than their authors intend. But with the first-rate it is surely a self-defeating cleverness to prefer our own theories (literary, psychological, sociological) of what their authors reveal without knowing it to what they are deliberately enabling us to understand. I think the reader will find that what the authors of these novels teach us deliberately is worth our attention.

He will find too that they are profoundly akin. I don't mean they are alike. On the contrary, it is a large part of the pleasure they give that they are different from each other; the insights to which they were led by their own worlds and characters will make for the reader a rich variety. Goethe is secular, for instance, and Dostoevsky is Christian. Mann exposes the odd, fruitful connection between the artist's strength and his weakness. Gide and White show the importance of the self, Eliot of our community with others, and Hawthorne the danger of trusting either the self or the community. And the fact that I can enjoy and value both Bellow and McCarthy has been a puzzle to some of my friends, for the man usually appears an out-and-out romantic, encouraging us to honor our feelings, while the woman is just as clearly neoclassic, dramatizing the need for the cool critical intelligence which sees through them. My subjects can be regarded, indeed, as evidence of the irreducible complexity of human experience, proof that if we really listen to people of talent and insight, we must learn to say yes to truths which contradict each other—or seem to.

And yet, since these novelists have all "reached" me so intimately, it ought not to be surprising if, in spite of their variety, they have something significant in common. In fact, they come together in the most important thing they have helped me see and say. Underlying and supporting their many insights is the one persistent insight that experience, in its idea-defying complexity, is the touchstone of ideas.

How in particular this shared bent of mind is expressed in their work, creating both their differences and their similarities, will be revealed, I hope, in the essays themselves. Enough to add here that in each of these novelists it results in a mistrust of ideas which experience has not tested, validated, made necessary. Each recalls us again and again to a humanity which is deeper than our thought. What I wrote of McCarthy, Bellow, and Lionel Trilling in my essay on the first is true of all the writers I discuss: "Different though they are in so many ways . . . they stand together against the intellectual's tendency to value chic ideas more than the human experience or the human ends they are supposed to serve, or, worse still, to conceal from himself, with the help of such ideas, realities he prefers not to see." Of course, this meaning which underlies my writers' many meanings is an underlying theme of literature itself, and its application extends very far. To know, as it is one function of literature to help us know, that experience is the touchstone of ideas, is to be on guard against all the theories that presume to tell us finally what man is and how—and sometimes whether—he ought to live.

Goethe's *Wilhelm Meister's Apprenticeship*

An enthusiasm for this novel, which first appeared in 1795–96, is not, nowadays, an easy thing to share. Unless one moves in circles professionally devoted to German literature, its title is likely to call up among literary people the following notions: that T. S. Eliot did not approve of Goethe, while nineteenth-century England did, both facts still, to many, rather discouraging; that the *Bildungsroman*, of which Goethe's novel is the great example, is a sloppy and self-indulgent genre—there is no form, since it just goes autobiographically on and on, nor any proper commitment to experience, which the self-obsessed hero only passes through; that this one might be full of "wisdom," perhaps, but that here is precisely its greatest fault, for what can wisdom be but smug "Victorian" moralizing or analyzing or generalizing, mere simplifying abstraction at best, and the death of all actuality, complexity, and charm. Nor is it fashion alone which accounts for the novel's virtual disappearance from our intellectual landscape. No, even when it is read, it tends to be disliked. Press it on the up-to-date intelligent reader, the reader who devours the Russians or Stendhal or Flaubert or Proust with joy, and more often than not—such has been my experience—he will find it repulsively cold-blooded, even frivolous, in its treatment of human affairs. It is sometimes admitted that what happens in the novel, at least after the rather long flashback at the beginning, ought to be interesting enough. But, the complaint is, one is hurried through even the big scenes at a pace that is shockingly sprightly. There is no sign that the author feels anything or wants us to feel anything. One is hurried on, moreover, to no particular purpose. Instead of "adding up," the story rambles in the most outmoded way. And so forth.

In view of attitudes like these—and the silence about Goethe in our nonscholarly literary magazines indicates that the coolness to his work must be general—it seems worthwhile to examine the novel again. For the fact is, they are terribly wrong. *Wilhelm Meister's Apprenticeship* is not only, as Yeats said, the wisest novel ever written, wisdom being ideas about life that do not betray its complexity, but express it, ideas that bring us closer to fact and that can have the poignancy of fact; it is also one of the most enthralling and beautiful of novels. It surely ranks with the greatest novels in the world.

If this is true, why do modern readers on the whole find it so unappealing? One reason, already suggested, is that current tastes have been shaped by novelists very unlike Goethe. (And though the writers most admired today certainly differ among themselves, they share, as I will try to show, something important which in Goethe is absent.) But a deeper reason, I think, is this: that the novel's form and its qualities are the products of an attitude to life which, while always hard to reach, has been especially alien to us of the twentieth century. It will be best to begin, therefore, with a sketch of what the story is about, what questions it asks, and how it answers them. To bring the idea of the book to light is not, of course, to prove that it is a good novel. But it may for some readers open up the possibility. For it may then be seen that its method, though different indeed from the fictional methods we are used to, is at least proper to its matter and rises out of this as its precise expression. It will be seen too, perhaps, that the Goethean insights which the novel embodies are, even as the nineteenth century declared, worthy of attention for their own sake, and that the novel's wisdom need not be held against it.

But first, to make clear what kind of problems the book presents, it will be helpful to take a look at its opening episodes. Our hero, Wilhelm, is the young son of a well-to-do businessman, but his tendency to dreams and strong feelings, given a particular direction by a childhood interest in puppet shows, has resulted in a passion for the theater—and for an actress named Mariana. These two loves, that for the theater involving also an ambition to write plays and poetry, seem to be two aspects of a single attraction. Together they pull him away from his father's business world, a world he feels to be altogether ugly and barren. One day, he thinks he discovers that his mistress has betrayed him. Since this is a genuine first love, the kind into which is poured, with none of the reservations of maturity, one's whole being, the supposed betrayal prostrates him. Even his literary ambitions now seem based on illusion, and in a perverse and agonized revulsion from his dearest dream, he burns most of his writings and devotes himself to his father's business. It is clear that his zeal is precarious in its excess. Yet he starts out honestly enough on a business trip for his father. It is only gradually and by steps he is hardly aware of that the original purpose of the trip is pushed aside, and he finds himself yielding again to his basic inclination and staying longer and longer in the company of certain wandering actors.

He is drawn to them first by a pretty woman, one whose merry flirting seems full of unmistakable promise. But immediately after his encounter with Philina, so gay and so feminine, he meets a solemn creature of about thirteen whose sex seems oddly ambiguous—he takes her at first for a boy—and whose exotic appearance makes an inexplicably deep impression on him. Gazing at her, he forgets the world about him until Philina rouses him from his "half-dream" (Bk. II, Ch. 4).[1] Her name is Mignon, and she belongs to a company of acrobats staying in Wilhelm's hotel. Later, seeing the child mistreated by her master, he buys her freedom and she soons becomes his loving servant, never ceasing to move him, by her presence and also by her melancholy songs, intimately and intensely.

He knows he should go on about his father's business, but Philina and the child, each seductive in her own way, hold him fast. He gives himself up to the pleasant pursuits of his new friends, whose number is increased by the arrival of several other itinerant actors. Now, at the time of his love affair with Mariana, he had met in the street one night a mysterious stranger, a man who had known him and his family and who, in a brief but profound conversation, had opposed Wilhelm's tendency to rely on fate as certain to bring about the fulfillment of his dreams. Such a stranger crosses his path again while he is on a picnic with his theatrical friends. This one joins amiably enough in their games, but his identity is never disclosed and he departs with odd abruptness. Before leaving, however, he argues with Wilhelm in a way that recalls that earlier talk. Instead of relying on a fate which operates through chance and can lead us astray, he prefers the guidance of a human teacher. As an example of fate's dangerous workings, he speaks of the bad effects which puppet shows can have on a child. Our hero is startled and, after the man's disappearance, imagines his face was familiar.

One more influence is soon added to those which keep Wilhelm drifting with his new companions. After an uproarious evening with the actors—they begin by reading aloud a play, which gives them a sweet feeling of virtue, and end in the most degrading drunkenness—Wilhelm is vexed to find in the morning that his horse has been hurt by his new friends beyond recovery. Circumstances thus take the matter of his immediate departure out of his own hands. He stays, buying presents for Philina, and that day, they are joined while dining by an old bearded man who carries a harp. The man sings to them for a glass of wine, and does so with such feeling and such art that though the others would have liked something more gay, Wilhelm, captivated, promises the man his patronage.

Meanwhile, at least one member of the group is making practical plans, a certain Melina. To this shrewd man, the theater, in which Wilhelm hoped to find a means both to employ his own highest powers and to benefit society, is simply a way of earning a living, and he has been plaguing Wilhelm to lend him the money with which to set up a company. Wilhelm has no intention of doing so; he is even angered by the man's clumsy importunity. He is on the point, it would seem, of breaking away from them all when Philina stops him in the street and begs him not to leave her to die of ennui among people like Melina. To his embarrassment (at which she laughs), her persuasion takes the form of hugs and kisses. And it is while, enchanted, he is following her to her room that he gives in to Melina. The man stops him in the hall, apologizes for his former rudeness, and renews his plea; and Wilhelm, wild to go after Philina, suddenly turns good-natured and promises him the money. Having thus allowed weakness and sensuality to commit him to the actors, he is prevented from joining the woman by the return of a youth who had loved her and had recently gone off in a jealous pique. This boy makes Wilhelm vividly aware of his own degraded condition, for Philina now turns her attention to a new arrival, throwing the boy into a state of hysterical jealousy. Looking on, Wilhelm sees himself as in a coarsening mirror. He becomes aware that he has left behind all joyous hope and striving, and that he is lost in a confusion where the expected pleasures grow more and more scanty. "But he could not clearly see what insatiable want it was that nature had made the law of his being, and how this want had been only set on edge, half-satisfied, and misdirected by the circumstances of his life." And he struggles in vain to break away from this society whose terrible seduction is that it enables him to "cherish his darling inclination, content his wishes as it were by stealth, and, without proposing any object, again pursue his early dreams" (Bk. II, Ch. 14).[2]

Thus the story begins. And though in condensing I have no doubt suggested my view of the relevance to each other of some of these episodes, it must be certainly be granted that in the novel such relevance tends to be obscured by the sheer variety of characters and events, as well as by the author's cool, unempathetic manner, and that the difficulty increases as the story goes on. This, in fact, is a major reason for the current impatience with *Wilhelm Meister's Apprenticeship*. It would seem that it does not, like *Madame Bovary* for instance, or even like *Portrait of the Artist as a Young Man*, stick to a single conflict to which all the separate episodes are clearly connected and which they all help to bring to its resolution. It seems to contain rather an incoherent multiplicity of conflicts, of problem-raising developments and relationships. The hero appears to wander and drift as if this were a picaresque novel, in which he alone holds together episodes intended to be entertaining and meaningful in themselves; or as if this were mere fictionalized autobiography in which there is no particular reason for the next event except that it fell out so in the life of the author. Now *Wilhelm Meister's Apprenticeship* does resemble both genres and, as it were, makes use of them. It does hold the reader—if it holds him at all—by the urgency, convincingness, and charm of each adventure by itself; and the unity that binds them together is at least partly a mystery whose solution we must—and can—do without for much of the time. And Goethe, who called Wilhelm his "beloved likeness,"[3] does seem to have put into it, either directly or by way of symbolic characters and events, many of his own experiences. Strictly speaking, however, the novel belongs to neither genre. Its confusing multiplicity of events and relationships is, in fact, a necessary element in a work which is shaped with quite as much forethought as is required in such matters to dramatize a subject and embody a theme. The misleading air of innocence with which characters and adventures succeed each other, innocence of any author's intention to make us think and feel in some one visibly necessary direction, is wholly deliberate. And the problem of grasping what all that variety "adds up to," far from having been shirked by an author ill educated in the responsibilities of serious fiction (as hasty readers have supposed), is the main problem to which this novel addresses itself.

For if our hero is capable of seeing himself as wandering astray and of feeling wretched about it, it is precisely because he is not a heedless adventurer, undergoing experiences neither he nor his author cares to "add up." It is because he is one in whom the hunger to understand his life and himself, in order to cease being blown profitlessly about by illusions and temptations, is peculiarly acute. This is that "insatiable want" which is the "law" of his existence. As Wilhelm writes to a friend who begs him to return to the life of business: "What would it stead me to put properties of land in order, while I am at variance with myself? To explain myself in a word: the cultivation of my individual self . . . has from my youth upwards been constantly, though dimly, my wish and purpose" (Bk. V, Ch. 3). Such cultivation, as will grow even clearer further on, is to be understood in no narrow sense: it is education for living. And if this purpose is so often baffled, if that want is so hard to satisfy, it is because his story has been deliberately shaped to resemble the puzzling drift of life, so that the search for the lessons of it all will be opposed, both for hero and reader, by a difficulty resembling life's own.

The wonderful subject of this book—its central unifying conflict— is nothing less than the struggle of the human mind, in the face not only of the world's complexity but of its own subservience to vanity, sensuality, and sloth, to find the goals and attitudes that lead to satisfactory living. It is worth noting at once that such a subject, since the difficulty of the struggle is really presented, is extraordinary in its scope and in its pertinence to the life outside of books. Beside it, the subjects of most other great novels seem narrow and literary; they seem mere fragments of life's real problem, isolated and superficially conceived in order to support a partial vision or to make their stories possible. In *Madame Bovary,* for instance, to continue to refer to that model for our dominant fictional ideal, we see the struggle of the romantic temperament with the bourgeois world. This subject, as Flaubert conceives it, contains quite enough reality for high distinction, especially since its underlying conception is not all that makes for a novel's success. But one who aspired to match a life—any life—in its complexity, could hardly come to rest on such a view of it. Sometimes that will seem to be the problem of a life (and something like it does, in fact, resemble Wilhelm's youthful notion), but sometimes it will not. The question of how the problem is to be conceived is in actual experience one of its most puzzling elements. For at any given moment we are likely to find ourselves not so much at a fork in the road, where two opposed paths of thought or action offer themselves, and where one is clearly right or where it is clear that neither is, as at the center of a labyrinth where all is doubtful. Moreover, it is not enough to have decided that one path is the right one, the one most clearly indicated by what we think we are, by what we think we want, by how we think life goes. Too often the attitudes on which a "right" decision has been based will, in another context or another stage of our growth, lead us astray. Or else we find that a path offers a mixture of gains and losses, so that though we choose "right" according to our best knowledge of the moment, we may come out no better than if we had chosen "wrong," while choosing "wrong," we may find ourselves showered with undeserved blessings. Indeed, that life is mysterious and that we grope in the dark forever seems at last the one certain truth, and the more deeply reflective among us have always been tempted to conclude that the problem of thinking and living properly is insoluble for limited man, and that our success or failure is always, in fact, in other hands than our own—in the hands, as we used to say, of a Higher Power. And Goethe would not entirely deny this. "Alas," says the Abbé, a character in the novel who plays Goethe's own role of teacher of men and who utters many of his author's central ideas,

> the man who thoroughly understands the endless operations of
> nature and of art which are required to form a cultivated human

being, or who takes a deep interest in the education of his fellow men, may well despair when he sees how madly people pursue their own ruin, or expose themselves thoughtlessly or intentionally to danger. [Note again that for Goethe "cultivation" or "education" means that which teaches us how to avoid danger and ruin, how to live.] When I reflect on this, life appears to me a gift of such uncertain value that I could almost praise a man who holds it in but small esteem. (Bk. VII, Ch. 2)[4]

But here we come at last to what is so alien to us in the author's attitude to his material—to life—and to what produces the book's unfamiliar qualities. In spite of a grasp of life's terrible difficulty that would seem to lead inevitably to the so-called tragic view, Goethe refuses to be tragic. As a man he regards life—and as an artist he pictures it—not as an unalterable state to be realized, and to be savored or endured, but as a problem to be solved. His bent is—of all things!—practical and constructive—I almost said optimistic. He believes in the possibility of progress. Now it is true that we are not unfamiliar with the tendency to take life as a problem to be solved. But on the whole, this has been the attitude of those who have seen the problem of life as too easy to solve, and who have presented as the problem and its solution such gross simplifications that the very faith that life can be lived satisfactorily has fallen into disrepute among the sophisticated. At any sign of such a faith, these are nowadays apt to smile ironically, as though about to hear the voice of Lewis's Babbitt or of a "radical" of the thirties, or the like. The dominant alternative has been the opposite, the "tragic" view, which is that the problem of life is too hard to solve, that irreconcilable conflict, loss, and defeat are life's ultimate realities. Religion, of course, though itself affirmative, has always been intimately related to this tragic view, presupposing as it does man's inability to live right, either at all while on earth, or at least without supernatural assistance; and it is surely the current weakening of our faith in man that has revived our interest in religion, reminding us of the profound sense in its skepticism of man's powers and earthly possibilities.

Goethe, then, is that oddity, a great writer, a mind learned in life's dangers and difficulties, who affirms that it is man's proper business to discover how to be successful in what he does and to be happy. And to what has been said of the novel's subject so far we must now add two points. The first is that its author has reproduced the bewildering problem of life not merely to show how it bewilders, but to make of his story an adequate vehicle for his solution, that is, for his widest and deepest understanding of it. This understanding we sense along the way as we might intuit the coherence that does, in fact, underlie the mysterious phantasmagoria of our own lives; and the concluding section of the novel, centering around the castle of Lothario and its inhabitants, is designed to bring it home to us. We discover, indeed, by the time we reach the end, that the separate adventures of the hero have come together not only in their meanings but as a plot, and that mystery and accident (Who are those philosophic strangers? Why does the countess resemble the "Noble Amazon"?) have turned out, as so often in life, to be only the names our ignorance gave to a connectedness that life's variety and complexity work always to keep hidden from mortal eyes.

And the second point is this: that the struggle to understand which the novel dramatizes (to understand meaning not to luxuriate in feeling, but to know how to act) is the struggle of a "darling of nature"—so Goethe calls Wilhelm in one of the rare glimpses he permits us of his deepest intentions (Bk. II, Ch. 1). This no doubt means many things. One friend observes of him, for instance, that he has that "noble searching and striving for the better, whereby we of ourselves produce the good which we suppose we find" (Bk. VII, Ch. 4). And I suspect too that it means he is lucky—lucky, that is, in his circumstances as well as in his character. Nature's "darlings," in other words, are probably those for whom *all* things, both within them and without, are happily constituted. And if such a reference to luck seems to contradict the point already made about Goethe's understanding, to imply that some things must always lie outside that connectedness seen by the wise, it can only be admitted that however much our author understands, he does not profess to understand everything. That description of his hero certainly means, in any case, that he is to come out all right. In fact, Wilhelm's story is the story of a success, and the wisdom which the novel embodies is precisely an insight into the nature of success in living, and of how—by what attitudes as well as behavior—it is to be won, if it is to be won at all. It is in the light of this subject, then, that *Wilhelm Meister's Apprenticeship*, at first sight so formless, is seen to have a perfectly definite development and conclusion. Exactly what these are can be made clear by a brief examination of several characters who play important roles in Wilhelm's destiny.

Mariana, as we have seen, is a pretty representative of the world of the theater, who seems to the youthful Wilhelm worthy to stand at his side in the glorious future toward which his talents are surely leading him, just as the theater seems to him a worthy medium for those talents and certain to bring both glory to himself and blessings to the nation. But we understand from the start that it is he with his passionate dreams who creates the nobility of Mariana. The truth is she is an entirely ordinary woman, who falls asleep at his lofty talk, loves presents, yields easily to pressures and temptations—a reality which the self-obsession of youth prevents him from noticing. And the course of events teaches Wilhelm that those ardent dreams of his have led him into exactly the same error with regard to the theater, which so resists his efforts to impose on it his high purposes that he gives it up at last in disgust.

If Mariana represents his youthful folly, Felix ushers in his maturity. Felix is a little boy who turns out to be Wilhelm's son, and what he means in our hero's life is made explicit in the climactic scene at Lothario's castle. In this scene, which follows Wilhelm's abandonment of the stage along with many of the illusions that had been bound up with it, the strangers who had been haunting him reappear to hint at his life's meaning and direction. (They are a small group, headed by the Abbé, whose "hobby" is the education of promising youth, and whose half-playful—yet ultimately significant—fancy it is to shroud their activities in mystery and romance.) And when Wilhelm demands to know whether Felix is his son, demands it with an excitement which shows the birth of a genuine paternal emotion, he hears the joyful exclamation: "Your Apprenticeship is done: Nature has pronounced you free!" Later we are told: "Everything that he proposed commencing was to be completed for his boy: everything that he erected was to last for several generations. In this sense his apprenticeship was ended; with the feelings of a father, he had acquired all the virtues of a citizen" (Bk. VIII, Ch. 1). And it is like a good "citizen" that he turns his attention to the management of his property. A pattern thus discloses itself, though I need hardly say that the rich narrative does not present it quite so simply. (It must be added, indeed, that Wilhelm does not remain, any more than the rest of us, in perfect possession of his virtues.) Wilhelm has left behind the youthful state—"romantic" is the familiar word for it—in which he was sure that his private dream made him superior to the world around him (his father's world, the world of commerce); sure that passionate feeling and high aspiring thought were their own justification, so that he was always following the lead of feeling into a fresh tangle, or the lead of thought into a realm where he lost contact with people and things as they are. He has shifted his attention outward—to his son—and has by that son been drawn into the life of common humanity, and to ends, attitudes, and activity less lofty but more necessary and profitable than those of his dreaming self-centered youth. There, he learns, if anywhere, lies happiness, as the name of his son suggests.

As Wilhelm's new attitudes differ from those of youth, so Natalia, the woman he loves at the end, differs from his first love, Mariana. The bride of his maturity, Natalia is also a symbol of it. He meets her first after a disastrous adventure with robbers; she has been passing on horseback and dismounts to come to his aid. (He thinks of her for long afterward as the "Noble Amazon.") Fainting from his wounds, he seems to see her ringed by a halo as she approaches. And this halo is a hint, which all that follows will bear out. Not only is she more genuinely noble in mind and sensibility (as well as birth) than his first love, whose nobility was all illusion. When he meets Natalia again much later, he finds her to be the embodiment of selfless devotion to others, a devotion it is her distinction to express always in useful, practical ways. Selflessness and practicality, these are exactly the characteristics he has himself been painfully approaching, and not as mere a priori ideals, but as essential to a satisfactory life. That we are to see his marriage to such a woman as thus significant, the novel's last page makes unmistakable. His silly but destiny-fraught flirtation with Philina, which long ago had bound him to the actors, had been initiated by a young man who, at her request, had asked Wilhelm for a bouquet he was holding. This young man turns out to be Natalia's brother, and at the end, laughingly urging on the marriage, he says to Wilhelm: "When we first scraped acquaintance, and I asked you for the pretty nosegay, who could have supposed you were ever to receive a flower like this from me?" "Do not," Wilhelm replies, "at the moment of my highest happiness, remind me of those days." "Of which you need not be ashamed," the brother continues, "any more than one need be ashamed of his descent. The times were very good times; only I cannot but laugh to look at you; to my mind you resemble Saul, the son of Kish, who went out to seek his father's asses and found a kingdom" (Bk. VIII, Ch. 10). In a conversation with Eckermann, Goethe himself, though denying that the novel's "rich, manifold life" was compressible within the kind of theme most people were seeking, pointed to this sentence as its truest key.

But the sentence leads us further than may at first appear. If our hero's story has been a progress to maturity, we are not permitted to see it as a progress from mere error to simple truth, from wrong ideas and conduct to right. If this were all, there would be the less reason for the novel's variety and vividness along its lengthy way, for its "rich, manifold life." One must not be ashamed of one's descent—is it not by way of our past that we reach what we have? If Saul had not gone to seek asses, he would not have found a kingdom. And though the brother refers to Philina, there is a proof of this point which even more dramatically and meaningfully joins the end of the novel to its beginning. The child Felix who, by leading Wilhelm to turn his gifts to account in the world of reality, becomes his salvation, this child is the child of Mariana! And Mariana—do we not know her as precisely the embodiment of that world of the theater in which Wilhelm "wasted" his youth? The implication is clear that neither of his youthful passions had been a waste. For as his love for the woman produced the child who made him a man, so his love for the theater spurred him to exertions that drew forth and developed all his powers. This is why, though he finds in his maturity that he was wrong to despise his father's world of commerce, an old commercial friend is nevertheless amazed at the vast improvements which Wilhelm's theatrical experiences had wrought in him. By comparison, the friend feels that his own exclusively practical life has left him withered and shrunk. So in youth the lucky ones, by the ardor of commitments which grow out of love (and however "wrong" they may later appear to have been), plow the ground and plant the seeds that will, for their maturity, bear fruit. Incapable of passionate error, they would give birth to far less in themselves and their world. "Dim-sightedness and innocence" like those of the youthful Wilhelm are compared by one bitterly wise character to "the beautiful hull upon the young bud. Woe to us," she continues, "if we are forced too soon to burst it" (Bk. IV, Ch. 16).

But the richest expression of the novel's meanings is to be found in Mignon. Mignon is a strange creation, who seems different in kind from all the other characters, less realistic, more a lyric extravagance unrelated to theme, and mysterious because entirely arbitrary. In fact, however, her lovely peculiarities end by being sufficiently accounted for, sufficiently at least for all but the most pedantic of realists, and what is more interesting, we learn at last that it was her wealth of meaning rather than her lack of it that made her mysterious.

Wilhelm meets her, remember, at about the same time as he meets Philina, that charming invitation to life's easiest pleasures; both appear, that is, on the threshold of the world of his apprenticeship. And we see at once that she is a kind of opposite of Philina, her first dramatic role being to pull him away from all that the other pulls him toward. Where the merry woman is preeminently a sexual attraction, Mignon is so sexless that she puzzles him at first as to whether she is a boy or a girl. Indeed, physical passion is death to her: her fatal nervous illness begins when she accidently witnesses the physical union of Wilhelm and Philina, which the woman had tricked him into. Philina wants him to be an actor, adding sensuality and vanity to the deeper forces in him which impel him toward the stage. But Mignon hates the theater and always pleads with him to leave it, and her ravishing songs induce in him a kind of dream that lifts him away from the coarse life about him. Finally, we must note that she sings often of Italy, her native country for which she incessantly yearns—a land, her song tells, where both nature and the works of man are noble and beautiful.

Mignon, the sweet and troubling familiar of Goethe's "beloved likeness," seems to be a daring introduction into the story of his own highest ideal, human and aesthetic, an ideal whose home was indeed, for Goethe, Italy. His yearning for Italy too was a passion, and what he found there when he made his famous flight from the court of Weimar—this preceded the final version of the novel—transformed his hitherto realistic, emotional art into an art less freely personal, more classic, an art of harmonious essentials. And it is because Mignon is such an ideal—an ideal representing what mind or spirit contributes to art, what works "against" and purifies mere matter—that she could not but draw Wilhelm away from the comparatively vulgar stage.[5]

But it will be remembered that she also kept him away from his father's world of commerce, that world despised by Wilhelm in his "erring" youth, but *not* in his more open-eyed maturity. The fact is, she would draw him away from everything real, and this is why the very steps that bring him to his maturity literally kill her. Her love for him is passionately possessive, and as he enters more and more into the common, practical, *necessary* life of man, welcoming the now dead Mariana's child as his own and planning on marriage, Mignon's illness grows continually worse. Her fatal convulsion comes when she sees him embraced by a woman who calls him husband. It is not for nothing that Wilhelm, observing her near the end beside the robust Felix, reflects that it is like heaven and earth embracing. Thus Mignon too must be regarded in more than one way. Representing as she does an impossibly lofty and unqualified ideal, she keeps alive in him, while he struggles amid the vulgarities of the theatrical world, that which lifts him above them. But his progress must finally be a descent out of the clouds of thought—the "half-dream"—where she would keep him, to the earth, where man's real work and lasting satisfactions are to be found, and so she must die.

And even that is not all we learn from Mignon. This ennobling ideal out of Italy is not only above the vulgarities of the theater and above the realm of practical activity; she is also "above" the world of Judeo-Christian morality on which the family and society in the West are founded—and this too is why she must die as Wilhelm takes his place in that world. She was born, we learn at the end, of an incestuous union: her parents were brother and sister. Her father is none other than the old Harper, her fellow singer of sad and beautiful songs. And this father had put quite plainly the significance of his "criminal" behavior: in his passion for his sister he condemned the moral order altogether and declared that passion justifies itself, that nature is indifferent to morality, which is imposed on it by society cruelly and arbitrarily. He is right about the cruelty. The bliss of the lovers and their potential bliss as parents were converted by the Church into guilt and madness.

The mother died and the father, obsessed with the vague memory of some terrible crime and with fear, went wandering about as a singer of life's pain. But Goethe, though he grants the sense in the Harper's pagan amorality, though he shows that it can produce unearthly loveliness—can produce Mignon—sees too that it is at war with the essential conditions of fruitful living. It belongs, for instance, to the Harper's madness that he fears he must always bring trouble to those who befriend him. Is it not true that the life of freely indulged passion must lead to continual trouble? He fears too that a little boy will cause his death—and, in fact, his death does come about because of Felix. Does this not tell us that the life of unregulated passion must end when the family and family feeling begin? For Goethe, as we have seen, it is best that it should end at last, for where such passion tends to the self-indulgent dissipation of energies, it is in building for the family that our energies are set properly to work and are most likely to bear fruit.

It must be added at once, however, that Goethe's tribute to the teachings of religion—at least of Christianity—is a qualified one. It is precisely in order to make this clear—that is, in order not to leave unexamined the great *other* idea of how life should be lived—that he interrupts the adventures of Wilhelm with a long story of an aunt of Natalia's, a story called "The Confessions of a Beautiful Soul." (This chapter also serves the purpose of showing the relationships among the apparently separate characters of the novel, of clearing away mystery and tying up the plot.) The aunt is a kind of Christian saint, selfless in her dealings with others, but convinced that men are born sinful and must war forever, with the help of God, against the world, the flesh, and the devil. From the first two, in fact, like Gide's Alissa, she ends by cutting herself off almost entirely. Goethe has some sympathy for her, as he has some for the terrible Harper. We see this in her conversations with the great-uncle of Natalia, the wise head of the family who put the Abbé in charge of the children's education and who, like the Abbé, speaks always for the author. The uncle believes—and this, be it noted, is the very heart of Goethe's message to humanity—that "the whole world lies before us like a huge quarry before an architect, and he only deserves the name of man who out of this accidental mass can fashion with the greatest economy, ingenuity and durability some form the conception of which has arisen in his mind." And to the saintly woman he willingly admits, "You have sought to bring your moral being, your deep and loving nature, into accordance with yourself and with the Highest." To work for inner harmony, and for harmony in accord with a moral ideal, this too is a task worthy of the shaping spirit of man. And it is significant that of all her nephews and nieces, it is Natalia, the novel's ideal woman, who most resembles her. "Nevertheless," the uncle adds, "we are not to be condemned for seeking to understand the whole race of reasonable men, and to bring their powers into harmony" (Bk. VI),[6] a remark echoed by the Abbé's teaching, "Mankind is composed of all men, and all powers taken together make up a world" (Bk. VIII, Ch. 5). And we see that his praise could hardly be acceptable to the devotee, since her way is honored simply as being proper to herself, and as adding but one element to the myriad which make up a complete humanity. The uncle, indeed, for all his kindness, has ruled that she is to have no contact with her nephews and nieces, and Natalia grows up entirely free of her aunt's life-condemning Christian mysticism, resembling her aunt only in those "Christian" characteristics that can help life toward its richest earthly fulfillment.

Nor should we be misled by the honor finally paid to the "virtues of the citizen" into supposing that Goethe ends by growing "respectable." If it is fruitfulness that matters, then right and wrong, good and evil, become irrelevant as criteria of attitudes or behavior. What is important is that an individual's attitudes and behavior be such as to elicit and make productive his own unique capabilities; the right may therefore differ from person to person and even from one stage to another of a person's development. It is always when Wilhelm is led away from "his natural mode of thought" or from "wholesome consistency" (Bk. V, Ch. 1) that he grows miserable. And the Abbé maintains, in a key passage worth quoting entire,

> that with man the first and last consideration was activity, and that we could not act on anything without the proper gifts for it, without an instinct impelling us to it. "You admit," he used to say, "that poets must be born such; you admit this with regard to all professors of the fine arts; because you must admit it, because those workings of human nature cannot very plausibly be aped. But, if we consider well, we shall find that every capability, however slight, is born with us; that there is no vague general capability in men. It is our ambiguous, desultory education that makes men uncertain: instead of forwarding our real capacities, it turns our efforts towards objects which are frequently discordant with the mind that aims at them. I augur better of a child, a youth, who is wandering astray on a path of his own, than of many who are walking upright upon paths which are not theirs. If the former, either by themselves or by the guidance of others, ever find the right path, that is to say, the path which suits their nature, they will never leave it; while the latter are in danger every moment of shaking off a foreign yoke, and abandoning themselves to unrestricted license." (Bk. VIII, Ch. 3)

The virtues of the citizen, then, are for Goethe a means and not an end: they are the means whereby the freedom to realize the possibilities of the unique self is prevented from degenerating into the license by which the self's energies are wasted. Goethe is, in fact, as little respectable as his modern disciple André Gide, whose insight is Goethean through and through—as little respectable as Gide, but also as little *merely* rebellious.[7]

It may be objected of Goethe, as it has been of Gide, that his teaching is really no teaching at all. (Natalia herself speaks so of the Abbé's methods: she prefers that the young be more firmly guided.) And it can be pointed out as proof of this that the mysterious strangers who, under the Abbé, are the educators of the novel and who sometimes give the impression of being responsible for Wilhelm's development actually left him more or less to his own impulses, simply uttering aloud now and then the lessons he himself was learning or would soon be forced to learn. There is a certain plausibility in this charge. I would suggest, however, that if the strangers guide so delicately, often so imperceptibly, and if they leave the individual so free to find his own path to fruitfulness, it is because they aspire to teach as nature herself teaches—as nature teaches those like Wilhelm who earnestly seek out her hints and are capable of following them. Their teaching—Goethe's teaching—represents no imposition on things as they are, no condemnation of them in the name of ideals derived from "above," but is the very voice of things as they are. That their role is indeed to utter and underscore the lessons of nature, of life as it actually works, is this not further implied in Wilhelm's bitter complaint that they seem to operate by indifferent whim, loving simply to separate what is united and to unite what is separate? For exactly so might nature's operations be described, especially at those times when we feel ourselves helpless and bewildered amid her irresistible currents. Nature's "darlings," however, do not stop in such complaint. Sooner or later, they do their best to discover what their parent is like and to live in harmony with her. We cannot be free of her jurisdiction, but, as Goethe learned from *his* teacher, Spinoza, we can have the freedom of doing willingly what she requires. It was precisely to show how her requirements are learned and what they are that Goethe, one of the most cherished of her darlings, wrote his book.

A full discussion of the book's meanings would occupy us much longer than this. There is hardly a point I have made that is not richly complicated by the story, as it would have to be in life, with which the story tries, with such staggering ambition, to be commensurate. But my purpose has been only to uncover enough to show a legitimizing reason for the novel's peculiarities. And what I would like to suggest by way of conclusion is that just as the story as a whole no longer seems formless when its chief meanings are grasped, so Goethe's handling of the parts may for some readers grow less unattractive. It may at least become clear that his narrative methods are not dated mannerisms impossible for any but scholars to respond to, but, as I have said, the appropriate and precise expression of the author's idea, the methods proper to a work which dramatizes, not so much one or another particular situation, as the struggle to learn the lesson of them all.

It must be admitted, to begin with, that the novel tends to leave unsatisfied two important demands we generally make on fiction. The first is that we will be seduced into sharing the emotional experiences of its characters. Since life is to be shown, not as a series of moods to be shared, but as a series of problems to be rightly understood and solved, we are given of character, scene, or event only what is essential to the growing tangle they create for the mind. The art of Goethe is a linear art. And it is the novel's paucity of psychological or sensuous detail that makes for that odd quickness of pace which, to readers saturated in fiction of another kind, seems so shockingly inappropriate in an account of life's troubles. This does not mean, however, that what we get is the abstract, the schematized, as in so-called problem novels. Goethe is interested in the adventures of the mind, but these emerge from those actual feeling-clouded, mind-defying complexities we struggle with in life. Though he handles his scenes with a unique economy of detail, they are nonetheless "realistic," and not merely symbolic of ideas. We are accustomed to a realism that shines the light on surfaces or on emotions, but there is also Goethe's kind, which seeks to illuminate rather the essential structure of life's most significant developments, that in them which makes the problems we try to solve.

The second reason for our disappointment in the writing is related to the first. Not only are we not especially led to feel with the characters, we are also deprived of the guidance that comes from knowing the feelings of the author. Goethe *has* no familiar "human" attitude to what goes on, of the kind which other novelists, however slyly, are always inviting us to share with them. He writes as that Olympian he has often been called, who knows what is hidden from his suffering characters, who knows too that it must be hidden, and who cannot very well vibrate in sympathy with or indignation against their shortsightedness. He writes, that is, as one who regards the emotions and attitudes which ordinarily direct our judgments from the point of view of the great whole, of which they are misleading fragments. Beside detachment like his, the famous "objectivity" of Flaubert is a mere literary device, and a device in the service of the most transparently passionate involvement. Beside irony like his, that of Flaubert seems the angry disappointment of a persistently youthful mind. The French artist is ironical at the expense of a world which has violated ideals hotly cherished. But for Goethe, all ideals are forms of error—or, if you prefer, "working hypotheses"—which are more or less appropriate in certain situations. His ideal, that of fruitfulness, is only a kind of test of the varying rightness of all others. This is an irony so thoroughgoing it requires no emphasis—emphasis would imply that something else would be safe from his irony, which is untrue—but merely the calm tracing out of that life process which leaves all passionate convictions gradually behind. It is like an atmosphere which ceases to be noticed because it bathes everything alike. And what *is* noticed is that failure, so annoying to some, to lead our sympathies in any simple or clear direction.

There is for many readers great beauty in an economy so richly meaningful, as well as in that expression of Goethe's detachment, his cool, dancelike sprightliness of manner about serious things. But it is true enough, as I say, that in choosing his subject and evolving for it such qualities, he had to do without certain major sources of interest. He had apparently resigned himself in advance, however, to interesting a smaller public than that which wept—or killed itself—over *The Sorrows of Young Werther*. He tells us in the later novel: "The rude man is contented if he see but something going on; the man of more refinement must be made to feel; the man entirely refined desires to reflect" (Bk. II, Ch. 3). Now it would not do to be impolite to those readers who, in spite of all efforts like the present one, will persist in being bored by his marvelous novel. Let the formula serve to suggest not that the third category of readers is the most "refined," but only that it exists, that there *are* readers whose tastes this book is shaped to satisfy. And what must be emphasized at once is that these are not necessarily readers who would be content to find a philosophic tract substituted for a work of art. No, it is only that they do not automatically disqualify as art a work whose "aesthetic" effects are made out of "intellectual" materials.

For those who share Goethe's interest in the meanings of experience, it is hard to see how the novel can fail to be as fascinating, as full of suspense, as a thriller. Is not this pursuit of wisdom a chase after a most precious prize—freedom from pain and, if one is lucky, happiness—a chase as fraught with danger and difficulty as any chase of man or woman? The problems with which the hero and the reader are presented are after all problems like the following: Is Mariana true? Are Wilhelm's dreams of glory delusions? How can he disentangle himself from degrading but seductive relationships? Is the boy really his own? Does it matter? Why is he so wretched? What should he do next? They are the problems of experience at its most intense, and since this is a work which offers no simple solutions, but focuses always on the mind's actual difficulties, these problems are forever being brought dramatically to birth and engendering action which leads to further problems. Nor is it only inside Wilhelm that difficulties arise. They come too from his contact with a thickly peopled world, a world in which social classes as well as individuals stand forth sharply in their essential nature. So urgent, however, is our hero's quest for understanding that, far from objecting, some of us are grateful when a little light is thrown into dark places by way of explicit comment or by the discussion of interested and intelligent characters. Indeed, strange as it may seem, when Wilhelm is presented, in that spooky scene in the castle where the end of his apprenticeship is announced, with a scroll full of profound maxims on the nature of art (for he begins as an artist) and of life, these maxims are a real story climax, they have dramatic force as well as meaning, and we devour them with as lively a sense of their importance to the gripping narrative as in another kind of thriller we would read the long lost will that restored our beggared hero to his dukedom.

In fact, the novel's resemblance to the tale of romantic adventure is quite marked, though here the effects involved are shown as belonging to life rather than merely to "stories" which help us "escape" life. There is, for example, the effect already mentioned, that of mystery. It is interesting to note, indeed, how much of darkness this apostle of light has deliberately brushed into his canvas. But it should not be surprising; Goethe does not, as I have suggested, think we can understand everything, and who is more likely than the man of deep and active mind to grow aware of the limits of human understanding? In *Wilhelm Meister,* this awareness is dramatized in two ways. The first is by an almost Gothic mystification, the sort that comes with Mignon, the Harper, the inhabitants of the castle. (And though all our common-sense questions are finally answered, it cannot be denied that once or twice, as in those stories devoted most shamelessly to our "entertainment," we feel a bit cheated: the answers seem incommensurate with the portentousness of the original effect.) The second kind of mystery is less theatrical. It comes from that refusal of our author, mentioned before, to make prematurely clear the full meaning of his episodes. Goethe will interpose generalizations, but he will only guardedly reveal essential secrets; and since these secrets, that is, the insights which his developments embody, are complex, they do not fall into familiar, easily grasped meaning-patterns. We read him as we live. We may be interested, and even fascinated, all the time, but complete understanding of how things go together and of what is truly right and helpful, or the reverse, is the prize only of a flexible insight working on a complicated experience—it is not handed to us on any silver platter. It is our narrow view of life's possibilities that the novel mystifies—and then enlarges.

And here too is a source of interest for some readers—I mean the quantity and depth of insight into the way life goes and how it should be lived which the novel presents to us. This is to be seen not only in the large organizing ideas traced out here but also in every episode along the way, however innocent of meaning it may appear on a first reading. There is not one of Wilhelm's adventures that does not turn out on reflection to have put in terms of his life and character some common pattern of human difficulty or development. And the work is full of general remarks, coming not from the author alone, but from characters who are painfully learning sense or have already thus learned it, which have an electrifying pertinence to our own lives, and would surely help us if we could be helped by others at all.

One final point. It is true that this novel appeals chiefly to the reader who "desires to reflect." And yet there is an emotion of which the multiplying adventures of Wilhelm Meister become the "objective correlative," an emotion made richer rather than violated by all the novel's implicit and explicit thought. Suppose a deeply conscious man who has lived long and undergone much and who pauses to look back over the crowded vista—will not this man think a thought so complex that it is a feeling, that it is, as it were, the taste of life itself on his tongue? This is what the novel evokes in us. It is the feeling of the larger view, the feeling of wisdom. No novel ever written gives us at last so vivid a sense of the whole bittersweet tangle of human existence, and of the mysterious unity beneath its apparent chaos. Only a work which joins, as this one does, a lifelike variety of experience with a matching depth and scope of insight could have provided us with such a feeling. No vicarious pains or pleasures are involved, as I have said. No pity or indignation. We are not "moved." Instead, the shudder of recognition. We understand and are exalted.

There are certainly other ways for a novel to be wonderful. If we were forced to choose between this one and *The Brothers Karamazov*, we might well have to let the German novel go. But why do we have to choose? Is there not, indeed, a certain narrowness in holding against him Goethe's failure to resemble our current favorites, as though we had nothing to learn from outside the circle of our current notions and our current tastes?

Goethe's *Elective Affinities*

Though *Elective Affinities* (*Wahlverwandtschaften,* first published in 1809) for us today is the most readable of Goethe's novels, realistic and subtle in its psychology, urgent, swift, and mainly convincing in its plot, it may well seem at first less moving than such a tragic love story ought to be. The suffering it deals in is rarely given center stage; what we seem invited to attend to is the working out of a mysterious natural process whose meaning is our chief concern. And yet, oddly enough, the more we think about this novel—that is, the more we seek to connect and reconcile its contradictory elements—the more heavy grows the weight of the life-pain it has left us with, the more we feel it to be a kind of cry.

That the pain it deals in should here go along with thought, rather than oppose it, is a clue to the strange relationship of this novel of Goethe's sixtieth year with *The Sorrows of Werther,* the work of his twenty-fifth, and *Wilhelm Meister's Apprenticeship,* which he finished at forty-seven. The youthful novel gave itself up so seductively to the emotions of its love tragedy that, as is well known, it helped to romanticize a whole generation of readers and writers, some of whom found even the hero's suicide worthy of emulation. And it is because feeling predominates so conspicuously and, as it were, self-righteously over thought in that novel that the mature Goethe judged it so contemptible. Rereading it, he decided that "the author made a mistake when, having finished the book, he did not put a bullet through his head." It seemed to him positively dangerous "because in it weakness is delineated as strength."[1] And in fact, the idea that (as he expressed it later to Eckermann) "romantic" means "sickly" and "classic" means "healthy"[2] rules over the great novel of his maturity, *Wilhelm Meister's Apprenticeship.* In this work, passion and pain are symptoms of incompleteness of understanding, rather than primary realities in which life finds its real meaning. Observed coolly from the standpoint of one who surveys life as a whole, they are seen to have meaning only as they prevent, or contribute to, an education that leaves them behind and that enhances our powers for productive work. For, says a character who speaks for the author, "the whole world lies before us like a huge quarry before an architect, and he only deserves the name of man who out of this accidental mass can fashion with the greatest economy, ingenuity, and durability some form the conception of which has arisen in his mind" (Bk. VI).

Now, in *Elective Affinities*, which is sometimes regarded as Goethe's return to romanticism, we have, actually, a strange combination of the attitudes expressed in the other two. For instance, its story of the passion of a husband for his wife's niece and of the wife for her husband's friend duplicates the essential elements of the despised *Werther:* love, renunciation, and what can be called suicide. Moreover, there is no question here, any more than in *Werther,* of the agonizing experience "paying off" in a *Bildung* which leaves it comfortably behind. On the contrary, we are now shown that passion may have a force and persuasiveness impossible to refute, and that the conflict between its demand for personal happiness and the requirements of the human community, may, when both sides are given their due, resolve itself in disaster with a logic even wisdom must respect. Passion is thus seen once more, not as a stage in an upward progress, but as a permanent element of the human condition, a clue to its fundamental character. And yet we also find here, in harmony with the teaching of *Wilhelm Meister's Apprenticeship,* a constant, and finally victorious resistance to passion and its claims. The fact is that Goethe has dramatized in this novel, which he described, with some misgivings, as the only one of his larger works constructed to embody an idea (Eckermann, p. 206), the justice in the claims of both passion and the human community, and the profound ramifications of their conflict in man's life. For he sees them as versions of the conflicting claims not only of the part and the whole, but of those other polarities, nature and spirit, and the human and the divine. And the novel shows how certain rare, tragically gifted types, who respond to both with equal force—and precisely because they respond so to both—may attain a beauty, suffer a martyrdom, and exert a power over our feelings which shed light on the meaning of Christianity. If the novel finally seems a kind of cry, it is not, like *Werther,* the cry of a boy, but of a sage. And yet—for the words "and yet" are forced on us again and again by the novel's persistent ambiguity—it is a cry. Or, to put it more soberly, if it is classic in its romanticism, it is equally romantic in its classicism.

It is Goethe as classicist, however, who is mainly in control of the novel's art. We see this first in the title, a scientific phrase of his day for the crisscrossing recombination of joined elements, when two pairs are brought together as a result of the irresistible chemical attraction of the individuals to their opposite numbers. Goethe has thus chosen for his story of adulterous passion a title that draws us oddly—some would say grotesquely—away from the sphere of passionate experience to that of science, and of underlying principle. We see it in the storyteller's manner, which is always detached and economical, always hurrying us coolly past the moments of poignant feeling. We see it in the constant interweaving with such moments of details, episodes, and, above all, general reflections that remind us of what lies beyond the moment and force us out of feeling into thought. (Indeed, he goes so far as to characterize his passionate heroine Ottilie by means of a journal of philosophic maxims, her own or those of others, quite worthy of the author.) And Goethe's coolness of manner is never mere understatement, that apparent avoidance of feeling which is only a trick to intensify it by enlisting the imagination in its service. No, in this novel, we are still, as in *Wilhelm Meister's Apprenticeship,* in the hands of a writer who remains too conscious of the whole to abandon himself, or us, to the perspectives and responses of the part.

But more important, we see the classic Goethe in the substance of the novel and, to begin with, in his continuing concern with education and productive work. Again and again we might be reading the lessons of the earlier novel as to the way in which true education and the increasingly fruitful use of our energies and gifts in which it shows itself are at war with the romantic ego's demand for immediate gratification. The niece Ottilie, for instance, is forever being outshone at school by her aunt's brilliant daughter Luciane because the latter, greedy for prompt applause, is quick to imitate mere external results and indifferent to what leads up to them. Ottilie, on the other hand, in the words of the intelligent Tutor, can grasp nothing which "does not follow from something she has already learned." The easiest things are hard for her if "she cannot connect [them] with any former experiences, but as soon as one can find the connecting links and explain them to her, nothing is too difficult for her comprehension." In short, "she does not learn . . . like a pupil but like a future teacher."[3] Real understanding is thus a grasp of *connections,* of the relationship of the part to the whole. And such understanding is required of the teacher not only because he cannot teach without it, but also because the teacher is one who prepares others for life, and such a grasp of the connectedness of things is the basis of moral discipline.

As for productive work, this, chiefly in the form of the improvements on Edward's estate, is so important an element in the story that we might almost call it a story of the conflict between such work and the passions that interfere with it or exploit it. It is true that some critics have seen in the work on the estate only another example, less obvious than the elaborate games of the shallow Luciane but just as frivolous, of the aristocracy's way of fighting boredom. But this is to blur differences in attitude that are significant elements of the novel's meaning. The job itself, whether it is in the service of life-enhancing beauty (as art) or of utility—in both ways it affects the nearby villagers as well as the estate's aristocratic owners—is presented as a perfectly adequate occasion for the exercise of Goethe's favorite virtues: industry, skill, taste, wisdom. What we are invited to note is how differently this work, as well as other kinds, is pursued by different people, or by one person in different states of mind. Thus, the Captain, the Architect, above all, Ottilie, characters clearly valued by the author, show their quality as much in their mastery of the work they do as in their human relations. For the same thing is required for decent performance in both—indeed, it is the same thing noted before as required for proper learning—that is, the capacity to subordinate immediate gratification to one's sense of connections, between the self and others in the moral life, and, on the job, between present actions and future objectives. Also required, of course, is the gift to conceive of that good which is other and more distant than immediate gratification, as well as the skill to pursue it effectively. And as these three—the Captain and the Architect in improving the estate and the chapel, and Ottilie, first as a student, and then as her aunt's housekeeper—as these three are pointedly shown to be masters at their work, so the way the novel's two romantics relate to work (their own and that of others) is shown to be positively destructive, for all their cleverness or their occasional fits of enthusiasm.

The case of Luciane, as I say, is obvious. She tears up costly dresses and strips the buds—the productive future—of carefully nurtured plants for an hour's entertainment, or takes over the cure of an emotionally disturbed girl with a self-glorifying haste and publicity that drive the girl into madness. But Edward's work on the estate is only a more extended, subtle, and varied exposure of the same romantic temperament. It takes the Captain to instruct him in the necessity of keeping the "firmness" and "clear sequence" required by "business" in order to be able to afford the liberty appropriate to the time of relaxation. The Captain's days, unlike Edward's, "were always devoted to an immediate purpose, so that every evening showed that something had been accomplished" (Bk. I, Ch. 4). He learns a related lesson when the Captain turns a hitherto unsatisfactory clerk of Edward's into a surprisingly useful worker by noticing and adapting to his character, instead of treating him as an appendage to himself. (It turned out the man worked well only when he was permitted to finish one job before being given another.) But the climactic demonstration of how Edward handles a job occurs when, intoxicated with love and at increasing expense and risk, he hurries the work on the lodge and the new dam in order to be able to celebrate their completion on Ottilie's birthday. Though others have been forced to work harder than ever to pay, as it were, for his pleasure, the dam is not solid enough for the crowd of observing villagers, it gives way, and a boy is nearly drowned. And that is not the end of the demonstration. Against the wishes of his wife, and even of Ottilie—for the job has been botched and the villagers are disappearing—he gives the signal for the fireworks display planned to cap the festivities, and the explosion of colored lights writes his drunken folly large against the sky. Finally, to complete the picture of his slavery to the present moment and its feelings, he hands a gold coin to a beggar because of his joy in Ottilie's presence, though the man had once angered him with his rudeness and he himself had instituted heavy penalties for begging on that day.

But of course, it is in the tragic double love story that the difference between the romantic temperament and the other is most fully revealed. As Edward's iron whim brings the Captain and Ottilie into the home that his less greedy wife had been enjoying quite enough alone with her husband, so he is the one who yields most quickly to the new attraction. Then, after those easy-going adulterers, the Count and the Baroness, have made light of marriage during a visit, and Edward, chatting with the Count of past sexual adventures, has led him to the woman's bedroom, Edward forces himself on his wife, whom he finds preparing for bed, because he is full of desire for Ottilie. It is true that Charlotte, as she yields, finds herself dreaming of the Captain. But later, when their hidden longings burst into the open and require a decision that will affect their whole lives, the husband and wife react very differently. After Ottilie unconsciously reveals her love in copying for him a document over long hours, and in a handwriting uncannily like his own, Edward embraces her in rapture, and then pushes on that celebration in the drunken way we have seen. But when the Captain, carrying Charlotte from a stranded boat to shore, suddenly kisses her, she stiffens against her own desire. She tells him they must change their situation, since they can't change their feelings, and back in her room, "where she could not help feeling and remembering that she was Edward's wife . . . her character, strengthened by the many experiences of her life, came to her aid," and soon "consoling thoughts of friendship, affection and resignation passed through her mind" (Bk. I, Ch. 12). It is the climax of this same indictment that Edward, forced into a long exile during which his son is born, is, in part, the cause of his child's death when he returns. For, deciding to insist on the divorce and remarriage of all four, he cannot wait for his wife's consent, but seeks out Ottilie where she is walking with the child near the lake. He inundates her with arguments: the child was born of a mental adultery, this is a reason the more for atonement by his true marriage to Ottilie, Charlotte herself will surely agree to a divorce. And Ottilie, already introduced to the idea of divorce by the Count, accepts the thrilling possibility and returns his kisses. It is because she is thus delayed in bringing the child home by Edward's agitating embraces that she risks a shortcut by water, and the child slips from the boat and is drowned.

And yet. This indictment of the romantic is not the whole story. The novel has also shown us things that at least mitigate Edward's guilt, and may at moments make it doubtful. The love between him and Ottilie, like that between Charlotte and the Captain, but far more strikingly, is not a case of irresponsible seduction—indeed, it is hardly thought of at first as romantic love—but rises out of an innocent response to genuine affinity. Both couples feel and act in an instinctive harmony, like that of dancers, not available with their proper partners. Then there are indications that such love may issue from and result in what is good, and not merely self-indulgence. It may be related to our power to see beauty and meaning not only in one other, but elsewhere as well. Edward's discovery, for instance, that loving one person makes all others lovable cannot be dismissed as romantic foolishness, since the Captain immediately applies it in a way we must honor: "I think the same thing is true," he says, "of the feelings of respect and admiration. Only after we have had a chance to experience such feelings in respect to one particular object do we learn to recognize what is really valuable in the world" (Bk. I, Ch. 12). And later, Ottilie notes in her journal how love fills life with "connected meaning": "Life without love, without the presence of the beloved, is only a bad *comédie à tiroir*. We pull out one drawer after another, push it quickly back and hastily try the next one. Whatever good or of importance may occur, has little connected meaning. Everywhere we have to begin all over again and everywhere we should like to end" (Bk. II, Ch. 9).

But the main arguments against simple rejection of the claims of passion are dramatically summed up in Charlotte's response to that very tragedy which, from another point of view, seemed to complete the indictment of Edward. Charlotte herself, in her first agony, interprets the evidence otherwise. "There are certain things on which Destiny stubbornly insists," she tells the Captain as she agrees at last to a divorce. "Reason and virtue, duty and all that is sacred to us oppose them in vain. Destiny wishes something to happen which to it seems right, but does not seem right to us; and in the end Destiny will be the victor, fight against it as we may" (Bk. I, Ch. 14). And if "destiny" has a less honorific sound than "virtue" and "duty," may we not read this nevertheless as a reminder that life, in the power of its irreducible particularity, can exert a claim which general principle can never touch? In fact, a moment later Charlotte throws additional doubt on the legitimacy of renunciation, remembering that her loyalty to this marriage has perhaps been loyalty to a mistake that should never have occurred. She and Edward had hoped to marry in youth, but had been persuaded into practical marriages to others. Though both had been set free by their partners' deaths, Charlotte, accepting the changes of the years, had decided that Edward should marry her niece. And that he refused to be led in this direction, she now thinks, may not have been due to real love, but to his mere obstinacy in clinging to the youthful dream, an obstinacy that blinded him to the truer affinity.

But if Charlotte has only now awakened to these two disturbing possibilities—that passion may be a power that has to be respected, and that devotion to principle may look suspiciously like inability to appreciate reality—the reader has already had evidence of both. The first we see in concentrated form in the tale told by the visiting English lord of "The Amazing Young Neighbors." The second we see in the portrait of that irrepressible fountain of moral precepts on the sanctity of marriage, Mittler.

The tale is a miniature version of the novel's own situation but one in which the lovers win instead of lose. For the lovers here too pass each other over at first and learn only after a mistaken bond has been formed—the girl's engagement to another man—that they need each other for their life's happiness. In the tale, however, the "wrong" marriage has not yet taken place, and the passionate girl is saved from the pain of renunciation and self-chosen death, as Ottilie and Edward will not be, by the miracle of a second chance. It is true that after the two mothers' mere delight in seeing that their children, the girl who had tried to drown herself and the friend who had tried to save her, are alive—"Who is that?" is their exclamation—the fathers' "What is that?" registers a moral question at their reappearing as lovers. But as the pair fall to their knees and beg forgiveness and a blessing, the narrator concludes, "Who could have the heart to refuse it?" (Bk. II, Ch. 10). Who indeed, especially nowadays? Would it not be shortsighted and cruel to insist on keeping faith with a mistake, and in the face of a love that has shown itself, by a near suicide, to be valued more highly than life?

Mittler, of course, runs about defending marriage, not necessarily engagements. But this former minister, whose zest for preaching is such that he takes over a christening he is supposed to be only observing and drones on, oblivious, while the elderly, officiating minister has a seizure and dies, is surely Goethe's acknowledgment that even that defense can come out looking wrong. There is no doubt that Mittler, a mere bachelor, "all breathing human passion far above," is an outsider to the problems he is always trying to solve. He has far more respect for general principles than for the needs and feelings of actual people, and in his insensitivity to others' feelings, he not only causes pain, but even defeats his own ends, repelling those he seeks to persuade.

And yet. With regard to the tale, we are told that Charlotte was disturbed when she heard it because she recognized it as a true story in which the Captain had been involved. He can only have been the man who was jilted. And if we have not remembered him before, this reminder of the poor bridegroom who, seeking his lost fiancée, "was almost beside himself" (Bk. II, Ch. 10), must awaken us out of the spell cast by the persuasive lovers. It is not mere stuffy principle they are doing violence to, but a loving human heart, whose pain will pay for their happiness. "Who could have the heart to refuse them?" is all very well, but the story at least grows ambiguous.

And just as we end by doubting that appeal for the rights of passion, so we must question whether Mittler is merely the satire on his own devotion to principles and to marriage that he often appears to be. Goethe, insisting on the truth of Mittler, declared, "There is not a line in the *Wahlverwandtschaften* that is not taken from my own experience" (Eckermann, p. 289). And in fact, this "mediator," whose nature it is to be "ever . . . hopeful and striving" (Bk. II, Ch. 15)[4] and who saw marriage and the family as a way, not of denying man's feelings, but of controlling them, through a sense of their "connection" with the human community, toward their own most lasting fulfillment—this Mittler does, in fact, resemble his author, who, for that matter, might also be charged with a rather chilling tendency to general views where the rest of us would be concentrating on particulars. The irony directed at Mittler is surely a kind of self-criticism. It is Goethe's acknowledgment that even the principles he most deeply cherished might seem cold and irrelevant unless accompanied by a full recognition of the cost of obeying them. For, looked at by itself, everything Mittler says is true, however untimely or irritating. At least, it is the application to marriage of a conception of the relationship between the individual and the larger world he must live in, the present moment and the future, which is surely entitled to respect. That final outburst of his which sends Ottilie to her death—his insistence that children should be taught not the wrongness of adultery, but the rightness of a loving marriage, which all men should try to help over the inevitable difficulties; his belief that "any obligation [or "duty," as the word *Pflicht* is usually translated] and particularly this obligation which joins husband and wife indissolubly, is the source of the greatest happiness" (Bk. II, Ch. 18)—is clearly Goethe's own view, and the reason he consents to give up to agony and death a creature so beautiful to him in every way as Ottilie. And the proof that the idea is his is that it is also hers! For it is she who has pronounced on herself, and is now by starvation ruthlessly executing, the sentence of death. Mittler's outburst is not for her a fresh accusation, but only a reminder of what she had briefly and unconsciously permitted herself to forget.

Ottilie is, in fact, the bearer of the novel's fullest meaning, and the polarities between which we have been moving with our "and yets" are, in her, combined into a unity. Edward, imitating her martyrdom with difficulty at the end, calls her a "genius." She is, indeed, especially gifted, and a chief element of her gift is that, like the artist who knows that the particular is nothing unless related to the universal, but that the universal is also nothing unless it is embodied in particulars, she is equally responsive to the immediate world of feeling and that more remote world of its connections and consequences to which we are directed by our moral imagination. This is the meaning of the Tutor's account of how she learns, of her need to grasp "connections." The love Ottilie feels, at first unconscious of what it is and where it might lead and later doubtfully yielding to it because of all the "reasonable" arguments she has heard from the Count and from her lover, is evidence that she can feel as strongly as any romantic Edward. But in her renunciation, when she learns that Charlotte is not ready to give him up, and in her final resolution to "atone" when Edward's embraces near the lake are followed by the child's death, she seems as ruthless against feeling as any Mittler. (To our current morality, the "sin" which requires her "atonement"—as distinct from the mere accident of the child's death—may be hard to discover. Still, if we grant the possibility that psychological subtlety may be applied in the service of our obligations and not only of our wishes, it is not really absurd for her to detect in her own yielding to Edward's arguments and kisses a secret complaisance, against deep-lying doubts, to her own desire.) Of course, she is neither an Edward nor a Mittler, for she is drawn with equal power, as I have said, not just to one of these warring opposites, but to both. And it is because she knows there is no other way to be loyal to both that she chooses to die. If Ottilie returns, among the others at the end, to the happiness of loving Edward as in the early days, it is only because she has earned the right to do so by that irrevocable decision. It is true that Mittler's last reminder turns out to be needed. But that reminder is not what kills her, as some readers have supposed. Mittler's outburst only sends her fleeing to her room, and it is there that, already weakened by starvation, she receives the killing blow. Her servant Nanny is in the room, admiring the dress Ottilie has been making for Edward's birthday out of the materials contained in his hitherto untouched love gift. "Look!" the child exclaims in delight. "It is a wedding gown worthy of you!" And immediately after, "Ottilie, hearing these words, sank upon the sofa" (Bk. II, Ch. 18). Goethe himself has alerted us to the importance in his novel of the precept "Whosoever looketh on a woman to lust after her hath committed adultery with her already in his heart,"[5] which does not, surely, imply any simple puritanical condemnation, but only reminds us of the subtlest forms that the novel's central conflict may take. It is because, after that first jostling by Mittler, Ottilie has been awakened by Nanny's exclamation to the hungry heart's profound duplicity—even hers, which is thus revealed to be dreaming of a wedding while the deceived mind prepares for a birthday—that she now hurries, as it were, into the only real safety from its irrepressible hunger.

Of course, that both lovers are willing to pay for their love so heavily seems by itself, whatever the hungry heart goes on dreaming, to change its moral quality, and to entitle it to the respect of even the strong and the wise. We see this moral change in Edward as, silent and starving, he follows Ottilie's road to death. When he occasionally breaks his silence or feels a wish to eat, he mocks himself as an ordinary man struggling clumsily to imitate what had been so easy for the naturally gifted Ottilie, and he firmly recalls himself to his chosen end. His very tone is thus different from the self-righteously demanding tone of his simple romanticism. And Charlotte, one of the strong and the wise, acknowledges what such love has earned and buries him beside the dead girl.

But Ottilie's martyrdom is not the same as Edward's. He chooses to die because his beloved is dead, while she has died to be true to both her love and her principles. We have yet to confront, however, the deepest meaning of this double allegiance which constitutes her special "genius." It begins to rise into view with an episode that the contemporary reader may have some trouble swallowing. In the madness of remorse at helping her mistress starve by eating her food, the child Nanny leaps from a window during Ottilie's funeral procession, is nearly killed, and a moment later is restored to perfect health and sanity by the feeling that the dead girl has touched and forgiven her. Thereafter, though many are skeptical, a few who share the child's faith in the power of Ottilie's holiness are similarly healed when they visit her coffin in the chapel. Granted that Nanny's cure is a bit excessive for current tastes, the episode does not really require us to accept miracles, I would suggest, but something much easier: the power over the body of even mistaken beliefs if they are sufficiently intense. And since the girl who induces such belief has acquired her hold over the feelings of others by that strange gift for uniting in herself the extremes of both passionate love and passionate devotion to self-denying principle, or, in the old terms, both nature and spirit, both the human and the divine, a meaning even more audacious than that of "miracle" now arises.

Is not Goethe suggesting that the Christian story itself is an embodiment of his idea? And though Jesus is the central image of that union of human and divine, whose double allegiance can fulfill itself only in death, and who brings blessings on those whom he inspires with sufficient faith, we need not think of Ottilie as simply a version of Jesus. For the novel has collected around her a number of details suggestive not only of Christianity, but of Catholicism (she alone felt at home amid the Architect's "early German" pictures of saints, angels, and happy believers; he and she help restore a chapel of that period, where, because he sees her so, he paints her face among the hovering angels). And Catholicism is the form of Christianity which gives us saints who literally unite in themselves that allegiance to both the human and the divine, who are, in effect, martyred by it, and who are thereafter a source of blessings to believers.

Now, in this view of the novel, nature is posed *against* spirit—except in Ottilie—and I have been reminded by a distinguished Goethe scholar[6] that in Goethe's own view they form a "continuum," that Ottilie's headaches in the vicinity of the underground coal deposits, her power to move the pendulum in the Englishman's "ESP" experiments, the resemblance of the baby to the two lovers of whom its parents were dreaming when it was conceived, are intended as evidence of the interaction, the oneness, of nature and spirit. I must agree that this is, in fact, a deep-lying element of the novel's meaning, and worthy of its own emphasis. And yet all that has here been said seems to me in harmony with it. For to point out that Ottilie feels the claims of nature and spirit with equal force is to acknowledge that for Goethe the "genius" does indeed grasp them as aspects of a complex unity. That idea, however, does not contradict the fact that in the life we live in the world (even the genius) they are, in effect, in opposition. It is because most of us can rarely honor one of them without neglecting the other that we fall into endless conflict or alternate endlessly between extremes. And this is why Ottilie's passionate fidelity to both at once is associated by Goethe with their miraculous union in Jesus and the saints, just as her suffering, her death, and the healing faith she inspired in some echoes the way their stories end. For us, in short, it is usually religious faith that makes possible the belief in a unity underlying the world of conflicting appearances, and only a belief of rare intensity can perform that literal interaction of nature and spirit exemplified in the cure, by the mind, of the body's ills.

Such "unrealistic" belief is not, of course, available to all. One example of it was bitingly rejected by Thomas Mann. He regarded the novel's last paragraph, that vision of the happy moment when the lovers, now lying side by side, will awaken together, as a sop thrown to the simpleminded.[7] Still, Goethe never quite rejected immortality, though he had his own idea of the form it might take. May not that paragraph be seriously intended both for those who can believe and for the rest of us, less fortunate, who cannot? For to dream that such lovers may be united in another world serves at the same time to remind believers of an age-old comfort and to emphasize for the rest of us the novel's pitiless conclusion, that here, where we live the only lives we know, they have not come together, and they never will.

It is because the novel's deepest meaning is that its conflict, in spite of all our desperate and ingenious struggles, can never be resolved in this world that the pain of the story grows as we reflect. The pain was Goethe's, and the novel is his attempt to understand it. Its author was not the vigorous man in his prime who had decided his inner health required him to leave Weimar and Frau von Stein's ethereal love for Italy, who did so, and who there enjoyed a pagan sensuality and a classic art most beneficial for body and mind—*he* wrote *Wilhelm Meister's Apprenticeship*. It was the aging man who had learned from the beautiful young Minna Herzlieb, and perhaps from others as well, of desires that could be neither fulfilled nor renounced. This Goethe created Ottilie and attained to tragedy.

Dostoevsky's
The Brothers Karamazov

> You say that Dostoevsky described himself in his heroes, imagining that all people are like that. Well then! The result is that even in these exceptional characters, not only we who are his kinsmen, but foreigners also, recognize themselves and their own souls.
>
> Tolstoy in his *Letters,* II, 492

I was very young when I joined those who called Dostoevsky's last novel (published in 1880) the greatest ever written, and I have long realized that assigning rank to works of art serves chiefly to give vent to our feelings. But having just reread it, I find myself driven again to the old extravagance. Accordingly, I begin as follows. If we go to novels to share in the experience of other human beings and in the insight that gives it meaning, then for me *The Brothers Karamazov is* the best of them all, its characters the richest revelation of what we are, the experience it gives the most intense and the most moving, and its meaning—at least in the exploration of issues urgently important to our lives—the most profound and the most grandly inclusive. With a work so vast one need not, I think, apologize for adding one's own view to the many already in existence, whether one offers novelties or only confirms with fresh emotion or from a fresh perspective what has been said by others. But it seems to me especially useful to keep renewing our intimacy with this novel because its main effect is to shock us out of the simplifications about human life that are nearly impossible for most of us to resist, and, in particular, to challenge the prevailing assumptions of modern culture.

That effect was Dostoevsky's purpose in writing it. The novel was deliberately composed to express with a culminating fullness his opposition to the "progressive" ideas which dominated intellectual life in his time and place—and still do in ours. In brief, it was written to refute the view that man's suffering and his crimes are caused chiefly by social injustice, and that a rational reorganization of society, eliminating inequality and hunger, would set men free to be good, as well as happy. But the novel remains a challenge—and even a shock—not only because that idea is still ours (though its fruits in modern history have somewhat shaken our confidence), but because of the other idea, the religious idea, it boldly proposes instead. Referring to the rationalistic, materialistic, progressive Russian intelligentsia (called Westerners because their ideas came from Europe), Dostoevsky said, "*I shall compel them to recognize* that a pure, real Christian is not something abstract but is graphically real, possible, obviously present, and that Christianity is the sole refuge for the Russian land from all its woes."[1] Nor are this novel's power, beauty, and truth attained in spite of such "retrograde" ideas; they are in large part made out of them. For Dostoevsky's art is an art that gives us ideas in their living state, as they come from, affect, or are qualified by character and experience; and if I, "liberal" and nonreligious (for that matter, a Jew as well), find *The Brothers Karamazov* so overwhelming, this is because it does, in fact, embody its author's Christian way of understanding human experience in a story and characters that "compel" assent.

But before we try to see how, it will be helpful to look at the tradition and the experience it came from. To begin with, *The Brothers Karamazov* has the advantage of being a nineteenth-century Russian novel. It shares with the otherwise very different works of Gogol, Turgenev, Tolstoy, and Chekhov a way of looking at people that makes them, on the whole, more intimately moving than those of other times and places. "All of us came out of Gogol's 'Overcoat,'" Dostoevsky was once supposed to have said. And though it now appears he never said it, he surely might have. For that tale dramatizes in its plot what is implied by its opening paragraphs, which tell us how Akaky Akakyevich Bashmatchkin, the comically named, comically poor, comically humble clerk, unable to bear the comic office teasing he naturally provoked, suddenly cried, "Let me be. Why do you do this to me?" and how a young newcomer to the office, who had joined in the teasing, "stopped . . . as if awakened from a trance. . . . And for a long time to come, during his gayest moments, he would suddenly see in his mind's eye the little balding clerk and he would hear the words 'Let me be. Why do you do this to me?' and within these words rang the phrase 'I am your brother.' And the young man would cover his face with his hands."[2]

That we feel the characters in nineteenth-century Russian fiction to be brothers means that, in spite of the way they look from outside, they are usually seen at last from within, from their own point of view. To see a human being from his own point of view is to see, under all that makes him more or less grotesquely other, a creature whose deepest needs we share, who became what he is by steps that are familiar to us because we have all taken them (if not always so far), and whose vices and virtues are often bafflingly intermingled. It is the sense of something like this under the oddities that compose the human surface that accounts for the unique reality and the unique beauty are of nineteenth-century Russian fiction. And that reality and that beauty are in Dostoevsky raised, as it were, to the tenth power—the reality because his experience was a peculiarly rich education in the painful secrets of the inner life; and the beauty, a beauty of "Christlike" compassion, because of his intense need for it and because of his own recoil into pity from a savagery he had found inside himself. In fact, no other writer (except Sade) focuses so deliberately on cruelty or evokes pity with such irresistible poignance.

The chief outer facts of his education by experience are well known. There was the supposed murder of his often harshly strict father by serfs when Dostoevsky was eighteen;[3] his epilepsy, with its psychic effects of euphoria before the seizure and depression and guilt afterward; his rapture of pride at being hailed as a genius at twenty-four by the great critic Belinsky for his first novel (*Poor Folk*), and the shaming disappointment of his comparative failure with the works which immediately followed; most important of all, his arrest for conspiracy at twenty-eight by Czar Nicholas's secret police (for, though always a Christian, he shared then the new dreams of a more just society); the mock execution by firing squad which he believed would be a real one up to the moment when the command of "Fire!" was to be given, and was withheld; and the four years of hard labor among criminals in a Siberian prison, and the five years of exile which followed. (Dostoevsky emerged from prison in effect to kiss the hand of the absolute power that had punished him, already the "reactionary" who was to produce his greatest works.) Moreover, that same Dostoevskian turbulence is to be seen in his experiences with women: with the Siberian woman who became, after she was widowed, his first wife, but who nearly gave him up for another man on the eve of their wedding (the rival was invited to the wedding and warmly befriended by Dostoevsky!); with the beautiful willful, "new woman" he later followed about Europe in a frenzy of desire even after she had cast him off in Paris for a handsome Spaniard; and with the sane, domestic twenty-year-old he married at forty-five, in the raging, jealous sexual passion for her he carried into his old age. And there was the addiction to gambling which compelled him once to take from his second wife, and lose, the last of their money, money he knew was needed for the baby's food. It is clear that, without going as far as his heroes—to rape, murder, madness, suicide—he knew at first hand all the extremes of feeling out of which came both the violence of his plots and, as he boldly pursued what such feelings implied, the complexity and sweep of his thought.[4]

But one kind of experience underlies Dostoevsky's fiction more than any other. This is not unusual. The imagination of most serious writers turns out to have been tethered all their lives to one powerful experience, their works, as they grow, exploring it from different angles and more and more deeply, until, among the best, it becomes a way of understanding the world. For Dostoevsky that experience was the ambivalence he dramatized in his second story, *The Double*, a work he called "a confession."[5] It is the ambivalence that results from humiliation. For the tale's hero, Mr. Golyadkin, obsessed to the point of mania by his total insignificance and powerlessness and the contempt he expects from everyone around him, a nightmare comes true. His place in the world is taken from him by the Other he longs to be, an identical Mr. Golyadkin who has all the gifts for succeeding among people which our hero affects to despise and who becomes his lordly conqueror, on the job and in society. What will recur throughout Dostoevsky's career is the weakling-victim's explosive mixture of abjectness and pride in the presence of the masterful humiliator, the hurt pride simmering below the abjectness, or an enfeebling certainty of insignificance waiting under the pride, and both perfectly sincere—so that when a parade of the one is suddenly, at some last straw, interrupted by an explosion of the other, it surprises even the weakling himself. Moreover, this seesaw of humility and pride develops quickly into another of love and hate. For Mr. Golyadkin and all his brothers and sisters to come, the shame caused by that powerful other is so agonizing that at the ineffable relief, or prospect, or just hope of a friendly word, hatred can vanish in a burst of even tearfully grateful love. Not that the love is to be trusted either. The "eternal husband," in the little masterpiece of that name, who tenderly nursed the lover of his dead wife through a day of illness, surprised them both by coming to his bed that night with a razor in his hand.

Then, in *Notes from Underground*, the post-Siberian work which is a kind of overture to his greatest novels, we see that same Golyadkin—with a sword-clanking officer as his Masterful Humiliator—but a Golyadkin richly conscious and well read and steeped in years of solitary brooding, and so, as is typical of the characters of those later novels, carrying what he is to hitherto undreamed-of extremes. We recognize him in the very style of his opening monologue, since in it he is hopelessly seeking, and rejecting, the love of the reader he claims to scorn.

And not only does sadomasochism now appear, his hero being "a man who tries to find pleasure even in the feeling of his own humiliation."[6] The moral ugliness this hero confesses to is now shown to be the underside, the inevitable accompaniment, of human freedom and all its beautiful achievements. For the contemptible weakling who retaliates for his own shame by horribly shaming the prostitute he has awakened to love is also the passionate champion of Dostoevsky's most cherished political idea—that the material welfare promised by the new Western theories is worth less to man than the freedom, even if only the freedom to seek suffering, it requires him to give up. His lofty wisdom can't save him from his ugliness, however, because, as Dostoevsky wrote to his brother, his hero was intended to demonstrate "the need of faith and Christ,"[7] that is, the need of what can save us from the ego-driven reason. The obsessive Dostoevsky experience of the "double" begins to lead very far. And why not? Isn't the experience of feeling oneself weak and shamed and of being compelled to compensating dreams fundamental in our lives—as children dominated by adults and as adults dominated by "reality" or, if we believe it, God. Then too, the one kind of ambivalence becomes a clue to others, to the great fact of a self hidden below, repressed by, and opposing the self of which we are conscious. There is thus material in such an experience, given, of course, the mind and the genius of Dostoevsky, for a whole world of people, actions, feelings, ideas—in fact, for *The Brothers Karamazov*.

Where earlier novels dramatized one or another aspect of the progressive Zeitgeist he opposed (*Crime and Punishment*, for instance, the unbearable isolation of a young intellectual who acts, by way of a "useful" murder, as if reason could be the supreme guide in human relations, or *The Possessed*, the political crimes and fatuities resulting from the same "nihilistic" break with the nonrational roots of our moral life), his last novel was a deliberate attempt to set forth the basic life-problem itself—that of human nature and the hell on earth it can produce—in all its actual difficulty, its resistance to rational, progressive solutions. Moreover, if the novel seems loose and improvisatory in the prose of individual pages—and perhaps too in its way of stitching its early scenes together by the rushing here and there of his "hero" Alyosha, sometimes on errands, sometimes purely on impulse—it is no "fluid pudding" in its structure. It is the story of a parricide, and of what leads to it and follows from it, and each of its four "parts" and the twelve "books" divided equally among them and concluding with an epilogue is as functional as the divisions of a well-made play. Not only do all the actions and relationships develop with a grandly simple logic from the opening situation, but the story being itself the answer to a fundamental question—what is man and how can he be saved from that hell of his own making?—and its major characters thinking as well as feeling people, each plot development is also, up to the last page, a development in the answer to that question, a further illumination.

The novel's logic of structure can be seen from the start. By the time of the meeting at the monastery where Alyosha, the youngest son, is a novice, a meeting arranged by his father in the cell of Alyosha's saintly teacher Father Zosima in order, he claims, to patch up his quarrel with the eldest son Dmitri, we have been shown the Karamazov family as an example of human nature's most dangerous possibilities. We have seen in the father the "ordinary sensual man" whom animal appetite carries to disgusting extremes. To such a father, the sons, abandoned in childhood when the death of his second wife set him free to bring a "harem" into the house, became, as they reached manhood, mere rivals (except for Alyosha, for reasons to be noted) for power, money, and sex. We have seen too that in the eldest son Dmitri that same raw appetite equals the old man's in intensity, and that the trouble promised by such a pair is exactly embodied in the primitive, the archetypal, conflict over money and sex raging between them. They are quarreling over an inheritance of which the son believes he has been cheated. And though Dmitri is bethrothed to a spiritually "noble" and beautiful heiress, he has been seized by a Karamazov passion for the far less respectable woman already desired by his father to the point of frenzy.

The clear function of that meeting in the monastery cell is to present both the first foreshadowing outbreak of the drama's central conflict, the conflict which is to expose the real problem of what we are, and a first statement of contemporary culture's chief ways of responding to the problem. So, for the former, we get the father's irrepressible "buffoonery," stirring up the rage he had ostensibly come to that cell to calm down, then Dmitri's "Why is such a man alive?" and the father's "Listen! Listen to the parricide!" and at last, in a startling climax which underlines the threat of tragedy, the dying old monk Zosima suddenly rising to bow to the ground before the wild-eyed Dmitri. And for the latter, to go first to the great idea the novel exists to answer, we get from Dmitri's half brother, the brilliant second son Ivan, the modern world's dominant way of thinking about the problem, the way of reason set free from religion and traditional moral assumptions, but that way carried by the young man's proud preference for truth over comforting error to what for Dostoevsky was its logical conclusion:

> That there was no law of nature that man should love mankind, and that if there had been any love on earth hitherto, it was not owing to a natural law, but simply because men have believed in

immortality . . . and that [without such belief] egoism even unto crime must become not only lawful, but even recognized as inevitable, the most rational, even honorable outcome of [man's] position.

Since Dmitri reacts to this justification for crime with the pointed exclamation, "I'll remember it!" it is clear that Ivan's idea is about to be tested by the unfolding drama.

But the dominant ideas of the Zeitgeist, which the time's best representatives grasp and suffer in their purity, are always parodied, as it were, by smaller minds, who exploit them for vanity or profit. So we are also introduced at the monastery to Dmitri's aristocratic uncle Miusov, "a Liberal of the 40's and 50's [i.e., of the socially conscious generation of Belinsky], a free-thinker and atheist," who is proud both of his advanced opinions and of the good breeding that enables him to hold his own in the elegant drawing rooms of the establishment. Miusov is not only angered by the disrespectful vulgarities of Fyodor Karamazov (which spoil the "civilized," ego-gratifying encounter with ancient superstition he has been expecting to enjoy), but quick to disassociate himself from Ivan's shocking extremes of free thought.

If Miusov is the Zeitgeist's mere froth, Alyosha's fellow novice Rakitin, who joins the constellation of intellectual positions ranged around the novel's problem a minute after that scene in the cell, is its true champion. For he must take life seriously. As a poor priest's son, who resents his poverty and his social inferiority, he is already planning to leave the monastery for a career more in line with his abilities and more likely to pay. And he is no fool: in filling in Alyosha on the novel's other love rivalry, that between Ivan and Dmitri over Katerina Ivanovna, Dmitri's soon-to-be-discarded fiancée, he makes comments clearly entitled to respect. Throughout the novel, in fact, we will find Rakitin representing in his character and tone, as well as in his thought, the attitudes that came to so many, and especially to the young Dostoevsky, by way of the radical critic Belinsky, who was for Dostoevsky first an influence, then, in their talks, an increasingly irritating opponent, and, after a final quarrel and for the rest of his life, the intellectual type he most detested. To begin with, Rakitin dismisses with contempt, as a rational materialist, the monk's "holy mummery." Zosima, he says, "tapped the ground with his head" before a man so obviously headed for violence because it was an easy way to get credit for prophecy. But then, as a liberal humanist, he also rejects Ivan's black view of man. In his opinion, to say "everything is lawful" is "an attractive theory for scoundrels," or at least for "pedantic poseurs 'haunted by unsolved doubts'. . . . His whole theory is vileness!" he goes on. "Humanity will find in itself the power to live for virtue even without believing in immortality. It will find it in love for freedom, for equality, for fraternity." We will not be surprised when Rakitin later dismisses Dmitri's religious-philosophic questions with "You'd better think about the extension of civil rights, or even of keeping down the price of meat. You will show your love for humanity more simply and directly by that than by philosophy," or when it turns out he is collecting data for an article to prove Dmitri couldn't help murdering his father because he was "corrupted by his environment." And surely, we mid-twentieth-century Americans must recognize that, give or take a nuance, these ideas are also ours.

The novel's answer to the Zeitgeist variously represented by Ivan, Miusov, and Rakitin will come from the youngest brother Alyosha and his beloved "father and teacher," Zosima. But Alyosha is a listener and not a talker, like his brothers, and he expresses his "position" mainly by what he is, a nature we will examine in a moment. Enough to say now that his youthful decision to live uncompromisingly for God is made convincing by the fact that he was drawn to the monastery by passionate devotion to its celebrated "elder." For what in Alyosha is unconscious or half-conscious impulse has in Father Zosima, as we will see, grown conscious and been carried all the way—to the point of genius; the two are, in fact, different versions or stages of that Christian answer to the novel's core question. And though Zosima's talk during the meeting instantly brings his genius before us, it is his electrifying action, his bow to Dmitri, that gives us most fully, because with the wide suggestiveness of a symbol, the novel's opening statement of the Christian answer. As he explains it later to Alyosha, "I bowed down . . . to the great suffering in store for him." Where Ivan has offered a chilling assertion of the ego's right, in the absence of any prohibitions the reason can respect, to whatever it wishes, and Miusov mere poses of enlightenment and worldliness, pertinent to nothing, and Rakitin, a confidence in man's reason and nobility that soared far above the real Dmitri, whom he despises, the monk, with his bow, showed that he had *seen* Dmitri, seen him in his actuality, and instead of presuming to explain or judge, gave him an intense, trembling sympathy.

But this beginning sets forth only the donnée which the novel will explore, and thereby too that surface of things we see on a first approach. And since, as I have said, what Dostoevsky's characters are is deeply related to what they think—since, moreover, it is a chief element of their supremacy as fictional creations that they are as misleading and contradictory on the surface as you and I—one way to get at the novel's ideas, as well as its quality, is to look back at them more closely. And this means that we must examine what Dostoevsky's clue of human "doubleness" enables him to reveal below their surface.

But before turning to the characters who dramatize the novel's problem and its two great contending solutions, we might note the inadequacy to that problem of Rakitin's rational progressive humanism. For it is an inadequacy Dostoevsky himself makes plain on Rakitin's first appearance, as well as on all his others. We see at once that his lofty views, which pretend to be the voice of reason and justice, in fact come from—and serve—a character which is not so lofty. Not only is it obvious that in his "shrewd" assumption of Father Zosima's duplicity, he is smugly simplifying what is complex and ascribing to another the kind of motives his needy careerist's ego knows best. His rejection of Ivan's "vile" idea of man on behalf of freedom, equality, and fraternity is expressed with a telltale heat and abusiveness that reveal a small mind's jealousy of a greater, as well as a social climber's of the higher social status of the Karamazovs. And we see the same Rakitin in the talk in prison that Dmitri reports to Alyosha, in his claim to be laying siege to a rich widow so her money can enable him to be "of great social utility," on which Dmitri comments: "They have this social justification for every nasty thing they do," or when he says that lowering the price of meat shows a truer love for humanity than "philosophy," and Dmitri observes, "Well, but you, without a God are more likely to raise the price of meat, if it suits you, and make a ruble on every kopeck." All this is a caricature, no doubt; we liberal secular humanists are not all so vulgar or transparent in our egoism. But the caricature clearly embodies a truth, the truth that our claim to acting on behalf of reason and justice—of liberty, equality, and fraternity—is always being mocked, and often without our realizing it, by the hidden reality of what we are, and that without a philosophy, a principle, or *something* to restrain the greedy, subtle ego, we may indeed find it hard to resist raising the price of meat if we actually, not just hypothetically, get the chance to do so.[8] And though we do have our own ways to restrain the ego—for example, the "checks and balances" of democracy—they confirm rather than invalidate what Dostoevsky shows us in Rakitin, and the rest of the novel.

But the error in Rakitin's progressive, idealistic assumptions about man is seen best in the portraits of Fyodor Pavlovich Karamazov and his eldest son Dmitri. In them Dostoevsky has most fully represented— one may say, confessed—the human mixture he found in himself, just as Ivan and Alyosha (Karamazovs also, as we are often pointedly told, and therefore aware from within of the appalling data) represent the two religious-philosophic views by which he was himself divided and out of whose conflict his great novels emerged. The Karamazov father is indeed a horrible old man, but he is horrible, after all, because of an excess of something not itself evil, that is, because the sensual appetite which life requires attains in him a vitality civilization is powerless to curb. He sired Smerdyakov, for instance, because, as he boasted, even the grunting, stinking town idiot Lizaveta, for whom his fellow revelers one night expressed only "lofty repugnance," had "a certain piquancy." As he later tells Alyosha, "To my mind there are no ugly women. The very fact that she is a woman is half the battle." Moreover, though his sexual lust can become sadism—he liked to act deliberately cold to Alyosha's mother and then reduce her to a "tinkling quiet, nervous, queer little laugh" by sudden passionate devotion, kissing her feet, etc.—we are not permitted to see him as a mere grotesque other than ourselves. "Nihilism appeared among us," Dostoevsky says in his *Notebook*, "because *we are all nihilists* [italics in original]. . . . We're all to the last man Fyodor Pavloviches" (p. 769). That is, we are all nihilists because, with the loss of our old religious and moral certainties, we no longer securely believe in what says no to sensual appetite. As old Karamazov says, "Sin is sweet. All abuse it, but all men live in it, only others do it on the sly, and I, openly." And if this suggests our own kinship with his "animal" nature, it should also remind us that he and his kind will probably share in our humanity. In fact, the novel is strewn with evidence of the old man's "doubleness," starting with the first chapter's concluding observation about the contradictory reports of his response to the death of his first wife, Dmitri's mother, that he shouted with joy and that he wept without restraint: "It is quite possible that both versions are true."

For instance, he knows and feels himself the ugliness of what he is. Though drunk, he is only half kidding when he tells Alyosha that if the devils have no hooks for dragging sinners down to hell, "il faudrait les inventer," for "if they don't drag me down what justice is there in the world?" Then, as Dmitri says to Rakitin in prison, "The Karamazovs are not blackguards, but philosophers . . . and though you've studied, you are not a philosopher—you are a low fellow." He means that philosophy comes from a zest for naked reality more in harmony with passion, even ugly passion, than with the shrewd self-control of those busily calculating what will pay. In fact, we see the old sot's interest in naked reality not only in his undisguised appetites, but in the oddly poignant intensity with which he, like his sons, discusses the fundamental questions. When Smerdyakov, showing off the freethinking he had learned from Ivan, "logically" refutes the elderly servant Grigori's simple faith, the father contemptuously dismisses such village-atheist cleverness as mere blindness to what those questions are about. And when to his thrice-repeated "Is there a God?" Ivan answers "No" each time and Alyosha "Yes," the suspicion that "most likely Ivan's right" *bothers* him—quite as if God and justice and life's meaning really matter. Finally, what is his theatrical buffoonery among the respectable if not that same doubleness in action? Father Zosima explains it during the scene in his cell. "Do not be so ashamed of yourself, for that is at the root of all." And we get an immediate demonstration of how this works in his rapid shifts from ecstatic gratitude for the monk's compassionate insight to mockery of both of them, the two responses coming together in the cry, "Blessed be the womb that bare thee, and the paps that gave thee suck—the paps especially." Such psychological "iridescence" (George Eliot's word), such rapid alternation of shame and defiance of shame, reminds us, of course, of Dostoevsky's early "confession," *The Double.* And I wonder if it is not precisely to hint that this late version of Mr. Golyadkin is also a confession that the author gave him his own first name.

But all of Dostoevsky's characters come from their author's inner life, and it is actually Dmitri, sharing the old man's animal appetite, but loving with equal intensity what opposes it, who represents that inner life most richly. "Man is broad, too broad, indeed. I'd have him narrower," Dmitri says to Alyosha in "The Confession of an Ardent Heart" (the title of the three chapters devoted to their talk) that follows that explosion in the monastery. And we see at once how much his broadness contains in the passionate gloss on Schiller's "Hymn to Joy," with which his confession begins. The poem tells us that the joy-fostered "force of ferment" by which nature "enticed each blade toward the light" and evolved "the solar systems" brings "To angels—vision of God's throne, To insects—sensual lust." "I am that insect, brother . . . " he goes on. "All we Karamazovs are such insects, and, angel as you are, that insect lives in you, too, and will stir up a tempest in your blood." But what creates his trouble is that, as he cries out after reciting the poem, "Though I may be following the devil, I am Thy son, O Lord, and I love Thee and I feel the joy without which the world cannot stand." Moreover, not only is Karamazov-man drawn by both "the ideal of the Madonna" and "the ideal of Sodom," yielding to Sodom even as he reaches for the Madonna, and continuing to adore the Madonna in the depths of Sodom. The two ideals are versions of one thing. It is "beauty" that he sees in each, even in Sodom. For "what to the mind is shameful is beauty and nothing else to the heart. . . . The awful thing is that beauty is mysterious as well as terrible. God and the devil are fighting there and the battlefield is the heart of man." We will see later that this first outburst of Dmitri, this celebration of the "joy without which the world cannot stand," but which draws man to Sodom as well as to the Madonna, is the key to much more than the Karamazov nature.

But the confession, as it goes on, leaves no doubt that Dmitri's metaphor of Sodom refers to a perfectly concrete reality. "I loved vice. I loved cruelty," Dmitri tells Alyosha, proving it with a lip-smacking zest that resembles his father's. And it is the "uncontrolled passions" of the "degraded sensualist" (his own words about himself) which produce the novel's interweaving lines of plot. They do so not only by issuing in the frenzy to keep Grushenka from his father which brings about the murder and the trial, but also by giving Dmitri—as an impulsive man of action, not an intellectual—the role of the Masterful Humiliator in two more versions of that obsessive Dostoevsky experience. In one he takes out his rage at his father on the pathetic Captain Snegiryov, his father's mere errand boy, pulling the man along the street by his beard in the presence of the man's horrified nine-year-old son Ilusha and the boy's classmates. The man's agonized veering thereafter between proud resentment of the insult and the dread of offending imposed by his poverty and his family's need of him, and, even more, Ilusha's shame amid his mocking classmates, provide the novel's most poignant example of life's "insulted and injured," as well as the occasion for its final demonstration of how Alyosha—and what he stands for—answer their need. But it is Dmitri's sadistic shaming of Katerina Ivanovna and her retaliation by "nobility" in the resulting battle for moral superiority that gives us Dostoevsky's most profound and most brilliant version of that obsessive experience, and it is therefore worth going over here in some detail.

The battle begins when Dmitri, annoyed at the learned beauty's initial coolness, offers her the four thousand rubles needed to save her father from disgrace if she will come for them to his room one night, alone. For what defuses his nearly overpowering lust to carry the spiteful joke to its sexual conclusion, or at least to avenge himself by some horrible insult against the nobility that makes him feel like a "bug," is his fear that she would emerge from the encounter his moral superior, he'll have "lost the game." It is as a brilliant move in that "game" that, mastering a hatred which was "only a hairsbreadth from love," he gives her the money with a deep respectful bow. And when she, growing "horribly pale," bows low in her turn and leaves, he is seized with a wild "delight," I suspect, because they have both—after a very close call—preserved their honor. But the battle goes on—with the passionate love letter she writes next, offering to be at once his slave and his savior, and most fatefully, with the three thousand rubles she asks him to mail to a relative knowing he'll disgrace himself by spending them on Grushenka. And the brilliance and power of this version of that relationship comes from the fact that it is based not only on what is false—the weakling-victim's "underground" fantasy of becoming her humiliator's beloved friend and savior, and the dream of the "bug," quickly abandoned, of living up to such "nobility," it is also *sincere.* Though Dmitri "involuntarily" exclaims, "She loves her own virtue, not me"—to account for her sticking to a "monster" like himself when she clearly ought to prefer Ivan, he immediately hates himself for such cynicism. "What if anyone does show off a bit?" he says. "Don't I do it myself? And yet I'm sincere, I'm sincere." And it is out of this ambivalence that her great explosions come. For instance, there is the scene in which the clear-eyed Grushenka rejects her passionately affectionate forgiveness with a sly insult, and the aristocratic beauty bursts into the coarse shrieks of a stranger. And there is the climactic explosion of ambivalence at the trial. She has come there intending to help the man she "nobly" persists in loving in spite of insult. But when Ivan suddenly confesses his own guilt and puts himself in danger, that shame-born fantasy-love is swept away by her real love of Ivan, and her hatred of Dmitri shows itself naked in a furious exposure of the letter threatening to murder his father Dmitri once wrote her when drunk. After which, having doomed him, she falls to the floor in hysterical writhings at her own treachery. But Dostoevsky "tops" even this in the dazzling chapter of their meeting in prison called "For a Moment the Lies Become Truth." When Katerina Ivanovna fearfully yields to Dmitri's plea that she visit him there after his conviction—and we see them both genuinely uncertain of how they will feel—what bursts out of both, the man whose insults tormented her into fantasies, and the woman whose hatred condemned him to Siberia, is *love,* a genuine passionate love they promise never to forget even as they tell each other that their real love and real life belong forever elsewhere. Because the pain they caused each other made them matter to each other so intensely (as in a kind of marriage), they now become aware, with surprising grief, that this is a farewell to a part of themselves.

But Dmitri's "uncontrolled passions," which thus produce the novel's crimes and suffering, lead also to the awakening "blow" he tells Alyosha his kind requires, the blow which turns those passions away from the "devil" and toward "God." When the blow falls, and Dmitri's frenzy has made him a near murderer and yet brought him also, during the nightmare of the preliminary police investigation, the supreme joy of Grushenka's love, he has a dream that, in his new state, becomes a clue to his deepest need. He dreams of starving peasants and of a weeping "babe," and asking, "Why are people poor?.... Why don't they feed the babe?" he awakens in "a passion of pity" that, in the months that follow, becomes for him a "sign." What the sign means we learn in his great prison conversation with Alyosha, where we are shown the other side of the Karamazov nature, the pity which recoils from the cruelty, and the love of life which, for Dostoevsky, goes with love of one's fellows. "It's all over with me now," he has begun by announcing to Alyosha, and what he means is not that he is doomed to Siberia, but that Rakitin has just persuaded him that man's life is the mere wriggling of nerves in response to external stimuli—and the redeeming beauty associated in his mind with a soul has vanished. But as the talk brings him back to his "good dream," Rakitin's life-reducing "science" falls away; and he cries, "It's for the babe I'm going," that is, to atone, if not for the murder, of which he is innocent, then for his own part in human guilt for human suffering. And foreseeing how much of that suffering he will share with his fellow convicts, he also foresees the fundamental human need it will bring home to them, the need for joy: "In our great sorrow we shall rise again to joy, without which man cannot live nor God exist, for God gives joy. . . . And then we men underground will sing from the bowels of the earth a tragic hymn to God, with Whom is joy." And, as if to emphasize that for Dmitri—and Dostoevsky—joy and life are the same, this leads immediately to one of the many echoes in Dostoevsky's works of that terrible mock execution he had undergone in his youth: "I think I could stand anything, any suffering, only to be able to say, and to repeat to myself every moment, 'I exist.' "

Telling Alyosha of what was foreshadowed in Dmitri's face, Zosima had added, "But everything and all our fates are from the Lord," and then uttered the saying of Jesus which is the motto of the novel: "Except a corn of wheat fall into the ground and die, it abideth alone, but if it die, it bringeth forth much fruit." We now see what he meant. Dmitri's passions and their terrible consequences have led him to his great affirmation, to a sense of life as joy, and of humankind as brothers, which reconciles him to the pain and saves him from despair.

But that "tragic hymn" is only the feeling Karamazov heart affirming what it needs. The *mind* of modern man must respond with the question, Is it true or false? And as Dmitri's need is Dostoevsky's, Ivan gives us their author's negative answer, the "furnace of doubt" which he lived in all his life and of which he wrote in his *Notebooks:* "Those blockheads [his progressive opponents] have never even conceived so powerful a rejection of God" (p. 769).[9]

Like Dmitri's, and, indeed, like all the novel's philosophic conversations, Ivan's outpouring to Alyosha after that scene at the monastery is first of all a dramatic revelation of character, the ideas emerging as elements in a whole with which they may or may not be in harmony. So, long before Ivan reaches his great negations, we have learned that he too is divided. In the monastery Father Zosima had already suggested this in an observation we were clearly meant to respect. "The question [of God and immortality] is still fretting your heart . . ." and "if it can't be decided in the affirmative, it will never be decided in the negative. You know that is the peculiarity of your heart and all its suffering is due to it." But since Ivan thinks he has already answered that question in the negative, we must examine his experience to see what Zosima means. Now, as the brothers' talk begins, Alyosha observes with pleasure that under his cool intellectual facade Ivan is just "as young as other young men of twenty-three," and to this Ivan happily assents. He expects indeed that, at least until he is thirty, nothing will be able to crush his Karamazov "thirst for life," a thirst which is the "centripetal force on our planet," and which "only some driveling consumptive moralists" would call "base." So, "though I may not believe in the order of the universe, yet I love the sticky little leaves as they open in spring . . . some people . . . great deeds." He foresees too that in Europe, though he knows it is only a graveyard, he will love even the relics left by the "precious dead" of "the burning life of the past," for such a way of responding to the world is "not a matter of logic or intellect, it's loving with one's insides, with one's guts." But even as Ivan confesses this youthful love of life, he makes it clear that one can indulge it with some "shadow of nobility" only by deceiving oneself. And such self-deception, on the great questions long waiting between them to which he now turns, his intellectual pride will not permit.

If God exists—and he sweeps aside the logic-chopping arguments for and against His existence as beside the point—Ivan must reject His world. For to accept the world as ruled by God—that is, to accept it as a kind of non-Euclidean order our hopelessly Euclidean minds can never see—is to be reconciled to what, in the world we can see, outrages our sense of justice. But no ultimate harmony of the kind religion promises to lure us into such reconciliation, no promise that we will eventually learn that all moves according to God's law, or even the law of cause and effect—should reconcile us now to undeserved human suffering and unavenged human evil. And, as is well known, he doesn't leave the suffering and evil an abstraction. "To make my case clear," he presents Alyosha and us with a collection of historically true anecdotes of the torture of children so horrifying that, to his question after one, "Well—what did [the torturer] deserve? To be shot? To be shot for the satisfaction of our moral feelings? Speak, Alyosha!" even the Christian Alyosha, "with a pale twisted smile," answers, "To be shot." And though Alyosha calls his own response "absurd," Ivan cries, "The world stands on absurdities," meaning, I suggest, that no system, religious or any other, can contain all that is, and what *is* is his concern. But he attacks religion directly. Religion says that man is presented with good and evil in order to be free to choose, and that all the suffering which results is part of a "higher harmony." But "Why should he know that diabolical good and evil if it costs so much?" Ivan demands. And as for "harmony," it requires that at last we see the reason for the tortured child's tears—and forgive the torturer—but Ivan has no use for such an "at last." "Is there in the whole world a being who has the right to forgive and can forgive? I don't want harmony. From love for humanity I don't want it."

But the rejection of God's world—that is, of the faith in a moral order under the horrible appearances—is only half of his negation. When Alyosha reminds him of the Forgiver and Reconciler he has not yet mentioned, Ivan, long ready for the challenge, goes on to the great remainder, his "poem in prose" of "The Grand Inquisitor."

This famous "poem," whose wealth of meaning can only be suggested here, ascribes the view of man that for Dostoevsky follows from atheism to the Catholic Church, which he regards as the great expression of "devilish" wisdom. It turns out to be because of the same love of humanity underlying Ivan's rebellion that the burner of heretics rejects the Christ who reappears one day in sixteenth-century Spain. For he knows that Christ's refusal of the three temptations—He would not turn stones into bread because man does not live by bread alone, or prove His divinity by a miracle because He wanted men to choose Him with a free verdict of the heart, or master all kingdoms with the sword because He didn't want for man the unity of the ant heap—that refusal to win men's minds in the devil's way was a compliment deserved by only a tiny elite out of all mankind, and an intolerable burden to the rest. Christ's error had been to assume that men were capable of living in freedom. The terrible truth is that freedom leads men to an inequality in the possession of bread, and to a variety of beliefs, to which they respond with "riots of blood," with "cannibalism." For men are children who want and need what the church gave them when, having understood that this life is all there is and that they can be happy only if deceived and controlled, it abandoned Christ for "the wise spirit, the dread spirit of death and destruction." It gave them a strong authority to take over and distribute their bread, and to serve also their need to worship since the giver of bread becomes their divinity. It gave them miracles and mystery to establish faith and end the torture of free choice. And it gave them the ant-heap unity which only force can preserve to end the equal torture of doubt-engendering differences of opinion. Nor was this mere cynicism, Ivan insists. For along with the many members of that elite who cared only for the church's power and dominion, there must have been some who began in the love of Christ and who took on themselves the painful duty of lies and crimes to give their fellowmen, children as they are, whatever contentment is possible for them before they die. (The brilliance of this poem as an account of political reality is well known. To catch a glimpse of it here, we have only to recognize the resemblance of the "church" of Ivan's poem to those twentieth-century states which also promise to lift from their people, in exchange for their freedom, their adulthood, the burdens of hunger, choice, and doubt. Indeed, we have only to consider how often we are tempted to agree with those views of the Grand Inquisitor—and must agree, for they are often true!)

Alyosha sees that the Grand Inquisitor's tone and his moved response to Christ's farewell kiss betray Ivan's own inner division, and that it is he who loves a Christ, a way of feeling and judging and being, which his mind rejects. And he sees too how much is involved in this rejection. "But the little sticky leaves, and the precious tombs, and the blue sky, and the woman you love!" he says to his brother in pain. "How will you live, how will you love them?. . . . With such a hell in your heart and your head. . . . " But Ivan is ready for this too. "There is a strength to endure everything," he answers "with a cold smile," and names it: "the strength of the Karamazov baseness." And in fact, Smerdyakov's observation that it is Ivan who is most like the father is intended to be believed: in him that Karamazov "thirst for life" is also dangerously unopposed because there are no moral restraints his intelligence can respect. This is why it is he, whom his father's death and his brother's conviction would at once enrich and set free from a sexual rival, who is the novel's real parricide.

In the conflict between this "base" Ivan and the lover of "sticky leaves," "great deeds," and the rest, Dostoevsky anticipates most audaciously the discoveries of depth psychology. For the life-loving Ivan can only recoil from the ugliness of such motives and such a murder. The murder must therefore be done in a way he can avoid knowing. In fact, it is performed for him by his admiring disciple Smerdyakov, who would also profit from it and in whom complacent egoistic rationalism is opposed by nothing. When Ivan plans the murder with Smerdyakov beforehand and then discusses it with him afterward, he does so without consciously knowing what they are talking about, that is, knowing and not knowing it at the same time. Hence, Ivan's eruptions of rage when the other's sly double-talk seems to hint to his innocent "conscious" mind that they are preparing a possible murder, or that mind's uneasy surprise at his own failure to strike the other for such insults, or later, Ivan's "odd" disquiet when Dmitri's guilt grows doubtful, and his "odd" relief when it seems certain. And hence, finally, his genuine outrage when Smerdyakov forces him to know the truth at last and his immediate demand that they confess and return the money Smerdyakov had stolen when the father lay dead. (It is surely because Smerdyakov realizes then that Ivan's innocence had not been the pretense of a "clever man," as he had supposed, but sincere, and that his master and teacher cannot stand behind the ideas he had given him to live by, that his life loses its point and he kills himself.)

But a chief key to Ivan's nature is his intellectual pride. We are told that he fights off brain fever as his hour to testify draws near because he wants to "say what he has to say boldly, and so justify himself to himself." (Isn't it to insinuate a sense of this pride that the author, who calls his brothers mostly Mitya and Alyosha, refers to him almost always as Ivan Fyodorovich?) And how can one who believes in "the new moral law" and respects his own intelligence sacrifice himself for his brother-rival—that is, enact such exploded moral ideals—without profound embarrassment? It is precisely this embarrassment that, just before his appearance at the trial, gives rise to the great dialogue with the devil with which his madness begins, a dialogue in which we get, again, a wealth of meaning whose main points only can be conveyed here.

"You are the incarnation of myself," Ivan tells his talkative visitor, scorning him as a mere hallucination, "of my thoughts and feelings, but only the nastiest and stupidest of them." But the devil retaliates by reminding Ivan, as he ironically echoes even his grandest ideas, that they too come from that same nastiness and stupidity. In fact, the devil's appearance, what he says, what he provokes Ivan to say—all of this is the expression of Ivan's brilliantly corrosive self-consciousness. For instance, that the devil appears to him as a "sponger," a typical semirespectable hanger-on at rich men's tables, suggests his repressed awareness that his own nay-saying reason, because it "sees through" everything, leaves him poor in the beliefs, affirmations, heart-felt relationships life requires. For these, he must "sponge" off those who are rich in such goods, who say yes to life, who love it and live. Then, the devil makes Ivan "moan" in a boredom which is really embarrassment at his stories of priests and the sexy girls who confess to them—that is, at this exposure of the ignoble pettiness which underlies so much of his lofty skepticism—and follows that by exposing the ignoble pettiness of his annoyance: "You are really angry with me for not having appeared to you in a red glow, with thunder and lightning. . . . How could such a vulgar devil visit such a great man as you!"

But the sting is worse when the devil grows "serious." After he echoes—and demeans—Ivan's idea that he provides the "indispensable minus," the evil, which, though it ruins thousands, gives the few their chance to choose good, he refers to "a promising poem entitled 'The Grand Inquisitor,'" and Ivan explodes in a shout of rage. And the climactic insult comes when the devil quotes Ivan's humane amendment of the nihilism of the time's "new men," who "propose to destroy everything and begin with cannibalism." Just as this voice of Ivan's ruthless self-knowledge had earlier, with pretended admiration, hinted at the irrational sentimentality of his intention of saving his brother by confession, so he now "admiringly" repeats Ivan's lofty dream of what human reason can achieve. "Nothing need be destroyed . . . , " he quotes, "we only need to destroy the idea of God in man." With God replaced by the man-god, men will not only conquer nature and make a heaven of earth, but, knowing they are mortal, will love each other all the more. "And so on and so on, in the same style. Charming," he says with his gentlemanly sneer. (In the monk's cell and with Alyosha, Ivan saw through this dream too, but Dostoevsky assigns it to him here, surely, because it *is* the inevitable dream of the humane atheist and so has to be hiding in a corner of his mind.) But of course, the devil continues, the man-god's next thought will naturally be that, since the dream won't come true for at least a thousand years and, as a man-god, he does after all live by his own laws, he may as well "lightheartedly overstep all the barriers of the old morality of the old slave man" and get his. "That's all very charming," the devil concludes, "but if you want to swindle, why do you want a moral sanction for doing it?" And at this final stab—à la Luther, but in the Russian style—Ivan flings at the devil his glass of tea.

That tormented alternation in Ivan between his illogical impulse toward human decency and his contemptuous skepticism of such impulses appears in the courtroom with the dramatic clarity of open schizophrenia. It is literally two Ivans who answer the court's president, the reasonable self-protecting one who, "almost stammering," says he has "nothing in particular" to tell, and the other, who turns back abruptly to confess his guilt. And this ambivalence is to be seen in the confession itself, which is a moral action performed in a state of raging Lear-like cynicism about human morality. For, just before he is dragged shrieking from the courtroom, Ivan cries, "Who doesn't desire his father's death?" and accuses the court spectators of nastily enjoying the spectacle of a parricide they pretend to condemn. And I ask in my turn, aren't such insults—such charges that morality can be a cloak for horrors—addressed to us, and aren't they—at some level, and in some degree—true? If so, we can understand why Dostoevsky, thinking of his answer to Ivan's negation, wrote in a letter, "If it succeeds, I shall have done a good deed" (p. 759).

As I have said, that answer is the Christian faith presented in its extreme form in the behavior and teachings of Father Zosima ("I proposed to make the sixth book, *The Russian Monk*, the answer to that whole *negative side*" [p. 761; italics in original], and in Alyosha as it would manifest itself in a young Karamazov and in the Karamazov world. And the reason Dostoevsky has in fact succeeded in his aim—and goes on even in our time compelling the assent of those who don't share his religious beliefs—is that the novel is actually full of evidence, and evidence supported by the letters, that its Christian symbols are to be read as forms of expression, and are properly understood only if we grasp the human realities they suggest. Dostoevsky tells us, for instance, that the novel "is not a direct point by point answer" to Ivan's negations, but the answer appropriate to "artistic realism" (p. 762). This means not only that it will be embodied in characters and experiences whose reality we don't need to be religious to recognize. It means too that we must expect to find the characters expressing themselves in ways their own lives have made natural to them, and be ready to *translate* to get at what they have in mind. So, of the monk's exhortations he adds, "Of course, they are absurd in the ordinary sense, but in another, inner sense they are just," and he had already written, "Though I completely share the thoughts he expresses, if I had expressed them as coming *from me* personally, I would have expressed them in a different form and a different style" (p. 760; italics in original). Moreover, if Father Zosima employs these forms of expressions at their most extreme, this is only because, like Ivan and many other Dostoevsky characters, he partakes of his author's genius and so, exploring the reality they symbolize, goes *all the way*, deliberately overleaping the obvious qualifications of "common sense." In fact, it is precisely to make clear how far Zosima is from a simply literal faith that we are shown the fanatically literal Father Ferrapont, who detests him and whose way of being a Christian is much preferred by the shallow visiting monk, a kind of Rakitin on the novel's religious side.

It may be admitted that, in his passionate will to be a Christian, Dostoevsky sometimes passes over or blurs the line dividing realistic insight expressed in religious symbols from a belief that the symbols are literally true. But those of us who find impossible a literal belief in the symbols may still assent to what they suggest. For it is an old story that our ways of formulating the infinitely complex reality we are part of can never be more than "fictions" or "myths" by which we point toward, but can't hope to describe fully, certain aspects of that reality vital to our living and thinking. And since this is the case even with our scientific theories, it should not be hard to grant that the Christian language of Zosima and Alyosha, whether or not they, or even Dostoevsky, intend some part of it literally, is always, in fact, such a pointing toward, which we are entitled to read more freely than they would. Of course, each of our myths selects out of the infinite complexity certain of its aspects and not others, and so Dostoevsky's answer to Ivan's negations is indeed Christian in being the kind of insight enacted and expressed by the Christ he loved and needed so intensely.

But even without Dostoevsky's warning against being misled by Zosima's monkish lingo, we must recognize him at his first appearance as a gifted psychologist, though one whose insight is in the service of a passion to help. We see it in the way he pierces through Fyodor Karamazov's compulsive buffooneries to the truth about them and, with the unoffended firmness of an adult to a child, speaks to the core of honesty in the old scoundrel that can hear and be touched. But we see it also when Zosima briefly interrupts that meeting in the cell to greet and bless the peasant women waiting outside. His ridding one of a "devil" who inhabits her is openly explained in psychological terms. But the intensely moving exchanges between him and the other three, for all his talk of "sin" and "God," are equally an expression of humane wisdom. And it seems to me that his exhortation to the young widow tormented by a crime against her cruel husband which she confesses in a whisper we are not permitted to overhear comes as the climactic last event in that scene because it states what for Dostoevsky is the deepest insight expressed by Christianity.

Addressing her torture of conscience and her fear of retribution, he says first, "Man cannot commit a sin so great as to exhaust the infinite love of God," and finally, "Think only of repentance, continual repentance, but dismiss fear altogether. . . . Forgive the dead man in your heart what wrong he did you. Be reconciled with him in truth. If you are penitent, you love. And if you love, you are of God. All things are atoned for, all things saved by love. . . . Go, and be not afraid." The Christian language that here so boldly flouts our materialistic common sense is only, as I have suggested, an invitation to us to be equally bold in recognizing possibilities in ourselves and the world which are usually closed to that sort of common sense. For whatever else it often is, the myth of a loving God in Zosima's teaching, and indeed, in our culture generally, is clearly a way of naming the unknowable whole of which we are a part and affirming it to be beneficent, that is, on the side of life and of what helps us live. And Zosima is reminding the suffering widow of a self which such a God would see and love, of a self which is not only the lustful, greedy one we all know best, because, in his healing wisdom, he knows that to be helped to believe in that self strengthens it, or may even, by selecting it from among our many possibilities, draw it into being. But more than that, he knows it helps one to forgive oneself, to give oneself another chance, in short, to *live*—just as to be helped to believe in that better self in others helps one to forgive them, and so to be released—by "love"—from the need for vengeance which keeps the chain of life-spoiling evils going.[10]

It is worth noting that Zosima does not deny human responsibility for human evil—the importance he assigns to penitence makes that clear. And so, when he later tells his fellow monks that "no one can judge a criminal until he recognizes that he is just such a criminal as the man standing before him," this is very far from Rakitin's "liberal" idea that the criminal is not to blame because he was corrupted by environment. Indeed, that idea is the exact opposite—and corrective—of the blindness to their own natures which make the Rakitins so complacent and so dangerous as judges of others. But, as Zosima explains, to exile the criminal from the human community by self-righteous punishment only hardens him, where the forgiveness of compassionate fellow-feeling can change his heart—if not at once, then when he is ripe for it, and if not his heart, then another's. And, to look ahead, it is in order to dramatize the contrast between this kind of judgment and that of the world we live in that Dostoevsky gives us Dmitri's trial in such detail. Both the prosecutor and the defense lawyer show us not only how reason, even at its best, can go wrong amid the complexities of human behavior, but that what makes for much of the error in this time and place is precisely the self-assured rationalism and liberalism of the Zeitgeist by which they are both infected. With regard to the defense lawyer, we see this especially at the trial's conclusion, where, after his persuasive pleading for forgiveness, he makes the fatal mistake of suggesting to the jury (some of whom are peasants) that it would be mere "mystical prejudice" to call Dmitri guilty of parricide, even if he did strike the fatal blow, because, by the standards of "reason," his father was no father to him. Their verdict of guilty, completing the chapter entitled "The Peasants Stand Firm," is clearly intended to show that the people's wisdom, though wrong as to fact, is right in principle. They have rejected the time's fashionable notions on behalf of Dmitri's—and his author's—own belief in a morality that is not at the mercy of each individual's self-serving reason.

After that opening demonstration of what the monk is, we are given, in "notes" by his disciple Alyosha, the story of his life, and then a summary of his exhortations to his fellow monks before he died (one of which I have just quoted). It would take too long to show how all the quaintly orthodox-sounding Christianity in what he tells them can be translated into wisdom. But a word or two may be in order about his life-story because it is a clue to the role of Alyosha in the world of the Karamazovs. Dostoevsky gives reality to Zosima's religious awakening, the possibility of which has been planted in him earlier by a saintly dying elder brother, in a characteristic way. It comes as the result of the recoil from its "opposite," from the life of a young officer in which lust and vanity have reached a climax. On the eve of a duel he deliberately provoked because his innocent adversary had won the love of a woman he wanted, he beats bloody the face of an orderly at attention. The next morning, in a passion of remorse that has, as it were, shocked him awake, he begs the man's forgiveness. And then, after submitting to his adversary's shot at the duel, he throws his pistol down and begs his forgiveness too. This action, accompanied as it is by his thrilled explanation of what he has awakened to—that "life is a paradise" if we would only realize it, and that men are brothers, all responsible to all—makes "society" laugh at him, but they laugh "kindly and merrily," the action touches them. And we see what his socially absurd action means when it draws to him a man who, though a respected husband, father, and citizen, had once committed a murder for which another was blamed a week before dying, and who, though now safe, is tormented by remorse and fearfully tempted by Zosima's bravery to a like bravery of confession. The two have long intense talks, and once the youthful Zosima expresses impatience at the world's slowness to see what they have seen. The murderer's view is that mankind must first go to the terrible end of a period of isolation. For, in the delusion that security lies in wealth, each individual is now given over to the pursuit of self-interest, of "the greatest possible fullness of life for himself," a pursuit which in fact leads to "self-destructive impotence." That "true security is to be found in social solidarity" mankind will remember only when "the sign of the Son of Man will be seen in the heavens." Until then, to "keep the banner flying," the one who understands, even if "his conduct seems crazy," must "set an example and so draw men's souls out of their solitude and spur them to some act of brotherly love so that the great idea may not die." This is the role of Alyosha Karamazov.

Dostoevsky calls Alyosha his "hero," and though he is overshadowed in the drama we have by Dmitri and Ivan (he would have loomed much larger in the sequel for which this novel was a preparation), his importance for Dostoevsky is easy to understand. Like Prince Myshkin of *The Idiot*, Alyosha is intended as a living example of what a Christ, our highest "ideal of man and virtue" (in the words of Zosima's friend Father Païssy), would be like in the actual world. "You will go forth from these walls," Zosima predicts after ordering him home to help his brother Dmitri, "but you will live like a monk in the world. You will have many enemies, but even your foes will love you. Life will bring you many misfortunes, but you will find your happiness in them, and will bless life and make others bless it, which is what matters most." And though we are often told that, being ideal, Alyosha's character can't convince, I confess that it is as convincing to me as any of the others. For, created by the same genius for seeing and evoking the realities of human experience, he too comes to us in actions and reactions immediately recognizable as human possibilities. For that matter, we have surely encountered all his qualities *sometimes*—in ourselves, as well as in others: the inner peace that sets one free to give rather than take, to help rather than judge; the intuitive psychological insight which is a recognition of kinship and which looks past offenses to the pain or need that caused them; the trust in people born of affection, not stupidity, and of the instinctive feeling that what is gained by such trust (for oneself and for them) is worth what is risked. We have seen too how such qualities often stir others to respond in kind. It is in just such recognizable action and reaction that they do so in almost all Alyosha's relations with others (not all, Rakitin they significantly fill with rage), and with special intensity and beauty in his talks with young people like Lise and Kolya, whose own quickness of mind and youthful warmth make possible a sort of running fire of moved and moving communion.

But Alyosha also convinces because his goodness is not the whole story about him, his nature has its own lifelike contradictions and holds its own lifelike surprises. For he is a Karamazov. Dostoevsky tells us early that his "hero" is not "sickly, ecstatic . . . a pale, thin, consumptive dreamer," but "a well-grown, red-cheeked, clear-eyed lad of nineteen, radiant with health," who, far from being given to "fanaticism and mysticism," was "more of a realist than anyone." This is a hint of the nature of his faith we will return to later. But it tells us too that it is the faith of one who responds to life with a Karamazov fullness and intensity. And this has to mean that he shares in all that belongs to the Karamazov nature. Sure enough, he betrays so quick an understanding of Dmitri's sensual obsession that Rakitin exclaims in delight, "You are a Karamazov yourself . . . a sensualist from your father, a crazy saint from your mother." And in his talks with the neurotic young invalid Lise, who loves and mocks him and to whom he is engaged, we learn that he can recognize worse things than lust. Lise is another of the characters who give intense life to a key element of the novel's idea. In her this Christ of the novel is challenged and tested by what, because he loves her, becomes his own share of human evil. For she is a brilliant girl who is suffering from that inner "broadness" Dmitri laments and is sick with the sickness of Ivan, that is, with a knowledge of the horrors of which human nature, in its freedom, is capable. Lise has seen those horrors in herself, and because she is rich and idle, and her mother is a scatterbrain, and she has no weapons to fight them with, Alyosha finds (after their happy

early talk) that they have begun to take over her mind. Loathing
herself, she loathes the world. She tells him she longs to destroy, to
commit crimes, that though everyone calls the parricide awful, "secretly they simply love it," and adds, "I for one love it." And of this too
Alyosha confesses a revealing knowledge, filling her with Rakitin's
delight at what is hidden inside this monk. It is interesting that the
climactic evil Aloysha is forced by her to confront and feel with is the
evil Ivan cannot forgive, the torture of children. What underlies her
increasing madness of self-loathing, and leads her to cry, "Aloysha,
save me!" is that, having read of a child being slowly tortured to
death, she finds growing under her anguish of pity the fantasy of
looking on in horrible pleasure while eating pineapple compote! "I
am awfully fond of pineapple compote. Do you like it?"[11]

But of course, what gives Alyosha his distinctive character is that in
him those darker impulses are feeble compared to all the rest, and that,
unlike the others, he is mainly in *harmony* with his own hidden depths.
Trusting God, which is to say, accepting trustfully all that is, he accepts
what he finds in himself, as well as in others. The surprises that emerge
from *his* depths tend to be recognitions of his kinship with others—in
everything, and so to serve as "direction" about what they are and need
from a source quicker and subtler than reason. This is why, though it
belongs to his Karamazov openness to life that he too will be reached
by its faith-destroying chaos, and we will see him "fall," we will see too,
in the chapter with which Dostoevsky said "the *spirit and idea* of the
novel will be completely filled out" (p. 761; italics in original), how that
trust in God saves him, and what it means.

His "fall" is caused by the outraging of a passionate love, the putting to shame of Father Zosima's corpse, to which crowds have been
drawn expecting miracles, by the speed of its putrefaction, its prema-
ture "stink." And this is not because he too naively expected and
wanted miracles; "it was justice, justice, he thirsted for." The "humiliation" of the elder he had adored as a living embodiment and proof of
his faith seems to show "Providence . . . voluntarily submitting to the
blind, dumb, pitiless laws of nature." And the seed planted in his mind
by Ivan now flowers in Ivan's sickness. "I am not rebelling against my
God," he deliberately echoes his brother "with a forced smile" when
Rakitin notes the angry irritability that has replaced his "famous mild-
ness," "I simply 'don't accept his world.' " But this fall of Alyosha is, in
fact, another "dying" of the kind that ends in richer life; and it leads to,
and "triggers," a great revelation.

Rakitin, malignantly pleased at the prospect of pulling the saintly
novice down to his own level, seizes this chance to earn the money
promised by Grushenka if he brought Alyosha to her. And Alyosha,

explaining later why he let himself be taken to that notorious woman, confesses, "I felt drawn to evil because I felt base and evil myself," and, "I came here seeking my ruin and said to myself 'What does it matter?'" Moreover, Grushenka wanted him there out of the same will to evil—in her case to get rid of the shame Alyosha caused her by seducing and laughing at him. But if life has made this woman spiteful, she too is one of Dostoevsky's "insulted and injured" in whom evil always has its opposition. In fact, she shares richly in the "earthiness," the sanity, which is the most attractive element in the Karamazovs. Seduced as a young girl by her own Masterful Humiliator, who had left her obsessed by her own torturing fantasy-love, she can break rapidly out of the fantasy when he comes back and she sees the petty fool he is and can turn gladly to the genuine love for Dmitri her genuine self has already begun to feel. (The scene in which Dmitri attains this supreme joy, and bending over her, sees her looking past him toward the police who have come to arrest him for murder, is, for dramatic power, one of the peaks of world literature.) So, when she learns Alyosha is just then grieving at his beloved elder's death, she jumps off his lap with such a burst of remorse and sympathy that Alyosha is, in his turn, shocked awake. And when he utters his moved gratitude and the new sense of what she is that his insight has leaped to, calling her "sister," she too is thus awakened, and, in her own remorse and her own gratitude, confesses her ugly design on him and the shame that drove her to it. They have thus "saved" each other from the "evil" by which they were tempted—"saved" is Rakitin's word, uttered in bitter mockery of that reversal of his expectations. And surely we must read the word "evil" here as the self-abandonment to those "pitiless laws of nature" which in man are loveless appetite and pure egoism. Their salvation is the perfectly recognizable psychological process by which the sort of insight and judgment of which Christ is one model can in fact heal us of such despairing self-abandonment.

Thus restored to himself, his heart full of "sweetness," Alyosha returns to the monastery room where Father Païssy is reading the Bible over his elder's body and finds that the body's stink has lost its power over his mind. And it is in what follows that "the spirit and idea of the novel" takes its place. As he kneels and prays and drifts into a dream, what Father Païssy is reading—how Christ changes water into wine for the marriage of Cana at Galilee—makes him cry out inwardly, "Ah, that miracle! . . . It was not man's grief, but their joy that Christ visited . . . . 'He who loves men loves their gladness too.' *He* [Father Zosima] was always repeating that . . . ! 'There's no living without joy,' Mitya says." And this thought is followed—illogically—by the other that in Dostoevsky's moments of spiritual exaltation always goes with it:

"'Everything that is true and good is always full of forgiveness,' he used to say that, too." And he dreams himself there at the wedding and sees his elder there, "joyful and laughing," and waking, goes out into the night and "stood, gazed, and suddenly threw himself down on the earth," embracing and kissing it, weeping, "in his rapture," even over the stars, for "there seemed to be threads from all those innumerable worlds of God, linking his soul to them." And again there is that same "illogical" jump from joy to forgiveness. "He longed to forgive everyone and for everything, and to beg forgiveness." And we are told, "It was as though some idea had seized the sovereignty of his mind—and it was for all his life and forever and ever."

That idea is the real religion of Dostoevsky. And it is not only Alyosha, the "red-cheeked" lad whose faith, we are told, is not mysticism but realism, the intellectual form, as it were, of his "radiant" health, who helps us grasp its inner meaning. As we have seen, the primacy of joy, which is the human version of the "force of ferment" by which nature creates worlds and blades of grass and which underlies even the insect lust of the Karamazov father, is the idea with which Dmitri's confession began and which we hear again in his "tragic hymn" in prison. And the inner division, the despair, of Ivan testifies to it as well. For he too feels in himself that "centripetal force on our planet," which only "some driveling consumptive moralists" would call "base." But, given over in his pride of intellect to the logical conclusions of his reason, he cannot *believe* in it, not in the face of the "facts," those horrors of life which make our joy in it seem a mere delusion, or a shameful acceptance, while we're comfortable, of the suffering of others. As far as "logic" is concerned, Dostoevsky agrees with Ivan. "My hero chooses a theme *I* consider irrefutable: the senselessness of children's suffering," he wrote (p. 758; italics in original). But, as Ivan admits ruefully to Alyosha, "One can hardly live in rebellion." And in fact, Ivan cannot live, he goes mad. Alyosha helps us see why the faith of Dostoevsky *must* bypass logic.

> "I'm awfully glad you have such a longing for life," cried Alyosha. "I think one should love life above everything in the world."
> "Love life more than the meaning of it?"
> "Certainly, love it regardless of logic, as you say, it must be regardless of logic, and it's only then one will understand the meaning of it."

Love must come first because reason is only an instrument, and is put in motion by what we feel and need, and for those who want to live, the feeling for life Ivan described as "loving with one's insides, with one's guts," is therefore its necessary condition and guide. Moreover, when applied to the human family, that love of life is also faith in man. For, as we have seen, the forgiveness of God which no crimes can ever exhaust is, in its "inner sense," the faith, equally easy to refute with "facts," that the evil we do does not make us unworthy of such forgiveness, of such another chance. Dostoevsky's religion thus turns out to be a dogged clinging, by way of the great symbols in which it has been embodied in our culture, to the "gut"-sense of our health that life and joy are one and the whole (including man) is good, the feeling which enables us to live. And the doubt which haunted him all his life and has always haunted honest believers is thus revealed to be at bottom something more than reason's doubt of the irrational or the supernatural, of God and immortality. It is the doubt we are all haunted by as we struggle to hold onto that necessary faith—the terrible doubt of Swift, who said happiness was the condition of being well deceived, or of Mark Rutherford, who called health a "divine narcotic." This is why the role Zosima foresaw for Alyosha was that he would "bless life and make others bless it," and why the elder concluded that this—this, surely, rather than the preaching of dogma—"is what matters most."

As an attempt to answer that doubt, *The Brothers Karamazov* is so compelling in part because of its modesty. For the claim Dostoevsky makes for Christianity's power to save the world is far less sweeping here than it is in his letters and his journalism. Alyosha's great "idea" does not save him from his own compromises with the world's evils. It is a kind of compromise that he consents to the "crime"—certainly to the lies and deceptions—of Dmitri's planned escape from prison because he knows his brother's faith will not survive the suffering and the parting from Grushenka. But it is in the beautiful speech of Alyosha to the "boys" after Ilusha's funeral, the speech which closes the novel, that we see how little—and how much—Dostoevsky's faith can do for man. Alyosha tells the boys that their memory of the love they now feel for their dead friend and for each other and of "having been kind and good at this moment" may not be able to prevent life from taking its course, or even, perhaps, prevent them from growing "wicked." Yet the memory will remain with them. "And if a man carries many such memories with him in life, he is safe to the end of his days, and if one has only one good memory left in one's heart, even that may sometimes be the means of saving us." And though they may laugh at it, each "will say at once in his heart, 'No, I do wrong to laugh, for that's not a thing to laugh at.' "

Does not this encouragement to face down our own worldly laughter at our own unworldly love of life and our fellows remind us of what drew that murderer to the young Zosima? In Zosima's "crazy" behavior after his sudden awakening he saw what can "draw men's souls out of their solitude and spur them to some act of brotherly love." And indeed, if such memories or actions won't solve all our problems forever, won't keep us altogether from our own wickedness, yet they "may sometimes," at some moment of crippling cynicism, restore in us the faith that helps us live.

It was as just such a "crazy" action, an action deliberately risking the laughter of his time's clever people (who are so much like our own), that Dostoevsky wrote *The Brothers Karamazov*.

Gide's *The Counterfeiters*

Though *The Counterfeiters* (published in 1925) is André Gide's most richly entertaining novel, it tends to be confusing to those who try to understand what it means. The reason for this is that the novel seems to have so many meanings, some of them in contradiction with each other. Ideas, truths, the formulas by which the human mind defines experience and prescribes for it—these are the materials of Gide's art. Now, it is a cliché of criticism that a concern with ideas must result in some violence to life's complexity. From such a result, Gide was saved, however, by the peculiarly Protestant sincerity with which he always examined a self too various and too much in motion for any formula that stood still. To this was due a mistrust of formulas equal to his interest in them. The conflict between these two movements of his mind may, in fact, be regarded as itself the formula for his entire career, many of his works being attempts to discredit some cherished principle of his own.

In *The Counterfeiters* this conflict receives for the first time its total expression. Unlike the works which preceded it (and this, perhaps, is why he called it his first novel), it examines not a single formula and the situation in which its truth may be tested, but a lifelike multiplicity of both. Moreover, following out to its extremity his own logic, he has provided the novel with a second level, a level below that on which the narrative we watch—the parade of its "truths"—takes place. On this level, that of Edouard's composition of his own *Counterfeiters*, we are shown the formula-making process itself. It is the function of the second level to cast doubt upon the first. *The Counterfeiters* tries to answer, then, by thus facing it head on, the ultimate question of Gide's intellectual life: in a world which the human mind can only grasp after subduing it to formulas, but in which both observer and observed are so complex and changing that none can do their relationships justice, what is the formula in which men *can* come to rest? We may well watch with suspense the result of such an experiment, since the problem was not only Gide's, but that of the modern mind in general, which his own, divided and self-distrusting, profoundly reflected.

The subject of *The Counterfeiters*, as Edouard defines it, is precisely this "rivalry between the real world and the representation we make of it to ourselves. The manner in which the world of appearance imposes itself on us and the manner in which we try to impose on the outside world our own interpretation, this is the drama of our lives." In other words, the novel's subject is no other than Gide's own struggle to write it, his own effort to understand his life truly, to find a unified structure of ideas which will permit him to transpose it without loss of value into coinage of the mind. How is this to be done? As I have said, Gide begins by denying himself the single insight—or homogeneous cluster of insights—which, conscious or unconscious, forms the core of all other novels and by which its material is organized in advance. To keep his novel true to its subject, he leaves it *open*, as, in fact, the mind which would preserve its relevance and justness must remain in life. "It is essentially out of the question for a book of this kind to have a plan," Edouard observes. "Everything would be falsified if anything were decided beforehand. I wait for reality to dictate to me." If the book's confusing variety sometimes suggests that it is in his narrative that Gide has left himself thus free, this is not, however, on the whole, the sense actually intended. Too many of the story patterns come out "right." The freedom Gide has chiefly made use of is the freedom to *change his mind*, to permit every new development to suggest some new measure by which people and events, true and false, good and evil, healthy and moribund are to be understood. This is what accounts for the novel's terrible difficulty. There is no one whose point of view it is always safe for the reader to trust—even Edouard is finally discredited—and no principle emerging as the moral of any particular episode and seized by the panting reader as a possible theme, which it will be safe to apply to all others. We do, it is true, come at last to one which seems durable. But it is so only because it is itself an open door to all others, and far from solving the endless problem, offers rather a touchstone by which to measure a given solution's varying adequacy.

I have said that the picture of Edouard's struggle must cast a doubt on the result of Gide's. That is not the only reason for doubt. Since the clash between reality and our formulas must necessarily be endless, how could Gide's attempt to write a book which will justly formulate his material ever come to an end? Edouard's does not. At the close of Gide's novel, Edouard's is still unfinished. In the *Journal of The Counterfeiters*, Gide suggests it will never be finished because Edouard is incapable of a "veritable devotion" to anything. "He pursues himself incessantly and through everything." But what is Gide's own peculiar distinction if not this incessant pursuit of himself, which is only a search for his true reactions to what is being observed? The other name for this pursuit is integrity. It is Edouard's extravagant integrity that will keep him forever at work. To stop seeking further at any moment of apparent understanding would mean a closing of his book to life, where the search is necessarily continuous, which would, precisely, invalidate it as an embodiment of his theme. Gide, then, has put a limit to his own integrity in stooping to finish the book we have. It is a betrayal by which its truth stands forever compromised. But if he has cheated us, as all novelists must, he has made up for it too. He has helped us to find him out.

The narrative of the book, then, is the realm of its (intentional) confusion, as Edouard's attempt to formulate it in a coherent novel is the source of its unity. But even for the confusion, or rather for the processes which engender it, Gide has found formulas to help us grasp them, and his chief symbols for these are the counterfeit and the devil. Without understanding the full, the developing import of each, it is impossible to understand the book.

The counterfeit gold coin begins, of course, by symbolizing the false, the inauthentic individual: a major preoccupation of Gide's career. "I should like," says Bernard, "all my life long at the very smallest shock to ring true. Nearly all the people I have known ring false." In the light of this, characters like Pastor Vedel, professionally virtuous, or the literary parasite de Passavant are immediately understandable as examples of the counterfeit. Nor do we see only "evil" pretending to be "good," but also the reverse, as when Armand, basically in love with virtue, apes out of despair a nastiness he loathes. And between these poles will be found many other degrees and variations of the process.

But the circle of suspicion widens. Even thoughts and feelings we entertain in all *sincerity* may be counterfeit, taken for granted once and for all because we believe, says the villainous cynic Strouvilhou, "everything we see in print." In literature, he tells us—and surely by extension in all the media from which we learn what to feel and think, as we learn the only language we know—"feelings may be as arbitrary as the conventions which the author believes to be the foundation of his art." They may "ring as false as counters, but they pass current . . . . A man who should offer the public real coins would seem to be defrauding us . . . . If I edit a review," he continues, "it will be in order to prick bladders—in order to demonetize fine feelings, and those promissory notes which go by the name of words." Though Strouvilhou is a monster, we may not shrink from the truth of what he says.

We come next to a complication more audacious still: the symbol ceases to be pejorative. Bernard has told us of his indignation at hearing a tourist boast of robbing the customs. " 'The State is nothing but a convention,' he said too. What a fine convention it would be that rested on the bona fides of every individual!" Though even the conventions upon which society rests are not so much true as believed to be true, like the counterfeit coin not yet found out, we are not therefore justified in denying them value. Their value is the value they elicit from us, which we unite to grant them. It is by such counterfeits that we organize the multiple possibilities of human nature in a desired direction. Objectifying thus the best in ourselves, we are sustained at the ennobling level by what we have created.

With the road thus opened, there is no place to stop. For Edouard, "ideas of exchange, of depreciation, of inflation gradually invaded his book." Whatever his mind rests on begins to appear to him, good or bad, as a kind of currency with questionable backing. Remember, indeed, how he defined the very subject of his book. What emerges at last is the suggestion that *all* the ideas and images by which we represent reality, and by which we must perforce live, are a species of counterfeit, waiting like Bernard's gilt-covered coin of glass to be seen through and discarded. The real culprit is the human brain which cannot with the best will in the world truly represent reality. When, in the light of this, we turn back to Bernard's description of the false coin, every modest phrase swells with meaning. "Just hear how true it rings . . . . I was taken in by it this morning, just as the grocer who passed it on to me was taken in himself, he told me. It hasn't quite the same weight, I think, but it has the brightness and sound of a real piece; it is coated with gold, so that all the same it is worth more than two sous; but it is made of glass. It'll wear transparent. No, don't rub it . . . . One can almost see through it as it is." For coin read the ideas, indeed the axioms, of any epoch or any individual, which, until time has rubbed their value away, ring wonderfully true, and are passed, innocently or not, from grocer to customer to whom you will, and on through a whole society. If we had not arrived at the point from another quarter, we would see from this that the chief counterfeit with which Gide presents us is the novel itself, as he is the chief of its counterfeiters. The novel pretends, as fiction must, to represent reality, a pretension to which it is itself designed to give the lie. And the failure of Edouard to complete his own is due simply to his unattainable desire to make of it a coin of solid gold.

Gide, however, is no mere skeptic. Though he shirks none of the difficult obstacles, he insists always on moving beyond despair. There is a chink in the darkness of Bernard's description. The coin "is coated with gold, so that all the same it is worth more than two sous." There *is* a way of being true that our counterfeits possess, even if that truth, with rubbing, must prove impermanent. The formula for it will be the same as that by which we outwit the devil, and we will come to it in its place.

"I should want one [character], the devil," Gide wrote in the *Journal of The Counterfeiters*, "who would circulate incognito throughout the book." This character is, indeed, the most important of all. If we examine a few of his appearances, we will find that he gives himself away.

It is the devil who leads Vincent to gamble with the money intended for Laura, and then helps him to invent an ethic to "legitimize" his behavior. For Vincent "continues to be a moral being, and the devil will only get the better of him by furnishing him with reasons for self-approval." Edouard, in confiding little Boris to old Azais as for an interesting experiment, has allowed curiously flimsy reasons to conceal dangers he should have foreseen. His sophisms "must be promptings of the devil, for if they came from anyone else he would not listen to them. . . . There often lies hidden behind the good motive a devil who is clever enough to find his profit in the very thing one thought one was wresting from him." And, "Have you noticed," asks the wretched La Perouse, "that in this world God always keeps silent? Or at least, at least . . . however carefully we listen, it's only the devil we can succeed in hearing." Finally, in a fragment of dialogue in the *Journal of The Counterfeiters*, we learn that though one can only regard the devil as a childish substitute for the rational solution of certain psychological problems, "the devil himself would not speak otherwise; he is delighted; he knows that he hides nowhere as well as behind these rational explanations." And his first words are bound to be: "Why do you fear me? You know I don't exist."

The devil thus delineated is the *self*. He is the voracious, sly, inextinguishable self, whose sole motive in every situation is the free gratification of appetites, but who must adopt, to overcome a variety of fears and scruples, an appropriate variety of disguises. This metaphor is complemented by an earlier one of Gide's. I do not love man, he said, but only that which devours him. What devours the self is a love of and aspiration toward something *other*, by which the self is used up, and which subordinates the gang of its clamorous, shortsighted appetites. For the self's immediate gratification, these appetites would destroy each other, destroy their own power of enjoyment, destroy the man. We need not be told, after the labors of depth psychology, how wonderful is this devil's cleverness. There is no principle, however self-denying, that he cannot find a way either to outwit or to turn to his own advantage. Indeed, the freezing suggestion of La Perouse is that every audible voice is his, that we are incapable of hearing—in a selfless motive—the voice of God. Why does the devil delight to be regarded as a fiction? Because those who leave him out of their calculations, leave out, that is, the immeasurable subtlety of their selfishness, will perforce accept those reasons which the devil provides to "legitimize" their behavior. On this account, scientific explanations are, of course, best of all. Screened by such authority from the gullible conscience, the liberated appetites may proceed to gorge themselves in perfect peace. As the case of Edouard showed us, however, reasons need not be ironclad if they come to grant us our desire.

In the novel, we are presented with four kinds of relationships to the devil—two based on denial of him and two on his recognition. The virtuous and the simple are his victims through denial. The first (Vedel and Azais), because they are convinced that, though he exists for some, he has no place in behavior like theirs, are covered by all the rules of virtue. They yield to him with all the gusto of self-righteousness, having equated their desires with the will of God. The simple, on the other hand, like Douviers, whose "goodness" is so sincere and modest Edouard feels cheap to treat it with irony, yield not out of pride in their virtue, but because they lack the imagination to suspect their own good motives, to fear another, a darker side to every act and profession.

The second pair begins with the Passavants and the Lady Griffiths, who may well be considered to grant the devil's existence since they deny rather the possibility of any other master. These are less his victims than his infatuated votaries, votaries, that is, of their own untrammeled appetites. They demonstrate, moreover, how dangerous are those appetites, is the merely liberated self, leading to the absolute inferno of ennui and ultimately to self-destruction. Finally, there are the wise, to whom Edouard, like most of us, can belong only intermittently, and whose nature the previously quoted dialogue makes clear. The wise are those who acknowledge the existence of the devil as adversary. Granting his existence, they are in possession of a clue with which to penetrate an infinity of disguises, a clue which prevents the natural carelessness of equating him with one or two of his forms. Too often we lull ourselves by such equations into believing that these forms are all we have to fear, whereas to know the devil who is their protean essence is to beware of him everywhere, in every form, and even the least likely. We are put on guard against *all* our reasons, that is, against ourselves.

In the *Journal of The Counterfeiters*, Gide writes: "The renunciation of virtue through abdication of pride." The wisely virtuous man must give up the pride of confidence in his virtue. Suspicious of himself, he is at least free at every moment to modify his behavior when, in spite of the handsomest justifications, he finds himself doing evil. Skeptical of reasons, he learns to judge by results. He is forearmed against the danger that his most disinterested profession may only mask the selfish motive, the devil, which renders it other and less than it appears, which renders it *counterfeit*. It is thus the two metaphors come together in organic—not arbitrary—unity. The devil is the glass beneath our gold.

One thing remains to be said. We have seen that though the devil is evil, it is positively wisdom and health to get to know him. Moreover, the speaker in Gide's dialogue expresses approval of Goethe's insight that the profoundest genius must be partly demonic, and in his *Dostoevsky*, Gide himself coins the maxim: "The Fiend is party to every work of art." This is no contradiction. Electricity too is a murderer unless recognized and controlled. Is not the artist preeminent among those who see through the counterfeits of word and deed to the hidden self who is their true author? And what gives him the clue to this *other* side, if not an intimate acquaintance with the devil in himself. It is precisely the artist's knowledge of the horrors that lie potential within his own breast that provides his art with its third dimension.

At the moment when Bernard, wholly self-liberated, must decide in which direction to proceed, an angel comes to hint that the devil's is not the only path before him. The principle which accomplished his liberation, that the self has a higher authority than whatever would prevent it from knowing or being itself, has begun to grow equivocal in its implications. Freedom alone provides no measure for the value of his acts nor any guide for his aspirations. For reasons which will grow clear, the angel cannot bring such a measure or such a guide, but what he does is more important: he awakens a desire for them.

Look again at the story of the angel. You will see that from the moment when he appears with a foot so light it might walk on water— *like the foot of Jesus*—his every act and effect involves sympathy for others. Further, it is when Bernard is seized by a contrary feeling, contempt, that the angel temporarily disappears. The angel is that in us—or elsewhere—which opposes the devil-self and would make of it a sacrifice to God. Jesus provides the form of this angel for many, and a chief sign of his influence, as in the novel, is love, generosity, the substitution of another's self on the altar where one had worshiped one's own. Actually, however, the form of every man's angel is unique, adapted as it must be to the unique self it will oppose; this is the reason Bernard cannot see the other angels wandering in the church. In their night-long wrestling, neither conquers. Not Bernard, because, as this chapter's significant first sentence tells us, he is one "for whom there is no greater joy than to rejoice another being," that is, because his self-ishness can never wholly conquer his generosity. And not the angel either, because selfishness is after all inextinguishable. Yet the *conscious* struggle accomplishes the highest object one may hope for from it: it brings Bernard to maturity, which means to an awareness of the issues and challenges of life, in short, to a knowledge of good and evil. His struggle is that of every young man evolving, after the self-absorption of childhood and against his own "interests," a conception of virtue, and a goal more worthy of his gifts than personal aggrandizement.

But the angel's gift of maturity is not an answer; it is a question. The next day, seeking a definite rule for his life, Bernard goes to Edouard for advice. The ensuing dialogue contains the ripest Gidian wisdom. The novelist has nothing definite to offer. All he can say, when pushed at last to rock bottom, is this: "It is a good thing to follow one's own inclination, provided it leads uphill." Indefinite—but the little sentence is far less modest than it looks. For even an angel who brings us the knowledge of good and evil cannot be expected to define a goal whose pursuit will guarantee our virtue. Of what value is a single fixed goal for men who are various and in constant motion? My goal will not be yours, and the goal which led me upward today will tomorrow hold me back. Dynamic to match the dynamism of life, Edouard's formula is, in fact, the only one which can keep us moving forever in the general direction of a God necessarily and properly impossible to pin down. Both its elements are essential, the first, that the self—yes, the devil-self—be frankly consulted, and the second, that the result lead uphill. Whenever the two are at war, the devil wins an advantage. For just as the heedless gratification of the self means the devil's triumph, so does the most virtuous program which involves its falsification or denial, since the self will only explode at last into rebellion against all virtue. (The fate of Armand brought up by the blameless Vedels.) Every right act, in short, must be a collaboration between the devil and the angel.

This concluding formula has implications as wide as the skepticism which preceded it. Though every image of reality is counterfeit, we don't have to despair, there remains a basis for choice among them. That basis is the self's needs, honestly acknowledged. Not absolute truth, but relevance to man's changing needs determines the value of his mind's coinage, as it is the growing irrelevance of that coinage, through changes in men and their situations, which rubs away the layer of gold and enables us to see through it like glass. The bringer of a new truth is simply the man who has become aware of needs which the old was not designed to satisfy. His will not be more permanent (insofar as it pretends to be it is a counterfeit like all the rest) but only more suitable. It is proper, then, that each age and each man, in some degree, make counterfeits of their own for the solution of their own felt problems, provided only that they are restrained from capitulation to unbridled appetite by endless care that the solutions lead always uphill. When will the often wearisome necessity for such care, for continuous fresh examination and evaluation, come to an end? When can we find rest in currency of pure gold? Never. For then change should have ceased, which is to say, we should be dead.

But *this* truth at least, the formula Gide does arrive at, this is gold, is it not? Alas, no. It is only the ultimate truth of the novel's first level, that of its material, of Gide's life. But the book's subject was precisely the impossibility of representing life truly. The only answer it gives us then is this: examine this final coin for yourself. Has the gold rubbed off it yet? Not yet? Then you don't know yet that it is false. Apply to it, as you must to every principle, the test itself advises. And when it ceases to conform to your personal needs—or to lead you upward— throw it away.

That formula (the conclusion of its first level) and this willingness to grant that it too is provisional (the conclusion of its second) is the moral of Gide's great novel, and the final equilibrium of the conflict in his thought with which our examination began. But as Gide's problem is the portion of free minds everywhere in our tormented self-conscious epoch, so its solution too extends in relevance beyond the book. It is such a moral, if any, that can be for all of us at once the safeguard of our freedom and the guarantee of its health and fruitfulness.

Gide's *Theseus*

André Gide often remarked that most writers produce too quickly, that serious work should be allowed to ripen. More than any of his tales, *Theseus* provides an example both of the process and of its justifying result. The first mention of *Theseus* in his journal was in 1911. It was not published in France until 1946. The result is, we have a retelling of the myth that is brief in compass and simple unto apparent casualness in style and that yet manages to be at the same time a spiritual autobiography and a complete summation of his thought, of his unique contribution to the wisdom of our time. This is what happens when a good writer waits. His means shrink and his meanings multiply. *Everything* is converted into symbol. The process could hardly go further than it has done in *Theseus*, of which every reading discloses the crucial significance of details the reader might at first have been content to regard as imposed by the original myth alone or intended merely to enliven the story surface. For this reason, what follows must be limited to the main line of meaning and the most important episodes. A detailed examination would have to be much longer than its subject.

The theme of *Thesus* is human progress. "Humanity," says its hero, "can do more and deserves better." What is involved here is not the nineteenth-century faith in progress which has long been in disrepute. That faith was after all a faith that material progress alone would make all other kinds unnecessary. Without despising material welfare (demanding it, rather), Gide was concerned chiefly with the continuous inner development by which man transforms and transcends himself. But such progress, the realization of man's endless possibilities, is an endless struggle, in which literally everything and everybody in the world may on occasion become his enemy. Think of whatever you like that might seem man's certain ally in this struggle. Rule out in your sophistication those allies who wear deceitfulness like a sign, and turn to the others who have, in fact, brought you thus far. It is of *them* Gide says beware. The time may come when exactly these will be the subtle enemies of your further progress. This was the central torment and insight of Gide's career. True, he was dedicated to personal development at any cost. But what are his successive works, and his journals too, if not a record of the dangers that lurk on every road toward such a goal? That direction is wrong, says *L'Immoraliste*. But *La Porte Etroite* replies, Look what happens when you take the other. (Hence, of course, Gide's insistence that his books be understood together rather than individually.) Everything can fail you except one thing: the infinitely resilient and fertile spirit of man. Let this be your oracle, says Gide, and listening, shut out every conflicting whisper. Theseus, then, tells the story of that struggle, which is man's but which was more particularly André Gide's, and of how the hero, Theseus-Gide, vanquished his enemies and escaped their traps.

The story is told as a rather chatty autobiography, of the kind to which a "man of action" (so Gide characterizes his hero) might turn his hand when the time of activity had died away into that of thoughtful reminiscence. There are, no doubt, many advantages to such a method. But the most obvious is that it solves at one stroke the problem of compression, selection, and rearrangement that looms first when one approaches the myth. In the chief sources, Plutarch and Diodorus, there are numerous versions of every episode and their chronological order does not necessarily correspond to an order of meaning. (Of course, the myth was selected because of the degree to which its events *were* meaningful and required simply, as it were, the proper lighting.) With the aged Theseus himself as our narrator, browsing over his life and remembering of each epoch only what is appropriate to a motivating idea, Gide makes everything in the crowded, confused history available when and as needed, leaving himself free by the same device to omit the irrelevant.

That the story is not an autobiography of Theseus alone is suggested by the character traits Gide chooses to mention here and there. Theseus remarks, for instance, that others have been more intelligent than he. "But people give me credit for good sense. The rest is added with the determination to do well that has never left me. Mine, too, is the kind of courage which incites to desperate enterprises. On top of all this I was ambitious." Just so did Gide deprecate his own intelligence, but with a modesty more apparent than real, since it is less on intelligence than on what follows in this quotation that great achievement is generally based. To intelligence "the rest" is added. Nor is it a contradiction of this that Theseus is described as a man of action. Gide too was a man of action, both as an artist whose works were acts, in which ideas were submitted to the ordeal of life, and as a man who lived his ideas and suffered their consequences.

Theseus begins, appropriately enough, with his education, his relations with his elders. Gide makes a slight change here in order to keep father and son in contact and the education of Theseus exemplary. In the myth, Aegeus, after getting with child a daughter of Pittheus, hides his weapons under a great stone, tells her that if the child is a son and he grows strong enough to reach them, he is to bring them to him in Attica, and then leaves for good. In Gide, Aegeus himself is in charge of the boy's education, of which the stone-lifting is a symbol. It is he who tells him of the hidden weapons (hidden, he says, by Poseidon), and who sets him to recover them by lifting the stones about the palace. But when Theseus, after overturning all the stones in the neighborhood, is about to attack the flagstones of the palace in his zeal, his father stops him. The story of the weapons, he explains, was only a fiction designed to develop his strength. Handing them to his son, he continues, "Before giving them to you I was waiting to see you deserve them. I can sense in you now the ambition to use them and that longing for fame which will allow you only to take up arms in defense of noble causes and for the weal of all mankind." Now this speech might be intended to be taken literally, and the fact that the reader does not see that readiness for the "good fight" mentioned by the father might be regarded as due to a vagueness in the story characteristic of myth. Not so: education and family have here received a characteristic and savage thrust. It is by lies that the father has stimulated his son's development. This development, however, following its own laws, gets out of hand, until at last the father's very palace, the world which warms and shelters him and in which he reigns a king, stands suddenly in danger. At this, hastily, his smile surely rather forced, the father calls a halt and says it was all a joke. He gives his son the weapons (the freedom and strength he has in fact already won for himself) and with an unction and a flattery typical of the frightened elder, tries to bamboozle the powerful youth into turning his strength in another, a socially acceptable, direction. The thrust, as I say, is characteristic. It was Gide who declared, "Families, I hate you!" and whose development was forever overturning the flagstones, and not only the flagstones, of the palace of intellectual and moral conventions in which his elders uneasily slept.

That this episode is, indeed, seen as conflict is borne out by the fact that immediately after it, Gide anticipates his narrative by some years, and, as if in passing, mentions how Aegeus died. Theseus, as Gide's predecessors have also informed us, was to have announced his safe return from the encounter with the Minotaur by replacing his vessel's black sail with a white one. He neglected to do this, disturbed by thoughts of Ariadne according to Diodorus, and according to Plutarch distracted by joy. As a result, Aegeus, seeing the black sail, was maddened by grief and flung himself from a cliff into the ocean. According to Theseus-Gide, he simply forgot. "One can't think of everything. But to tell the truth, and if I cross-question myself, a thing I never much care to do, I can't swear that it was really forgetfulness. Aegeus was in my way." One begins to see with what delighted recognition Gide must have read the original fable.

Our hero's next struggle is with the monsters and criminals who make the highways of life a place of terror to our elders and against whom they feel it their duty to warn us. He has, of course, refused their advice to take the safe route to Attica, fired by the example of Hercules, as talented youth is forever stimulated by his great predecessors to feats of intellectual and moral daring and self-assertion, self-discovery. Is this Theseus talking or Gide? "No one can deny it. I think I have performed some notable services; I've purged the earth once and for all of a host of tyrants, bandits, monsters. I've cleared up certain dangerous byways on which even the bravest could not venture without a shiver." What are these tyrants, if not the ideas and conventions, outworn but still reigning, which prevent our free movement along the road of self-development? And much more is signified than the sexual convention which figures in Gide's most spectacular tyrannicide. His hero's adversaries are not all secular. "Whatever was inexplicable was put on to the gods. Terror and religion were so nearly one that heroism often seemed an impiety. The first and principal victory which man had to win was over the gods."

We learn from Plutarch and Diodorus that Thesus delighted to seize his opponent's own weapon and turn it against him. So he handled Corynetes, the club bearer, Sinnis, the bender of pines, Procrustes, for whose bed all seekers of polemical metaphors must forever be grateful. When Gide repeats this information, adding that only by such tactics can we be sure of final victory, the mythic fact suddenly fills with meaning. Whether in matters of sexual ethics or philosophical debate, one can properly meet a challenge only by accepting the problem as presented, the realm of discourse in which it is stated and exists. To shrink from one's adversaries' weapons, terms, problems, is to leave the challenge not truly faced and the enemy never truly bested.

We come next to the most elaborately treated episode in the brief tale, that of the adventure in Crete. Here are embodied and dramatized the most basic and subtle opponents of man's development. As Plutarch and Diodorus have told us, Thesus refuses the protection of his status and volunteers as one of the seven young men who, with seven maidens, must periodically be offered to the Minotaur. Gide's Theseus explains his volunteering in a statement which is also to be found in some form in Gide's journal. "I care nothing for privilege and claim that merit alone distinguishes me from the rest." For Gide too renounced the safety his wealth and position might have afforded him and threw in his lot with the outcasts, the victims and the explorers of culture. Many versions of this adventure are given by his predecessors. In some Theseus overcomes not a bull-man, monstrous issue of Pasiphaë, the queen of Crete, and a bull, but a surly athlete named Taurus in the athletic games held by King Minos. In Gide the animal-man remains, but he takes the fact of such games and places Theseus before them as a spectator. There the Grecian observes the effeminate sensual culture of Crete; there he is seen and loved by Adriadne and sees and is struck by the child Phaedra, her sister. Every detail now begins to contribute to a meaning which emerges fully later on. The meaning is this: Crete is the realm of self-indulgence, chiefly but not only sensual, with all its nourishment for growth and all its traps and curbs for it. As such, it is also the realm of art, whence costly and beautiful objects had long flowed into Attica, exciting our hero's youthful curiosity.

After the games, Theseus, as a young prince, has dinner at the palace. Here, in a private dialogue with Pasiphaë, he is introduced to the rationalizations which rise to sanction fleshly or any kind of self-indulgence, and which, sympathetically heard by one who should judge and restrain—in her case, Minos—corrode his certainty and render him impotent to perform his duty. Pasiphaë, whose history, appearance, and manner proclaim her the arch-slut, declares herself, fondling Theseus' pectorals, to be a lover of heavenly things alone. "The difficulty, you see, is one never can tell exactly where the god begins and where he ends." If admonished by Minos on the subject of her peculiar tastes, she asks, "What about your mother?"—Minos himself being the son of Europa. Moreover, Minos believes with a "praiseworthy" tolerance which Gide thus audaciously questions that one can't be a good judge until one has experienced everything, either oneself or through one's family. And so his family is only furthering his career by its various errors of conduct. That Gide was not a puritan we know. Here we see that when the *enemy* invites to license, he could become one. In conclusion, she pleads with the young man not to harm the Minotaur, but to become friendly with him, "and so end a misunderstanding which has done great harm to our two countries." If the Minotaur, as will soon become clear, is the heart of the symbol which is Crete—that is, the seductive flesh—then this friendship she desires may well have a meaning deeper than a mother's solicitude. (Gide often gives his adversaries good arguments.) It is the fruitful union of flesh—Crete—with spirit—Greece (or use any terms that are more congenial and up-to-date), where exclusive devotion to either cripples both.

Throughout this dialogue, Ariadne has been waiting impatiently for our hero on the terrace. When he appears, she fastens herself upon him with a promptness and a volubility that fill him with misgivings. Ariadne is an amusing cartoon of the sensible, managing mate. Possessive, practical, keeping her aspiring man's two feet on the ground by her mere clamorous existence, it is she who will save him in his struggle with the Minotaur. But her narrowness! And the enormous price she exacts! A man like Theseus can only begin at once, while he uses her, to figure out ways of welching on his suffocating bargain. Listen to her: she has warned him against trying to fly out of the maze like Icarus: "That I don't dare to recommend to you; it's too risky. You'd better get it into your head at once that your only hope is to stick close to me. We shall be together, you and I, from now on in life and death." Etc. Etc. Later, Theseus tells us she was always saying, "You promised." Granted that one must be practical and careful as it is Ariadne's eternal role to inform us, there is such a thing as being too much so and failing to reach one's proper limit. Sure enough, Theseus, allowing her her usefulness by putting one end of the famous thread in her hand, takes the spool himself lest, if she had it, she refuse to unwind it as far as he wishes to go.

But the fact is this type of woman is not capable of being responsible for the hero's salvation, except as an instrument. Indeed, she yields so readily that Theseus can hardly believe himself "to have done the work of a pioneer." It is not in this particular hero and his salvation she is interested, in other words, but in a man, the fulfillment of her own destiny. Not she, but Daedalus instructs him in the dangers he faces and how to overcome them.

Gide ignores what his predecessors mention of Minos's anger with Daedalus for helping Pasiphaë consummate her perverse passion, as well as the flight of father and son caused by this. Daedalus is here as symbol of the pedagogue and scientist, and his son, the lost flyer, is a metaphysician carried away from earthly life by unanswerable questions. The jealousy-murder of his rival Talos, as Daedalus here tells the story, becomes only a "difference" due to a significant philosophic conflict. Talos's images of the gods kept them in rigid hieratic posture; Daedalus—and this is borne out by Diodorus—preferred to bring them closer to men by showing them with their limbs in motion and their eyes open. At the same time, by science he wished to bring men closer to the gods.

What follows is Gide's rich illumination of the two chief symbols of his tale: the labyrinth where the hero undergoes his most profound ordeal, and the thread which is his salvation. The labyrinth is a place difficult to escape from because—happy notion!—it affects the *will* to escape. Moreover, it is filled with vapors which not only act on the will and put it to sleep; they induce a delicious intoxication, rich in flattering delusions, and provoke the mind, filled as this is with voluptuous mirages, to a certain pointless activity; pointless, I say, because it has merely an imaginary outcome in visions and speculations without order, logic or substance. The effect of these gases is not the same for all of those who breathe them; each is led on by the complexities implicit in his own mind to lose himself, if I may so put it, in a labyrinth of his own devising.

Which of us, shrinking from the labor of realizing some cherished purpose, has not also wandered in this labyrinth, where "without order, logic or substance" we could dream its accomplishment? And as we wander thus, our very strength becomes our weakness. For each of us, to use another metaphor which Gide is fond of, the devil assumes a different disguise, the one most congenial and seductive. Indeed, the very thirst for progress, for self-development and fulfillment, which is the condition of all that is best in life and culture, may, unanchored, send us soaring away from the earth on which all real progress is made.

How, then, can we guarantee to our aspiring thought order, logic, and substance? To return to our story, how is the hero to escape a labyrinth so ingenious? Hear Daedalus:

> "Your will alone may not suffice . . . and so I have thought of this plan; to link you and Ariadne by a thread, the tangible symbol of duty. . . . Be always determined not to break it, no matter what may be the charms of the labyrinth, the seduction of the unknown, or the headlong urging of your own courage. Go back to her, or all the rest, and the best with it, will be lost. The thread will be your link to the past. Go back to it. Go back to yourself. For nothing can begin from nothing, and it is from your past, and from what you are at this moment, that what you are going to be must spring."

Thus we see that the reality with which we must keep contact for all actual progress has two faces: one is tradition and the other is duty. These alone, however they may seem at times to slow us down, can save us from dissolution in self-indulgence. For the past is our earth, and like any plant, to grow upward we must have roots in the earth beneath us, the deeper and stronger, indeed, the higher we would reach. And those roots are duty, by which the past at once restrains and nourishes, teaching us what we are and what the world is, with and from which we are to build. And thus we are shown too (as Gide had long since warned us) how dangerous it would be to understand our author too quickly. As the pursuer of every sensual fulfillment became before our eyes the acid judge of sensuality unbridled, sensuality corrupting, using for its own purposes the resources of the spirit, so the arch-rebel, the adventurer, drawn always toward and over human boundaries, emerges here as the justifier of precisely those forces against which rebellion would seem necessarily and ever to struggle.

Moreover, is not Gide's tale itself a living demonstration of this insight from which it flows? That the completion of such a work—and all its fellows—was an enchaining and laborious duty by means of which a fertile mind was prevented from dissipating its seed need not be insisted upon. It is also a lesson in the meaning and uses of tradition for the human spirit, devoted as it may and should be to the unknown. that is the future. By thrusting hard against an ancient myth, Gide was able to leap to his own new meanings. For what is myth? And here we must drop our metaphor of the past as the earth beneath us, for, in fact, it is more than this, it is also the air we breathe and the heaven of our aspiration. It seems beneath or behind us as we struggle away from it toward the truth that lies beyond, but when at last the truth is reached and we hear its voice, what it utters is always an echo. And perhaps what it chiefly echoes will be myth. Daedalus has called his son into the room, and Icarus, lost in the anguished theological speculation which was the inner labyrinth of *his* devising, gives Theseus an example of the danger he runs and then withdraws. Theseus is surprised to learn that Icarus is dead. "There is another truer plane on which time does not exist," Daedalus explains. "On this plane the representative gestures of our race are inscribed, each according to its particular significance. What happens in the case of a hero is this: his mark endures. Poetry and the arts reanimate it and it becomes an enduring symbol."

One word more about the invaluable Daedalus. Gide sees around him too, sees, as with others, the defects of his virtues. Like so many teachers with their theories, and scientists with their instruments, he has a respect for his tools that Gide regards as excessive. "Man's personal strength can effect nothing," he says. "Better a good tool than a strong forearm." But men like Theseus—or Gide—have a kind of pride which such a remark is likely to irritate. Precisely because of it, Theseus determines to enter the maze without weapons and to fight the monster with his bare hands. For Gide, it is man that counts, and all theories, like other tools which restrict us to *their* way of conceiving and solving problems, are expendable on behalf of the new possibilities of which man is the inexhaustible reservoir.

Theseus goes into the maze, finds and conquers the Minotaur, and then, hated for it at the time by his intoxicated fellow Grecians, forcibly rescues them from their delicious captivity. The struggle with the

Minotaur is left peculiarly vague. The monster himself is—surprisingly—beautiful. Far from leaping to devour them, he is found lying languorously amid flowers, while the eye he sleepily opens at the approach of Theseus is completely witless. Like that of the labyrinth in which he dwells, his power lies in attraction rather than force. How Theseus conquered him he cannot or will not recall. He mentions only that there was something voluptuous about the victory, and to leave the garden in which it occurred hardly bearable. But we may ask, how did Gide in his own life conquer such enslaving seduction? Why, by *yielding* to it. The symbol is surely apt: since hunger of the flesh can enslave the minds of those who keep it forever unsatisfied, to yield is at least one way to set oneself free. It was certainly Gide's—and not as easy a way as it sounds to one brought up like Gide to Protestant self-restraint. As his journal reveals, he had to drive himself toward pleasure, long after he had begun to question the Protestant mistrust of it, as another might toward self-denial.

In the events that follow, Gide slightly alters the myth, in which Phaedra is given to Theseus in marriage much later by her brother Deucalion. Here, Theseus takes her with him, stealing her away by trickery, on the voyage back which results in Ariadne's abandonment on the island of Naxos. The question may arise why our hero prefers the unripe child to the mature woman. Perhaps, though Theseus in fact disavows the fondness for boys which is precisely a Cretan custom, his choice of one who is not yet a woman keeps his image a faithful one of his author. Perhaps too we are here being told, as Gide has told us elsewhere, that the pleasures of sex are purest when unadulterated with other considerations. An Ariadne would force recognition and acceptance of more than her body, whereas his delight in the childish Phaedra could be undistracted, and leave his mind equally undistracted in the pursuit of its own ends. Whether this peculiarity of Gide's thought is less general than private in its validity is a problem that would carry us far afield. The episode does, however, yield a meaning clearly general, and a meaning that seems at first glance wholly repulsive. Theseus found it rather disagreeable to have thus to deceive his host Minos, who, after the adventure in the labyrinth, had given him his entire confidence. Gide spares no inflection to make this episode appear unworthy of his hero. And how is it justified? Flatly, thus: "But it was not, and indeed it is never a part of my character to allow myself to be stopped by scruples. The voices of gratitude and decency were shouted down by the voice of desire. The end justifies the means. What must be must be." Then even decency can become our adversary in this struggle—even cunning and duplicity our necessary allies, as well as, on pleasanter occasions, the courage in which we can take pride? Alas, yes. When desire is strong and sure, it may be fatal to withhold fulfillment until we can elaborate a structure of justifications or find sanctioned means. (*Desire,* remember, not some cold-blooded theory of social welfare.) For after all, the inner life is of a complexity that may make it impossible anyway to know all that is involved in the relation of a cause and an effect, all the steps of a human process. Without knowing why, we may *know* that health and safety demand behavior it would be impossible to explain and justify on the rational conscious level. All this is dangerous—granted. In such matters, we play with dynamite. But it can't be helped. We must simply try to be careful. And we must remember on behalf of Gide that in admitting the occasional validity of a principle, he by no means gave it his total and permanent allegiance.

We come next to Theseus as a statesman. In Plutarch he is shown to have unified the many small quarreling city-states of Attica into one, Athens, containing three classes, nobility, husbandmen, and artisans, all equal in the dubious sense that each excelled the others in some one respect. Athens becomes a democracy in that the nobility govern it as equals instead of a single tyrant. Finally, its stock of human wealth is wisely increased by an invitation to foreigners to settle there and enjoy the rights of Athenians. Gide's Theseus simply destroys all privilege entirely and brings about complete equality among the citizens of Athens. When his friend Pirithous warns him that inequality is inevitable and will reestablish itself, he says he knows it well. But the new state will be an aristocracy not of wealth but of intellect. Gide's hero too invites foreigners to Athens "to increase her power and importance." All were to have the same rights as Athenians to begin with. "Any necessary discrimination could await the proofs of experience." What we get here is not simply a model state, it is a description of the proper conditions for the flowering of culture, for growth toward intellectual "power and importance" on the part of individuals. There must be an initial equality, not only among men, but among ideas and ethical codes. There must be receptivity toward foreign influences. "Any necessary discrimination could await the proofs of experience." In fact, Gide's Theseus does finally admit differences, a hierarchy, because it helps the state to function better. That is to say, for proper functioning both social and intellectual processes will demand such organization (consider the means by which we attain to inner unity), though it may conflict with some ideal of the perfectly just and rational. But by his efforts to make human values the principle of social organization, Theseus—as Plutarch too informs us—won for Athenians the name of "people," that is, raised them to full humanity.

There follows a brief mention of the ill-fated love of Phaedra for his son Hippolytus, and their deaths—here Gide takes his cue from

Racine—and then the story closes with an episode for which the *Oedipus at Colonnus* seems to be Gide's precedent. Theseus is "surprised," however, that so little has been said of it. It is a meeting with Oedipus, a "moment at the crossroads when our two careers confronted each other." In this magnificent section, Gide poses against his hero, triumphant, a hero of the opposite kind, the defeated, against his idea of man's proper destiny its classic adversary, and thus finds an opportunity of summing up in conclusion the meaning of his fable. Faced with the blind wanderer, Theseus expresses a faint sense of his possible inferiority. "No doubt I had triumphed everywhere, but on a level which, in comparison with Oedipus, seemed to me merely human—inferior, I might say." It puzzles him, moreover, that Oedipus was not only defeated by life, but seems actually to have contributed to his defeat by putting out his eyes. Why? he asks. The answer is that, as Theseus is a kind of humanist, devoted to tangible triumph as a man and on earth, Oedipus is one whose life has taught him that the spiritual and the earthly are in conflict and that the spiritual demands for its fulfillment the renunciation of the earthly. He blinded himself to shut out "the falsehood in which I no longer believed . . . and this so as to break through to reality. . . . And at the moment when the blue of the sky went black before me, my inward firmament became bright with stars."

Theseus is ready to agree that the nontemporal world is important, but why, he demands, place it in opposition with the one "in which we live and act"? Because, Oedipus replies, what was dramatized in his own life, and now in the unhappy lives of his sons, is the truth that man is stained from birth, that he can break away from evil, the inevitable fruit of his original sin, only with divine aid—grace. And the chief road to this is through suffering and renunciation. It is by such means that Oedipus himself has attained grace in spite of his overwhelming sins. This was for Gide the great *other* idea, which he understood and for which he even felt a haunting sympathy, but which his whole life and work opposed. In Gide man is the measure, in all his fecundity and variety—not one part of him or another—and none of the great ideas by which he has in the past enabled himself to advance is large enough or strong enough to contain him forever. "I remain a child of this world," says Theseus, "and I believe that man, be he what he may, and with whatever blemishes you believe him to be stained, is in duty bound to play out his hand to the end." It was this faith that made Gide a truer heir of Goethe, that supreme apostle of man's divinity, than his contemporary, and indeed, his peer, who consciously wore the Goethe mantle: Thomas Mann. Both Goethe and Gide found life good—on the whole—and considered it man's chief duty to make the most of himself, never to linger, but always to "pass on" along the road of his own endless realization. We have seen that in Gide this is far from being the road of self-indulgence. What it amounts to, rather, is a call never to come to rest in any fixed structure of ideas, attitudes, beliefs, to remain forever open to the new experience or insight which may break up an old pattern, to keep to *oneself* the responsibility to judge and evaluate. In a time when many are reacting to the world's undoubted horrors with an abdication of this responsibility, a responsibility which is a condition of growth and which is man's ennobling opportunity as well as his cross, this is a faith it is good to have so greatly affirmed.

Of course, nothing that has here been said can convey the delicacy with which these ideas have been dramatized in their truest human context. Gide's style is the perfection of its type, a clean spare line drawn about his ripened meanings, and his wisdom emerges always as charm, wit, grace—entertainment in the highest sense—in a single word: beauty.

Thomas Mann's *The Holy Sinner*

It is not the least among the distinctions of Thomas Mann's novels that they are intensely enjoyable. This is worth mentioning because he has what might have been the handicap of being a philosophic novelist, and his tales are the deliberate embodiment of ideas. His characters are "real"—that is, they exist in their own right as convincing and recognizable human beings—and, more entertaining still, they are generally passionate. Indeed, they are often physically passionate, and few novelists convey more persuasively than Mann the intoxication of lust. Moreover, these characters always unfold their natures and their author's meanings in stories arranged for maximum dramatic effectiveness. Such pleasure does he take in his marvelous showmanship, in fact, that he is not unwilling to call attention to it, often announcing his big scenes with the complacent preliminary flourish of a performing magician. Add to this the fact that he is very funny, a fact to which we don't do enough justice if we talk merely of his celebrated "irony." It is true that most of his humor comes from his ironic doubleness of vision, his sly "seeing through" things. But irony does not always appear as humor. His does because this joke of another side to things, instead of making him weakly bitter, delights him—which means he has a tenderness, and even a relish, for the human mixture. (*The Magic Mountain* is essentially a comic novel—we hardly ever stop smiling, even where we are thrilling with awe.)[1] Mann gives us thus, for all his concern with ideas, the richest combination of fictional pleasures. And because of an economy which makes all his details mean a surprising number of things at once, these pleasures in his novels often come together. This intensifies them. A wonderful example is the climax of *The Holy Sinner* (published in 1951), a recognition scene in which the mysteries of both the human drama and its theme are simultaneously unveiled, and we are moved, we laugh, and our minds blaze with insight all at the same time.

Or rather, this has been true only of some of us. Though most of its readers find it entertaining enough, there has been a tendency to think that to its success in this regard has been sacrificed either general meaningfulness altogether, or at least that gravity *about* meanings which is apparently required as proof that they are deeply felt. It has been seen as too obviously written for its author's relaxation and its readers' amusement to be taken seriously. Or Mann is regarded as having "parodied" his characteristic insights, as having exhibited a "complacency" that destroyed their interest and their value.

Now I believe that, lively story though the novel is, a chief source of our pleasure in it is precisely intellectual—it is the constant and growing meaningfulness of every development—and that a theme *has* been adequately presented. And while there is no question that something like parody and something like complacency make for a great deal of the fun, to use the words pejoratively is to have missed the point, since these effects are part of it. For what *The Holy Sinner* aims to show us is that good and evil—holiness and sinfulness—are necessary to each other, and that the godlike foreknowing author—knowledge, in short—can hardly take evil as "seriously" as the ordinary man must, for he sees, even as his simple humanity shrinks from it, the good which it makes possible. Nor is this all: a descent from "proper" gravity also results from a meaning which goes deeper still. Not only are good and evil mixed to a point where simple judgment is confused and neither can be taken with full seriousness; the conception of life which, together, they represent is shown to be, like every conception, fundamentally arbitrary, an imposition on indifferent nature, from whose point of view it can sometimes look terribly silly. And these two ideas are the theme of *The Holy Sinner,* of which, however, as will appear, there is much more to be said. Far, indeed, from providing its author with relaxation after the profound philosophic labors of *Doctor Faustus,* this novel is a deliberate and clear extension of Mann's characteristic insights into areas they had never before so thoroughly explored. And there is hardly a detail on any page that does not provide us with the intellectual thrill of the double awareness: that of its deep, familiar roots and its startling new blossoms.

In order to see how this novel comes to mean what I have said—and somewhat more—it will be helpful to look first at its story. I will repeat it, but I will use as my source one of the medieval versions—that in the *Gesta Romanorum*—which served Mann for his. The two are almost identical, and it will also be of interest to catch a partial glimpse of the novel's origins.

An emperor, dying, charges his son to find a husband for his beloved daughter, but soon after his death, she grows heavy with her brother's child. Full of remorse, the brother accepts the counsel of a trusty knight that he set out on a penitential voyage to the Holy Land, while the knight's wife assists at the birth of his son. The young emperor dies abroad and his son, unbaptized, is abandoned to the sea in a cask. He is provided with rich garments and money, however, and near him is placed a tablet on which his high and sinful birth is revealed and his finder is requested to baptize, rear, and educate him. The doubly bereaved mother determines never to marry, and some time later, re-fusing the advances of a hot-headed duke, provokes him to a war which devastates her country and leaves her, for refuge, only a single fortified city.

A good story-teller, the anonymous author now drops the queen and her interesting trouble and turns to her son Gregory (Mann fol-lowing his lead here as elsewhere). The sea has cast him up at the feet of an abbot and his fisherman. He is baptized by the abbot and edu-cated at his monastery—where he soon surpasses all in knowledge—and he is reared as a son of one of the fishermen. One day, accidentally hurting a supposed brother, he learns from the angry mother that he was a foundling out of the sea. He declares to the abbot that he can stay no longer, but wants to go off as a soldier, and he begs in "intolerable suspense" some knowledge of his true parents. He cannot be moved by the abbot's promise that he will himself be abbot in time if he remains, and so the old man consents to his departure and shows him the tablet found in the cask. Gregory swoons with horror. When he can speak again, he asks to be made a knight so that he can "hasten to the Holy Land to do battle for the sins of the unhappy authors of my being." This is done, but contrary winds drive the ship in which he has set out onto the coast of his mother's city. There, he learns of the queen's plight, offers her his services, kills the duke, and restores her lost land; and finally at the suggestion of her steward that the realm needs such a man, is given the hand of the queen in marriage.

They are blissfully happy, but one day, while Gregory is out to the hunt, the queen is informed by a maid that he often emerges from his chamber in tears. She searches the room, finds the tablet, and con-fronts him with it, and though both struggle for a moment against full realization, the agony is not to be avoided and she cries out at last: "My son! For thou art so; my only son and my husband and my lord." We see that the old tale did not have to wait for Mann to grow disquietingly suggestive. The exclamation is followed by her question: "Why, O God, didst Thou permit my birth since I was born to be guilty of such wickedness?"—a familiar theological challenge, but surely especially pertinent here, that is, in a tale designed precisely to answer it and to show that her wickedness was essential to a process leading to the supremely good.

And Gregory says: "I thought to have shunned this evil, and I have fallen into the snares of the devil." We suddenly learn that he has considered the possibility that he unwittingly marry his mother, a very real one, of course, though improbable. No modern novelist, however, exposing unconscious knowledge and guilt, the old author does not pause to wonder whether Gregory's awareness that he *could* marry his mother means, as it might well, a suppressed awareness that the queen *could* be she. The fact of incest is bad enough, and forbidding the anguished woman to leave her throne, Gregory sets out the next day to seek penance on a pilgrimage that ends on a rock in the sea. To this he has been led by a fisherman, whose wife had persuaded the man to shelter him and who obligingly chains him to the rock and throws the key into the water.

Seventeen years later, on the death of the Pope, a voice from heaven declares that a man of God called Gregory is to replace him. Some messengers, in search of the chosen one, reach the fisherman's hut, and though he thinks the pilgrim must be dead, the key to his chains suddenly turns up in a fish's belly and this seems a good omen. They find their man on the rock, they bring him to Rome, whose church bells ring of their own accord at his approach, and Gregory becomes a great Pope, sought out for counsel and assistance by multitudes. Hearing of his sanctity, his mother goes to him to confess and be absolved. It is not till after the confession that they recognize each other. She weeps for joy, and we are told in conclusion that he founded a monastery of which he made her abbess, and that soon afterward both died.

Thus the old tale. Now in the *Gesta Romanorum*, each story is followed by an "application" or moral, which a recent editor has impatiently stripped away as an excrescence on the pure narrative. We can sympathize with him. The emperor, we are bluntly told of this one, is Christ, who gave the human soul, his daughter, to its brother, the flesh. "The son born of these is all mankind. The cask is the Holy Spirit, which floats on the sea of the world." The bad duke is the Devil—and so forth. The medieval application, in short, seems not so much to reveal meaning in all that sin, anguish, and triumph as to cancel out their actuality. Yet, as Mann will show us, the old monks were moving in the right direction. And to what has already been said of the theme we may now add that the tale *is* full of Christian meaning: it is precisely the relationship of Mann's familiar insights to insights embodied in Christianity that Mann's version is designed to show.

But the fact that the old tale is so perfect a vehicle for both that it need hardly be changed at all presents the novelist with his major aesthetic problem. The problem is: How to make us hidebound realists accept a medieval tale of Christian miracle. To solve this problem, he does two things. Not only does he bring the tale closer to us, making its characters and their crises "real"—this we would expect. He also brings *us* closer to the tale, by loosening our allegiance to the modern literary convention of realism. This is one of the two chief reasons for the monk who is his narrator and for the "rambling" reflections with which this monk introduces his story.

The convention is attacked head-on: Mann pointedly begins with the story's "grace-abounding end,"[2] the miraculous ringing of the bells of Rome. "Who rings them?" it is asked. And the answer is "the spirit of story-telling," a spirit which is "as air," "free," "abstract," "not subject to distinctions of here and there." We are thus reminded at the start, we who might object to the miracles to come, that any story, for all the tricks by which it tries to appear "natural," is essentially miraculous. "Reality" is as clay in its hands, to be molded to the spirit's purposes. But the narrator goes on. "And yet he [the spirit of storytelling] can gather himself into a person . . . and be incarnate in somebody who speaks in him"—and this somebody now introduces himself. He is Clemens, an Irish monk with all the limiting particularity of any actual person (we glimpse at once his funny jealousy, as an Irishman, of the Roman authority). To say that he "embodies" that spirit disturbs our monk, however, for the body is the domain of Satan. And yet, on the other hand, it is also "the vehicle of the soul and God-given reason, without which these would be deprived of their basis," and so one must regard the body as a "necessary evil." Now we shall soon learn that this remark has more than one connection with the novel. What is pertinent here is that it is another step in that instruction in the mysteries of art with which Mann has found it politic to begin. The "necessary evil" of the body is in this case a metaphor for the particular narrative conventions through which the spirit of storytelling must operate, but which are not identical with it, which, indeed, work against it by limiting the freedom that is its essential character. The implication is clear that though we must use a particular convention, we must not forget it is only a "vehicle," nor reject what the spirit may have to offer by other means.

So, throughout the story, we find the monk slyly discrediting the realistic convention which he perforce employs. "What know I of knighthood and venery," he interrupts his own vivid and enthusiastic description of the young prince's education. The technical terms "which I use with such apparent ease," he goes on, "I have just picked up. But so is the way and the spirit of story-telling which I embody that all it tells of it pretends to have experienced and to be at home in it." With realism itself thus shown to be mere trickery, the miracles to come should find us less stiffly "modern" in our response to them.

But we are still not done with the monk's rich first pages. He points out that the spirit of storytelling, though it has submitted in him to the limiting of incarnation, is at least embodied in a monk, Clemens, one who has "put off" with the grosser name of Morhold his fleshly self. In him, therefore, the spirit "has preserved much of that abstraction which enables it to ring from all the titular basilicas of the city at once." And he gives two examples of this "abstraction." First, his manuscript is not dated—he would make it impossible to say that it takes place at one time and no other. And second, it is written in a fluid mixture of languages (these are "Latin, French, German, or Anglo-Saxon," and we do, in fact, meet scraps of each later on) which all "become one—in other words, language." "For the thing is so, that the spirit of narration is free to the point of abstraction, whose medium is language in and for itself, language itself, which sets itself as absolute and does not greatly care about idioms and national linguistic gods. That indeed would be polytheistic and pagan. God is spirit, and above languages is language."[3] Have we not been told that the monk is here an artist, a man detached to some degree from the desires and fears in which he deals, his point of view deeper than common, more "spiritual"? And do not these two examples of the tale's "abstraction" define precisely the abstraction to which the artist aspires: timelessness and universality? We are to find, indeed, that the people in this tale (if not the way in which they express themselves) are not peculiar to one time, but recognizably human and, hence, possible always; and that the tale's meaning, its truth, though embodied in medieval Christian idioms and symbols is not identical with these, but only being expressed by them, as it can be expressed also by the "languages" of other cultures and religions. To think differently is, pagan-like, to bow to the mere vehicles—idols which incessantly multiply themselves—not to the Truth which they all attempt, with only partial success, to embody.

But, as I have said, there is another reason for this preface, as well as for the monk it introduces. These pages serve too as a characteristic Mann overture, foreshadowing the developments to come. That whole business of the distinction between spirit and body—or rather of the relationship between them—is also a way of describing the novel's plot, and is pertinent both to its concern with art and its concern with Christianity. And this is the second function of Mann's medieval narrator. Just as in his character of storyteller he shows how art works (weakening our faith in those conventions which the tale must violate), so, as a monk, he gives us the tale's Christian meaning. And thus he unites in a single person the novel's double intention.

Before we explore this directly, however, we must examine how Mann performed his second task, that of bringing the tale closer to us. For in fiction psychology must precede philosophy, and it is naturally

Mann's understanding of his people—of their experience—that will determine what he discovers their fate to mean. It will also, of course, reveal the permanent human significance of the Christian "language" in which the monk describes it.

Mann's basic method of making the story "real" to us is to expose the additional, the hidden, motives for every act. It is simplicity that is archaic; with a warring mixture of motives, we are instantly at home. So the dying father turns out to have left his daughter unmarried because he had loved her only too well, rejecting all her suitors as if they were hated rivals. Just such a rival, indeed, had the son, her brother, become, a fact the young man is aware of, if not "on top [where] the soul pretends," then "underneath, where truth abides in quietness"—a phrase used during the climactic confession, but pertinent throughout. For he dreams revealing dreams of the father's terrible animosity.

In Mann's version, Gregor (as he is called) does not have to wait for the discovery of his birth to feel beneath his apparent relatedness to those about him something that divides him from them, something both sweet and bitter as it both raises him above them and sinks him below. For his high and sinful birth has its counterpart—or result—in certain "gifts" which make him awkwardly different and which make not only his "father's" life as a fisherman seem impossible to him, but even that of cloistered scholar apparently no more suitable. He dreams of knighthood—of winning love and glory by rescuing the distressed. And when he leaves the monastery to seek out his parents and by such knighthood to redeem their sin, this comes less as the simply "logical" decision of the legend than as the realization of presentiments and wishes.

As for the mother-son incest, that unfortunate accident turns out to have been no accident at all, but a fate secretly willed by both. And this awful guilt is exposed first darkly in innumerable ambiguities that enrich from its earliest moment the narrative of their relationship, and then plainly at the end where Pope and Duchess (the queen of the old tale) confess their deepest secrets. The many little signs that he was her son which she had failed to recognize—though they had alarmed her and started memories of bliss and pain—their meaning *had*, in fact, been grasped "underneath," and it was her sinful desire for her own flesh and blood that both prevented conscious recognition and made the pretended relationship so wondrously sweet. Nor was the son less guilty, as the great Pope is to pain her by firmly insisting. Reason alone would have had to tell him that she *could* have been his mother. But feeling, he says, had made it unmistakable from the beginning.

Such mixtures, such ambiguities, occur throughout the novel. But it is in the character and fate of Gregor, the holy sinner, that we find the particular mixture that leads us most directly to its theme. An early statement of it comes when the Duchess, thanking her young champion for his conquest of her enemy, points out what seems a contradiction between his thought and his behavior. "Wherein does the humility and abasement of the Christian draw the courage, nobility and presumption of the knight?" "Lady," he replies, "all bravery and every daring emprise to which we dedicate ourselves, and on which we set our all and uttermost springs only from the knowledge of our guilt, springs from the fervid yearning to justify our lives and accordingly before God to redeem a little of our debt of sin." This explanation of Gregor's behavior, which makes it hard to know whether he should be blamed for his sin or given credit for his bravery and holiness, is a central formula in the novel, not only stated explicitly a number of times, but clearly defining the very plot. We know that if there had been no sinful birth to be discovered, he would never have left the monastery on that journey leading to the papal throne (indeed, he would not have existed). When, married to the Duchess, he becomes an especially good Duke, it is "only because he so urgently needed to be." And when the mother learns that the Pope is her son, she exclaims, "Grigorss, poor darling, how ruthlessly you must have done penance, for God to have set you so far above us sinners." Thus even his ultimate holiness is linked to a penance made especially severe because of a sinfulness especially black.

And this holiness is even further compromised. For the Pope, it is—"underneath"—a thing welcomed not merely as the necessary counterweight to all his sins, but also as the tool of a selfish motive. Mann's hero, no less than that of the old tale, sets out on his fateful journey in order to do battle for the sins of his parents. And his first words when, on that desolate rock, he is given the great name of Pope, and with it the keys to the gates of heaven, the power to bind and loose, are, "Sweet parents, I will loose you." Moreover, "has he not become so great a Pope," it is later asked, "in order that his fame should penetrate everywhere, and so to her ear as well?"

So, with the mixture at work in Gregor, we reach the first stage in our grasp of the novel's theme. But if we are thus led to "see through" the good to its dark other side, we are not left in mere cynicism. For this double nature of the Pope not only compromises his greatness, it also belongs to it—it is itself the source of the peculiar wisdom which makes him a blessing to his people. Our first example of this occurs immediate after his descent from the rock. In Mann too, the fisherman's wife had persuaded her husband to shelter the pilgrim. But the modern novelist reveals that when the fisherman gladly chains him to the rock, it is out of spite at his obvious nobility, a spite aggravated by the suspicion that his wife's generosity was due to the pilgrim's good looks. And lo, when the fisherman's wife kneels before the Pope seventeen years later, she confesses that her husband had been right. "Wantonness was at the bottom of the good I did you, depraved lost soul that I am." At this, in a decision foreshadowing many others of which we are to be briefly told, the new Pope willingly pronounces the words, "Absolvo te." For "seldom," he says "is one wholly wrong in pointing out the sinful in the good, but God graciously looks at the good deed even though its root is in fleshliness."

Now this "Christian" forbearance engenders problems—as we are instantly reminded. "The woman was blissful," the monk observes. "I suspect she derived from his absolution leave to feel still a little love for him in fleshly wise." Forgiveness of sin, that is, can sometimes work like toleration of it. Nevertheless, since "no one was worthy, and he himself on account of his flesh most unworthy of his dignity," the Pope chose thereafter to take the risk of "enforcing the divine mercy in cases where the Deity would scarcely have come on by Itself." For he believed that

> one should lighten the sinner's load, that remorse might be sweet to him. Justice is hard- and horny-handed, while the world of the flesh needs indeed firmness, yet gentleness. If one so zealously pursue the sinner, one may well bring more harm than healing. Too rash a penance laid upon a seeker for grace may make him lose heart, not bear it and again renounce God, spoilt as he is by the Devil, whose service he in reverse remorse takes up again. Accordingly it is statesmanlike to make mercy go before justice, since it creates the right measure in the life of the spirit by which means the sinner is saved and the good is constantly preserved, that the honour of God may wax mightily in the Roman Empire.

Here, then, is a theme for this novel, "entertaining" though it is, and one which surely justifies the "complacency," the lack of full seriousness, with which it takes its appalling sins. The greatness through which the chosen ones shed blessings on the rest of us is born out of weakness—they could not have become our fruitful superiors if they had not felt painfully the reverse—and *knowledge* of their weakness is, of their greatness, an essential ingredient. *A* theme, I said, for even this must submit to its author's irony, which will carry us deeper. But before we descend, let us pause to examine what the student of Mann will already have noticed: the fact that in the holy sinner, no less than in his monkish narrator, we find Mann's eternal artist, of whose character and fate the story is a kind of parable. It is, I think, no coincidence that the chapter devoted to the greatness of the Pope and the blessings he brought should end with the observation that, while part of his authority was due to his knowedge, part was due also to the fact that he was "very beautiful to look upon, as children of sin, for whatever reason, often are." For "he is gladly hearkened to, whom one loves." It is the artist's business too, Dr. Johnson—and not only he—has observed "to instruct by pleasing." Moreover, Mann showed us long before that such pleasure is a fruit of "sin" in that it comes from the lawless realm of desire and feeling—the artist is one afflicted with knowledge of this, a knowledge he shares with his happier ordinary brothers in beautiful form. At any rate, the story of Gregor abounds in evidence of the kinship.

There is first the fact that the sin which gives him birth (a sin fruitful at once, we are pointedly told, as his father's virtuous marriage had not been for years) and which, in his monstrous marriage, leads on to his final glory, is at bottom the sin of excessive self-love. Mann has changed the old tale precisely to enforce this view of its incest, for he has made the guilty brother and sister twins, and he has explicitly named the evil mating self-love more than once. Elsewhere, he had already spoken of the love with which the artist can regard his very hand. And in "The Blood of the Walsungs," the incest of a pair of twins is a kind of substitute for art, growing out of the same dangerous soil. Artistic sensibility there ends in sterile and destructive self-indulgence because self-love is not balanced by that love for the "others" which, in Mann's view, art needs in order to rise above mere Bohemianism and to grow productive. But in Gregor, the balance is present. Though the most frightful "self-love" is essential to his fate, he knows salvation must lie in turning to "other blood," as that earlier successful artist Tonio Kröger, drawn forever to the healthy blue-eyed ones (the "bourgeois," the "human"), knew it long before.[4]

There is above all Gregor's character, which any reader of Mann must instantly recognize. He is the familiar dreamer, gifted and lonely, irritating others with a superiority which he makes even more offensive by trying charitably to hide it, melancholy at last with a sense that even with his "rightness," that is, his gifts, so shady in their origins, "it was quite distinctly not right," and longing for a glory he needs in order to assuage his guilt and win others to him. Again we are reminded of Tonio Kröger, who becomes an artist because for him "there is no such thing as a right way," and who, pained to find that an officer he has been prepared to respect actually writes verses, cries, "I ask you: a lieutenant! A man of the world! He surely [did] not need to. . . ."

It is not only in the awkwardness of his superiority, however, but also in its nature that Gregor resembles the artist. He is one who in competition "came off better with his weakness than the others with their strength . . . because he understood better than they did how to pull himself together." To this power of concentration is added another, of which we learn when he conquers the Duchess's evil wooer, here a Duke named Roger. Instead of simply chasing and killing him, as in the old tale, he makes him a prisoner, that his power might be useful to the Duchess. And he does so by a trick which involves using the enemy's own strength to entangle him and then gripping his sword in one hand, though the weapon draws blood. The aptness of this struggle as a symbol for the life of art—and for more—will be examined further on. It is enough now to observe that this power of "pulling himself together" beyond the average and this "firm-holding hand" become Gregor's leitmotifs, the phrases recurring again and again. And surely these, together with the ambition born of his guilt, are essential characteristics of productive genius.

Finally, when Gregor first learns he is not the fisherman's son, he cries, "Since I know who I am not, only one thing avails; the journey after myself, the knowledge of who I am." He soon discovers his exalting and humiliating birth, and his journey becomes a struggle for redemption. But are not both motives involved in the fate of the artist? We hardly need, in order to see the bearing of the first, to remember Mann's own observation in the preface to his *Stories of Three Decades* that works of art are modes of self-realization, "stones on that harsh road which we must walk to learn of ourselves." And the bearing of the second motive the whole story has made clear. The artist, as Mann always showed him, is divided from the "others" by a self-consciousness which is born of extreme self-love and which means inferiority, as it makes for awkwardness in ordinary living, and superiority, as it makes for knowledge. And his achievement, in which he shares his hard-won knowledge with those others by making it easy to take, by making it beautiful, is also due in large part to the desire to atone for his guilty difference and to win their love.

I mentioned Mann's use of the leitmotif. For Mann, his notion of the artist is, of course, the basic leitmotif in the whole body of his work. And it functions in the same way as the smaller ones do in particular books. In these, it is a phrase which first rises naturally out of a particular human context and then recurs in others where it takes on a more general significance. This, we know, is a source of Mann's ironic humor. When the Pope, for instance, decides that a bastard can become a bishop, "if the illegitimate one was a true and religious man, and godly, and of a firm-holding hand," we recognize in that last phrase a memory of his youth and we smile to see through the pretense of impersonal wisdom. And yet we see more than the lowly personal origin of the generalization; we see also, with a small shock of insight, the general meaning of what began as personal. Just so do we see through the present tale of good and evil to Mann's familiar ideas about the artist, but with a smile not wholly ironical, for we have also learned these ideas can take in much more than we thought, their personal basis only guaranteeing the felt validity of the rest.

To all of which it must be added, however, that if Gregor is Mann's eternal artist, he is also a demonstration of how Mann's attitude had changed. Though he began his career by emphasizing what divided the artist from the others, he emphasized now what joins him to them, the social task his peculiar isolation and anguish enable him to perform. And this is why his artist came to be shown more and more—remember Joseph—in the role of leader and savior.

It remains for us to descend to rock bottom. The theme we have already found—that of the close and fruitful relationship of good and evil—is not, as has been said, the novel's only meaning, though upon it depends the actual story with all its shame and triumph. There is that other "opposition" I have mentioned, an opposition which is prior. Before we can have good and evil at all, we must impose a spiritual scheme on the chaos of Nature, who is herself supremely "indifferent." "He was a man and she a woman and so they [mother and son] could become man and wife, for that is all that Nature cares about," the monk tells us, "desperately" trying to justify the pair whose love and need have won his "Christian" sympathy. But "my spirit cannot find itself in Nature; it rebels," he goes on. "She is of the Devil for her indifference is bottomless." No, spirit cannot leave them simply man and woman, it must give them names—mother and son—and thereby replace their joyous indifference with notions of sin, and with pain. When the mother and son learn their "true" relationship and she in horror utters it by name, he shudders and holds up his hand. "Mother, desecrated one," he says. "Speak not so plainly. But yet do so. I understand why thou dost. We shall speak expressly and name things by name to our chastisement. For to tell truth, that itself is chastisement."

But this naming of things is also absurd. And of this absurdity Mann playfully reminds us—such is his mastery of his ideas and his art—at the very moments when it is causing its most moving anguish and exaltation. Here is another serious reason for his lightness and especially for his perpetual "kidding" at those climactic moments about the tangle of relationships which the sinful-fruitful matings have produced. "Since the father is the brother of the mother," the knight Eisengrin reproachfully explains to the first incestuous pair, "he is uncle to the child, and the mother, since she is the father's sister, is its aunt and fantastically carries her little nephew or niece about in her womb. Such a disorder and confusion have you unthoughted brought into God's world!" But what has happened after all? A young male and female occupying adjoining beds have responded "naturally" to the "natural" promptings of their flesh. And they have had such fun! And they are so ready to be happy with the baby that results! That confusion, which grows even more laughable when the nephew-son marries his aunt-mother, and, if he were to marry *their* children, would mean, as he says, "the defeat of thought," that ridiculous complication is not inherent in the act, but comes out of man's mind and would not exist if we would only leave the blissful pair unnamed. And this is what that "kidding" is meant to tell us.

But if man's naming of things, which enables him to distinguish and relate them (in spite of nature's indifference), can look silly, and if that silliness can becloud with guilt and anguish an otherwise delightful experience, there is one thing more to be said of it. Without it, there is no need to concentrate our powers, no need to struggle toward redeeming greatness. Without it, Gregor would never have been Pope.

Now what, precisely, is the spiritual scheme which makes possible the foolishness, guilt, and triumph of this novel? The question is answered in the monk's rueful observation that the aged Duchess, despite her sufferings, remained handsome and proud of gait, "the nobility of the flesh strangely reasserting itself against the abasement of the soul by reason of Christian consciousness of sin." With this, the deepest aspect of the subject and theme begins to grow clear. But Mann's ultimate audacity has still not been mentioned. When Gregor cries out that he is a "monster," set off by his monstrous birth from all mankind, the abbot thus reassures him. "But no . . . you are *a child of man,* and a very dear one, even although not in the regular order. God is full of wonders. Very well can *love* come out of evil, and out of disorder something ordered for the best" (italics mine). When the royal mother addresses heaven in a prayer on the eve of her marriage to her son, she prays not directly to God, with whose perfect justice she does not stand well, but to Mary, Queen of Heaven—to a picture of the Annunciation, where also a woman is on the eve of a most irregular union. She speaks in verse, as do certain other characters at moments of passion, as though poetry—art—were a device for throwing dust into the eyes of the reason. And her prayer has the strange air of a demand for special consideration, on the startling grounds that Mary must have a special sympathy with her sin.

> For thou [she says] art of the Highest child, as are we creatures all, and yet art thou His mother mild and thus He all must do that she doth say and her obey. Somewhat thou ow'st to me, with

woman's guile I said, that thou with God shouldst aid, since He for sinner's need in thy pure womb came in, and thee His mother made. Had never no one sin committed, ne'er had been what God with thee hath done, nor hadst thou everlasting praises won.

Finally: "A new task . . . have I to set your soul, but a merciful one," the Pope tells his mother at the end. "It is to grasp the three-in-oneness of the child, spouse and Pope [i.e., father]." And surely there, if not before, the breathtaking parallel should leap into light. Not only is this novel about the human habit of imposing a spiritual scheme on the indifferent chaos of nature; and not only is it more particularly about the scheme known as Christianity. *The Holy Sinner* is a secular version of the story of Christ, as the old commentator, though not perfectly accurate, had divined, and the meaning of both stories is the same.

Is not Jesus the child and—as He is God—the Spouse and the Father of Mary, Queen of Heaven? And though He is of high birth (none higher), is He not a child also of sinful humanity, without whose sin He would never have been born, and whose guilt He suffers His frightful penance to redeem? What, moreover, is the distinguishing character of His greatness? It is precisely Gregor's "bold way of enforcing the divine mercy in cases where the Deity would scarcely have come on it by Itself." This is a purpose understandable enough in view of His own questionable, mixed nature, and His "natural" desire to save His own parents. But if His holiness is partly "selfish," like Gregor's, it has also Gregor's justifying result. This is "to create the right measure in the life of the spirit," to mitigate for feeble man the crushing absoluteness of pure Deity, lest he despair—as well he might—and fall back entirely into the arms of the Devil.[5]

And does not this justification apply to art as well? Both art and Christianity exist to save us from the dominion of nature, of passions uncurbed by human law. These have their own joys, and even "dignity," but their realm, finally, is one in which the spirit of man cannot abide, for it is a realm of chaos. Yet the peculiar value of both art and Christianity is that while each stands firm against the chaos, they do not turn their backs on it completely. How should they? Not only would it be inhuman, for the human partakes of it; but each grows out of that chaos and lives on it—nature and passion are their "basis" and provide them with their special task.

And here we are ready to see that in one respect at least the tale's old commentator had been exactly right. That hotheaded ruler whom Gregor fought with over—or for—the Duchess, and whom he conquered by holding firm to the man's naked sword, Mann too has seen him as the Devil. And, indeed, if the woman represents humanity, both in the divine incest and in the novel (where, in her fleshly weakness, she speaks out for nature, or prays for indulgence of it, and where, at the end, the flesh retains its dignity in her in spite of the soul's abasement); and if Gregor represents Christ—holiness born of sinful man, whose guilt he redeems; who *else* would Roger be? For he was "a prince," the monk remarks, "such as for my life I cannot bear, a shameless fellow. Even at fifteen years he had a pointed beard, eyes like burning coals, eyebrows arched like his moustache, and was tall, hairy, quarrelsome and gallant, a cockerel, a heart-breaker, a dueller, a devil of a fellow, to me quite unspeakable." No woman "less than fifty" was safe from this "cock and stallion," whose lust for the Duchess, however, was the great motive of his life and who wished, we learn finally, to "increase his realm by adding hers." Gregor made him prisoner—and this is Mann's addition to the old tale, as has been said—because as such his power could be useful to the Duchess. Religion too, of course, would only harness the passions, not kill them, for it is they which give heat and energy—and even birth—to its higher purposes. And how does the Son and Champion of humanity fight His lawless Adversary? Brought into being because of sin and for sin, He knows the Devil well enough to turn His own strength and weapons against him, though He must undergo the risk of intimate contact with them, must hold the sword firm in His bleeding hand. Exactly the same is true of the artist, that dealer in the passions, who uses their dangerous power to ensure a triumph which means their conquest and control. And so it is not strange that our narrator, our good artist-monk with the feelings always comically mixed, should have preferred, as he frankly confesses, to write of the sinful brother-sister pair, rather than of another he might have chosen, saintly from the beginning.

No meaning! *The Holy Sinner* is at least about the absurdity, the tragedy, and the glory of Christianity and of art. And the rest of what it means I must leave to others.

And now, why shouldn't I share with the reader the letter about *The Holy Sinner* I received from Thomas Mann in response to the foregoing essay? It is dated May 5, 1954, and was sent from Kilchberg am Zurichsee, Alte Landstrasse 39, in Switzerland. After a pleasant expression of thanks, the letter goes on:

> The little thing is especially close to my heart and I am often remembering with a certain tenderness the time when I wrote it in Pacific Palisades, California. It was a *good* time and I was

amused in a rather deep and uncommon sense of the word. . . .
You are the first American critic who calls my books "enjoyable",
"humoristic", "funny" instead of "ponderous" and "pompous"
which are the epithets mostly given to them. What a terrible
misunderstanding! . . . . I assure you, in the German original
these books are still more funny than in English. My desire and
goal is to entertain and I am fully in sympathy with my Pope
Gregor when he answers to his mother and wife at the end of
their colloquy of confession: "Wir taten es, um Gott eine Un-
terhaltung zu bereiten." ["We did it to provide God with an
entertainment."]

Cordially yours,

Thomas Mann

Hawthorne's
The Blithedale Romance

Henry James was right. *The Blithedale Romance,* Hawthorne's fourth novel (published in 1852), is not only "very charming"; it is "the lightest, the brightest, the liveliest" of all his "unhumorous fictions."[1] It is also rich in his characteristic psychological subtlety and highly dramatic; it is written with such easy-seeming mastery of English prose music and such wit that its style is a pleasure in itself; and, dealing with a recent period of idealistic social experiment, as well as with the status of women, it is right now strikingly timely. Yet the novel has always had, and continues to have, a mixed press. A study of Hawthorne written some years ago shows the sort of case that can be made against it. After noting that Hawthorne at first vacillated among many titles for the novel ("Hollingsworth," "Zenobia," "Priscilla," "Miles Coverdale's Three Friends," etc.), this study's author goes on:

> Such indecision corresponds all too well to the indecisiveness of the story itself. . . . Hawthorne's customary equivocation about social and moral ideas has been extended to include such apparently elementary matters as his moral estimate of his characters, his notion of their feelings about one another, and even his factual knowledge of their previous lives. . . . [The novel] is just coherent enough to permit its critics to call it failed utopian satire or failed melodrama or failed autobiography. The necessity has rarely been perceived of putting the various imperfect parts within a single rationale that would explain Hawthorne's inability to make any one of them his focus of interest. . . . If Hawthorne has blurred all his portraits except Coverdale's, backed away from the simplest explanations of fact, exploited literal scenes for a cabalistic meaning that is lost upon the reader, and included episodes that make virtually no sense apart

from such meaning, then we must infer that Hawthorne, as well as Coverdale, is at the mercy of unconscious logic.

In that logic, *spiritual aspiration, reform of humanity,* and *romantic art* are interchangeable terms; each represents flight from mature sexual challenge.[2]

I quote the above at such length because it exemplifies both how and why Hawthorne's novel can be misread, and perhaps especially by contemporary scholar-critics, whose natural intelligence tends to be hampered by an appetite for expertise. For *The Blithedale Romance,* like *Moby Dick,* like *Wilhelm Meister's Apprenticeship,* like *The Magic Mountain,* like *The Counterfeiters* (like in kind, if not in stature), belongs to a class of what may be called wisdom-novels, novels whose texture and themes rise, not out of one idea of what is so or another, but out of the conflict between all ideas—indeed, between the truth-seeking human mind— and the complexities of experience. Such novels are written to explore this conflict in a given life-situation, rather than to treat the situation as a problem to be solved. But the object of expertise is precisely to escape from the conflict into the comparative simplicity of some problem-solving theory.[3] Thus the passage I quoted substitutes that "unconscious logic" of fashionable psychology for the difficulties of what Hawthorne is actually saying. And the trouble with going so "deep" is that one risks overlooking what the surface itself, to a mind free of theory and open to complexity, might be ready to reveal. The expert's way of understanding things is, in fact, the very opposite of the "intelligence" which James saw as a key to Hawthorne's special quality. It is also the opposite of that awareness of the mind's many, and often contradictory, ways of being right, that tentativeness—or serious play— with ideas, that continuous irony, that readiness, in Forster's formula, to say not yes *or* no, but yes *and* no, which characterize the "wisdom-novels" I have just named. For the reader demanding a yes *or* no, the novelist who says or, in his story, implies both at once will, of course, seem confused, and perhaps in need of therapy. But yes *and* no is exactly what Hawthorne, through his ironical narrator Coverdale, and under that, in his ironical treatment of this narrator, says or implies in *The Blithedale Romance.*

And, as in Gide's *The Counterfeiters,* the first and major object of irony (though it may be the last to be understood as such), is the art of storytelling. For, in spite of the interest we naturally take in the events being narrated, these are only part of Hawthorne's tale. Always qualifying Coverdale's account of them, and so, in a way, the real story being told, is the narrator's struggle, amid his own involvement, confusion, or ignorance, to understand and report them aright. Moreover, what is most useful for students of Hawthorne, we find that the struggle issues in a Hawthorne "romance." The novel is a quite realistic demonstration of the nature of such a romance, of what kind of truth it deliberately, or maybe perforce, does without, and of what other kind it is thereby enabled to achieve. And because every novel is, in fact, a romance—in its depths, if not on its surface—that of Coverdale can be understood as Hawthorne's ironical defense, not only of his own art, but of the art of fiction in general.

The author himself is sometimes misleading when he discusses his art. More than once, in half-serious self-deprecation, he suggests his novels are deficient in reality, the reality he relished, as is well known, in the novels of Trollope. But it should not be necessary to insist at this date that he is referring only to their artistic method, their lack of *realism;* or that, when he speaks in the Custom House essay of inviting us into a "neutral territory, somewhere between the real world and fairy-land, where the Actual and the Imaginary may meet and each imbue itself with the nature of the other,"[4] he is not confessing to an evasion of reality. To the nineteenth century, the imagination was not a mode of escape; it was our faculty for perceiving an order in reality's apparent chaos. For that matter, Hawthorne's work is too obviously full of life's real pain and difficulty. No, what gives his novels the special character which his term "romance" is intended to legitimize is their inveterate symbol-mongering, the way all his surface details turn out to embody meanings. Hawthorne's romance is simply fiction in which the real has become, as he says somewhere, "transparent," or, as Thomas Mann put it in describing his fictional goal, "a transparency for ideas." Such symbol-mongering is indeed dangerous in fiction, but not because it is unrealistic, since realism is only one of several methods of conveying reality. It is dangerous because it risks limiting a writer to ideas already familiar to him: the mind's true wealth emerges, as Emerson taught, only when we are stimulated in unforeseeable ways by the world outside. In *The Blithedale Romance,* however, Hawthorne escaped from that danger because, more than any of his other works, it grew out of actual experience. The novel is a kind of grappling with real memories—of his own youthful adventure at the socialist commune of Brook Farm, of the brilliant Margaret Fuller—less beautiful than the novel's Zenobia, but just as voluble—of that epoch's rage for mesmerism, which he earnestly warned his young fiancée to avoid, even of a female suicide whose horribly rigid corpse he once helped recover from a river.

It is true that incoherence can result from trying to fit too much "real life" into a story. But the title Hawthorne finally settled on, far from being a resignation to confusion about his subject, identifies exactly the subject he *had* arrived at during his labors. This subject is not one or another character, it is the Blithedale romance. That is, it is the Utopian experiment which is the story's setting, it is the story which takes place there and which dramatizes the essential problem of all such experiments, and, finally, it is the narrator's own struggle to grasp and convey the truth about it all. And what makes the novel a sufficient unity is that these are all, at bottom, examples of the same thing. The attempt to understand and give a meaningful shape to reality is an enterprise common to idealistic reformers and to narrators, both inside and outside of novels.

"Coverdale is an ass," wrote Mark Van Doren, who, for that matter, thought that Zenobia's tragedy was "trash" and that "few poorer novels have been produced by a first-rate talent."[5] He is wrong about all this, but one can sympathize with an impatience with Hawthorne's narrator. For Coverdale is an artist—a minor poet, but also the author of our novel—and in Hawthorne, this means practically the same thing that it means in Thomas Mann. (Mann and Gide keep coming to mind here because as will be seen, these three ironical self-observers have much in common.) It means a mixture of weakness and strength which must annoyingly frustrate any hunger for the unequivocal—of weakness hard to blame because it makes certain strengths possible, of strength hard to praise because it is the telltale fruit of weakness. Coverdale is the key to all, and we will return to him later on. It is enough to point out now that if, as he frequently confesses, he is defective in the power to commit himself wholeheartedly to the *purposes* of his fellows, this same detachment sets him free to understand them in their human complexity—to see what can be said for them, in spite of their faults, and what must be said against them, in spite of their virtues. His love is ironical and his irony is affectionate. This, and not Hawthorne's mere impotence to decide, is the reason for his narrator's "equivocation" about every important element in his tale.

Take, to begin with, the Blithedale experiment itself. Though Coverdale does show why the experiment failed, he rejects all easy cynicism at its expense. Here are both views in a single passage. The group of bright young visionaries who went to Blithedale "in quest of a better life" may not have found what they sought, since

> if the vision have been worth the having, it is certain never to be consummated otherwise than by a failure. And what of that! Its airiest fragments, impalpable as they may be, will possess a value that lurks not in the most ponderous realities of any practicable scheme. They are not the rubbish of the mind. Whatever else I may repent of, therefore, let it be reckoned neither among my

sins nor follies, that I once had faith and force enough to form generous hopes of the world's destiny—yes!—and to do what in me lay for their accomplishment.[6]

Carlyle and Mark Rutherford have also thus defended, as our true religion, those "impractical" dreams that save our inner lives from chaos and give them value. And yet even a vision that supports our inner life is likely, when we act it out in the world (still more when we impose it on others), to deny too much of external reality. It is the resistance of such reality that, as the days pass, Coverdale begins to acknowledge. The physical labor, for instance, that was to be, in an echo of Emerson, their form of "prayer"—a bodying forth of the Idea—turns out, except at rare, lucky moments, to be the *enemy* of thought. "The clods of earth, which we so constantly belabored and turned over and over, were never etherealized into thought. Our thoughts, on the contrary, were fast becoming cloddish. Our labor symbolized nothing, and left us mentally sluggish in the dusk of the evening" (VII, 66). Then, the very liveliness of mind and sensibility which brought the young Utopians to Blithedale was also a source of difficulties, "mortal tempers being so infirm and variable as they are. If one of us happened to give his neighbor a box on the ear, the tingle was immediately felt, on the same side of everybody's head. Thus, even on the supposition that we were far less quarrelsome than the rest of the world, a great deal of time was necessarily wasted in rubbing our ears" (XVI, 139). Finally, "I felt myself (and, having a decided tendency toward the actual, I never liked to feel it) getting quite out of my reckoning, with regard to the existing state of the world. I was beginning to lose the sense of what kind of world it was, among innumerable schemes of what it might or ought to be" (XVI, 140). So much so that he yearned for talk with "those respectable old blockheads" back in Boston and Cambridge "who still, in this intangibility and mistiness of affairs, kept a death-grip on one or two ideas which had not come into vogue since yesterday morning" (XVI, 141).

That danger at the core of all Utopian dreams is, in fact, what Coverdale's story chiefly dramatizes. This is why the center and source of his drama is the "philanthropist" Hollingsworth, why "he—and Zenobia and Priscilla, both for their own sakes and as connected with him . . . stood forth as the indices of a problem which it was my business to solve" (IX, 69). And this is why Coverdale's ambivalence about the noble error of the Blithedale dream is duplicated, but with the greater intensity of a deep personal relationship, in his attitude to that particular dreamer. (Hollingsworth's dream is not Blithedale's, of course, but his own, that of reforming criminals by appealing, amid pleasant surroundings, to their better nature.) With both, Coverdale begins by seeing what is worthy to be honored and loved. In Hollingsworth's case, it is a capacity for prompt sympathy with those in need and prompt action on their behalf. He is kind one winter day to the frozen newcomer Priscilla, while Coverdale himself is reacting aesthetically to the picture she makes; he is tender in nursing Coverdale through illness. Moreover, such a propensity for action comes from strength, both of mind and body—this former blacksmith is impressively made for acting on the iron recalcitrance of things to bring them closer to the good his idealism envisages. But therein lies the danger! A less attractive reality tends to hide under such idealism, to dilute it, and even to use it for its own alien purposes. In fact, the "deity" Hollingsworth serves becomes a mask for "all-devouring egotism" (IX, 70–71), a process which the very loftiness of his goal (a holy "end" which seems to justify any "means") prevents him from recognizing. We see the process when Hollingsworth cuts Coverdale off as a friend because he will not submit his mind totally to his cause. We see it when he plans secretly to take possession of Blithedale itself for his own scheme. But the climactic example of the idealist's unwitting self-worship is in Hollingsworth's relations to the tale's women.

He is loved by them both, the ethereal, will-less Priscilla and the robustly beautiful, intelligent, utterly autonomous Zenobia. But it is only when they are discovered to be half-sisters and Zenobia must give up to Priscilla the wealth on which he had counted to advance his Idea that Hollingsworth turns from Zenobia and declares it is the other he loves. This is the second of the two great scenes at "Eliot's Pulpit," scenes which remind us that Hawthorne, for all his "romancing," is one of our finest psychological realists. Challenged as to the sincerity of so opportune a declaration, Hollingsworth utters the words "I do love her" with "a deep, inward breath, instead of speaking them outright." And this hint that he is struggling not to know what hides under his own idealism is confirmed when the anguished Zenobia bitterly strips off his idealistic mask: "Self, self, self! You have embodied yourself in a project. . . . Your disguise is a self-deception." His next words give Coverdale the satisfaction of revenge. They are "Priscilla . . . come," and they are spoken in the "abashed and tremulous tone of a man, whose faith in himself was shaken, and who sought, at last, to lean on an affection" (XXV, 217–19).

But again, this negative view of the philanthropist never ceases to be qualified—or complicated. Coverdale observes in one place that the "too powerful purpose" which "utterly corrupted" him grew out of "what was noblest in him" (XIX, 157), and in another that *lack* of purpose had made his own life "all an emptiness" (XXIX, 246). Then, even the wronged Zenobia defends him. To an angry denunciation by Coverdale she replies, "Presume not to estimate a man like Hollingsworth!" (XXVI, 225). If this is love talking, we have no reason to think her love quite blind. And when the poet, in what is plainly a loser's undignified whine, calls it "an insufferable bore" that one man should engross both women (XIV, 126), it is hard not to conclude that Hawthorne, if not his narrator, is driving home that idea of Hollingsworth's superiority as a *man*, is suggesting that warmth of commitment in life, for all its dangers—and even when it does go too far—is what makes a man matter to women, and perhaps not only to them.[7]

With the third important male character, it is not by way of any hesitation in moral judgment that Coverdale's characteristic ambivalence shows itself. Though he regards the neighborhood gossip that calls Westervelt a demon as "all absurdity, or mostly so" (XXII, 188–89), he has no doubt that he embodies the evil which the word "demon" mythologizes. It is about *himself* that the poet grows ambivalent in this man's presence. Westervelt is the physically beautiful mesmerist, whose dazzling teeth, in a symbol not difficult to interpret, turn out to be false. It is he who invades with heartless theatrical professionalism the psyche of Priscilla, his "Veiled Lady," and who once won from Zenobia—or may have won (but Coverdale's guess seems intended to be believed)—a passionate love which his cold sensuality has turned into hatred. And if Hollingsworth cares too much for an ideal, and Coverdale merely "plays" with ideals (as, for art's sake, Hawthorne played, according to James, with Puritan ideas of conscience),[8] Westervelt shows still another way of relating to them. This is the "cold scepticism [which] smothers what it can of our spiritual aspirations, and makes the rest ridiculous." But "cold scepticism" must after all closely resemble scepticism of any temperature. Sure enough, "I detested this kind of man," Coverdale admits, ". . . all the more, because a part of my own nature showed itself responsive to him." Westervelt's "sceptical and sneering view . . . in regard to all life's better purposes" (XII, 101–2) issues in ironies directed at Blithedale and his friends there with which Coverdale finds himself agreeing more warmly than he likes, and which, indeed, closely resemble his own final conclusions about them. And is not the mesmerist's sinister profession a grosser version of Coverdale's own way of prying into and attempting to influence his friends' inner lives? A grosser version: the difference is crucial. But this affinity with the tale's shaping artist—and therefore with *his* shaper, Hawthorne—clearly rules out any simple yes or no to the activity of either.

It is to be expected, of course, that the novel will also suggest more than one thing about its women. But the most commonly noted ambivalence—that Coverdale shrinks from the dark, gorgeously sexual one his own sexual nature is drawn to, and that his attraction to the pale, passive other is somehow evidence of the same weakness—is not, in fact, what the story mainly emphasizes. If this has become virtually a critical cliché, it is because it is so convenient a notion for psychologizing critics who would rather "see through" a writer than perform the labor of understanding what he wrote.[9] In the novel itself, the women clearly convey something else: they show how their sex must fare among men for whom ideas or the life of the mind in general count for more than reality. Of the two, Priscilla is the sort whom each of the men—the poet, avoiding life's intenser commitments, and also the fanatical idealist, with his "all-devouring egotism"—are bound to prefer. And Zenobia is her opposite. She is not merely the sensual "dark lady" of the cliché. Far more to the point, she is the novel's most complete human being, wholly present both as a body and a mind, thinking boldly for herself and yet capable of giving herself with heroic generosity in love. Her role is to serve as a test by which Blithedale and its men are measured and found wanting. Nor is she a simple allegorical figure of excellence, for her completeness contains a touching capacity for small retaliations of malice when the narrowness of her world frustrates her intense vitality or when her love grows uneasy at Priscilla's rivalry. Even the "romantic" details of her portrait and her story bear out this "realistic" intention. The daily flower in her hair is only a frank underlining of her physical beauty—when the sex-shy poet, whom that beauty compels uncomfortably to imagine her naked, fancies it is some witchery, she laughs at his literary evasion of reality. And her hateful involvement with Westervelt, her partial responsibility for his exploitation of Priscilla: aren't these errors born of passion, and so also proof of what Coverdale calls the "rich and generous qualities of Zenobia's womanhood" (XIX, 157)? It is because a woman like her, feeling within herself the wealth of possibilities that constitutes our actual humanity, *must* join a group of Utopian simplifiers (however lofty their simplifications) as if joining in some game that Coverdale feels her presence among them makes them seem to be playacting. She "caused our heroic enterprise to show like an illusion," he tells us, "a masquerade, a pastoral, a counterfeit Arcadia, in which we grown-up men and women were making a play-day of the years that were given us to live in" (III, 21). And that is why, to his charge, back in the city, of disloyalty to the forms of Blithedale, her answer is, "I should think it a poor and meager nature, that is capable of but one set of forms" (XIX, 165). It is true that her end is tragedy, and a tragedy peculiarly unmitigated by Hawthorne's usual ironies: the horror of her drowned corpse is permitted to assault our feelings with a quite "brutal" realism. But this testifies not in the least to Hawthorne's sense of any fault in her which calls for retribution (as some readers have thought), but, on the contrary, to the intensity of his indignation against a culture not yet ready to permit a woman to be a complete human being.

That role of Zenobia's reaches its defining climax in the first of those two scenes at "Eliot's Pulpit." We are told that Hollingsworth has just delivered one of his occasional lay sermons from the lofty rock—the sermon's power, merely asserted by Coverdale, has little fictional reality—and then we are given a series of responses from Zenobia which not only make far more vivid her passionate intelligence, but which also serve perfectly the drama of the novel's approaching tragedy. Misunderstanding Coverdale's smile at her anger that women are not permitted to speak their minds with equal freedom, she hotly affirms her belief that "when my sex shall achieve its rights, there will be ten eloquent women, where there is now one eloquent man," and that "no woman . . . has ever once spoken out her whole heart and her whole mind" because "the mistrust and disapproval of the vast bulk of society throttles us, as with two gigantic hands at our throats!" Priscilla, who is shocked at such talk, is for Zenobia the type of womanhood fashioned over the centuries by man because he is "never content, unless he can degrade himself by stooping towards what he loves," though, "in denying us our rights, he betrays even more blindness to his own interests, than profligate disregard of ours!" (XIV, 120–22).

This unqualified assertion of feminism stings the novel's dominant male into an equally unqualified statement of its classic opposition. Women are admirable "at man's side," Hollingsworth declares. But without men as their acknowledged principals, they are "petticoated monstrosities" whom "physical force, that unmistakable evidence of [man's] sovereignty" should "scourge . . . back within their proper bounds" (XIV, 123). The response of the queenly Zenobia to this ferocity of masculine egotism is another of the novel's great moments. To Coverdale's "indignation," she replies as one "humbled," "Well, be it so . . . Let man be but manly, and godlike, and woman is only too ready to become to him what you say" (XIV, 124), and, as they move off together through the trees, Coverdale sees her take Hollingsworth's hand in both of hers and press it to her bosom. And yet, though such capitulation poignantly dramatizes that power to love which lifts her above the novel's men and also makes her so vulnerable, it does not actually give her woman's case away. "Let man be but manly or god-like," she has said. It is to man as he should be, not as he is, that she would be willing to sacrifice her autonomy—a sacrifice, one might well imagine, such a man would reject or make mutual. In fact, this portrait of Zenobia can stand, as a feminist argument, beside that of Hester Prynne, who also grew great as the men who hurt or judged her grew small and twisted, and who dreamt at last that "at some brighter period, when the world should have grown ripe for it . . . a new truth would be revealed, in order to establish the whole relationship between man and woman on a surer ground of mutual happiness."[10] Whatever he was elsewhere, in his novels Hawthorne was among the warmest champions of women in American culture.

Zenobia's fate must be tragic, then, because there is no man in her world who is her match in all that makes for fulness of being. But there is one, a "poor and dim figure in my own narrative," as he ruefully admits, "establishing no separate interest, and suffering my colorless life to take its hue from other lives" (XXIX, 245), who is her match at least in the richness of his understanding. Coverdale, sympathetically aware of so much, is a kind of mental counterpart of Zenobia's completeness of humanity—he too, after all, can never do more than "try on" for a time the simplified version of humanity required by idealists and reformers. This is why, for all their intellectual sparring, she does confide in him, and in him alone, as in one by whom she can count on being understood and valued. "You have really a heart and sympathies, as far as they go," she grants him at the end (XXVI, 226). But such approbation, that of the tragedy queen for her confidant, as she hints, is a rather left-handed compliment, for it implies he is of little account as a lover. The truth is, the scorn this life-worthy woman also keeps showing for the ballad-maker is very much like that which Hawthorne in that Custom House essay imagines his "stern and black-browed" Puritan ancestors would have felt for him. In both places, we are being told that those who take life seriously cannot take quite as seriously mere makers of "story-books."[11] In short, the yes and no in Zenobia's attitude to Coverdale is precisely that of Hawthorne to his narrator, to himself, and to his art.

Coverdale is as unsparing as Mann's Tonio Kröger (whose "serious" forebears also make him feel small) in exposing all the ways the artist is apt to go wrong.[12] He can go wrong, indeed, not only in the business of living, but even in his substitute occupation of understanding and reporting the lives of those he spies on. The novel's evidence for the former is plentiful. From the time when we find Coverdale so slow (where Hollingsworth is so quick) to help poor frozen Priscilla, through the demeaning picture of him as a voyeur of others' lives from hidden tree-bowers and hotel windows, to his complaint at the "insufferable bore" of watching Hollingsworth win all the available female interest, it is clear we are to regard him as deficient in manhood and a failure at living. As for his substitute activity, he makes us aware first that it leads to an invasion of the privacy of others' souls which is, as always in Hawthorne, a kind of "sacrilege" (XIV, 125). When he tries to prod the women into revealing what he imagines must be in their minds, their angry resistance is seen as justified. As I have said, the poet here resembles the devilish manipulator Westervelt, who thus serves to expose the darkest possibilities of his artist nature. Then, he himself observes that the mere study of individual human beings can be self-defeating, producing "diseased action of the heart" if the subject is oneself, and with others, in spite of small partial accuracies, inherently liable to error in the whole. "If we take the freedom to put a friend under our microscope, we thereby insulate him from many of his true relations, magnify his peculiarities, inevitably tear him into parts, and, of course, patch him very clumsily together again. What wonder, then, should we be frightened by the aspect of a monster, which, after all—though we can point to every feature of his deformity in the real personage—may be said to have been created mainly by ourselves!" (IX, 69).

"Thus," he adds, to nail in this reason for doubting the accuracy of his own narration, "I did Hollingsworth a great wrong by prying into his character; and am perhaps doing him as great a one, at this moment, by putting faith in the discoveries which I seemed to make." To top it off, "Had I loved him less, I might have used him better" (IX, 69); that is, he can go wrong not only because he is unable to see the whole truth but because he may not even want to—disappointed love may be making his friend's portrait darker than the reality. In fact, what is the reason for the rather anticlimactic confession in the novel's last line, "I—I myself—was in love—with—PRISCILLA!" (XXIX, 247), if not to remind us to doubt the "objectivity" of Coverdale's whole narrative? He tells us the confession "will throw a gleam of light over my behavior throughout the foregoing incidents and is, indeed, essential to the full understanding of my story." And though some readers are so sure he must prefer Zenobia (perhaps because that aforementioned critical cliché requires it) that they boldly declare his love for Priscilla "self-deception,"[13] the story itself, as it moves to its crisis, shows him more and more clearly as the jealous, hopeless lover of Priscilla.

Finally, Coverdale admits outright that some of what he is reporting is simply invented. In Moody's tale, his "pen has perhaps allowed itself a trifle of romantic and legendary license" (XXI, 181), but significantly, the process of invention is most flagrant when he reports a conversation between Westervelt and Zenobia which is of crucial importance to his story because it enables us to understand how these two and Priscilla are tied together and because it foreshadows the tragedy to come—in other words, he invents on behalf of the coherence and power of art. Coverdale himself forces on us the suspicion that what he tells us they said as he observed them from his tree bower may not be what they said at all—and not only because "I could hardly make out an intelligible sentence," but also because "what I seem to remember, I yet suspect may have been patched altogether by my fancy afterwards," for, "by long brooding over our recollections, we subtilize them into something akin to imaginary stuff, and hardly capable of being distinguished from it" (XII, 104–5).

What, then, are we to think? Is Coverdale, if not "an ass," at least a mockery of the pretensions of the literary artist to truth, and even worse—for distorting emotional needs, lapses of attention, of knowledge, of logic are the normal human lot—a nihilistic demonstration of the inability of the human mind to do justice to reality? Well, yes and no. The yes we have already seen: because their ideas meant more to them than reality, Blithedale was "wrong," Hollingsworth was "wrong," Coverdale was "wrong"—and Zenobia was destroyed. But Blithedale's and Hollingsworth's way of going wrong testified also to something right. What of the artist? The answer seems to be that if it is Coverdale's failure to be able to give us, in place of what actually happened, only a "romance," that he gives us a romance is also his success.

He succeeds as Tonio Kröger succeeds—as it is possible for the artist to succeed. It is Zenobia herself who indicates the way: "By all means, write this ballad [of what happened to them at Blithedale], and put your soul's ache into it, and turn your sympathy to good account . . . as poets must, unless they choose to give us glittering icicles instead of lines of fire" (XXVI, 224). He is saved as an artist by his power of sympathy, by that love of "the others" which divides him from Westervelt and which, as Tonio Kröger tells his Russian friend, will save *him* from sterile Bohemianism and enable him to write *his* "lines of fire."[14] Coverdale has already explained how sympathy becomes a power. "Was mine a mere vulgar curiosity?" he asks when Zenobia indignantly pulls down her curtain. "She should have been able to appreciate that quality of the intellect and the heart, which impelled me (often against my own will, and to the detriment of my own comfort) to live in other lives, and to endeavor—by generous sympathies, by delicate intuitions, by taking note of things too slight for record, and by bringing my human spirit into manifold accordance with the companions whom God assigned me—to learn the secret which was hidden even from themselves" (XIX, 160).

This sympathy of the artist is not sentimental. His office, like that of "the Chorus in a classic play," is not only to applaud or shed a tear, but "to detect the final fitness of incident to character, and distill, in his long-brooding thought, the whole morality of the performance" (XI, 97). And, as he tells us later, while none of the extenuating complexities of human error would go unrecognized, he would give his "full assent to the punishment which was sure to follow. But it would be given mournfully . . ." he goes on, "and with undiminished love. And, after all was finished, I would come, as if to gather up the white ashes of those who had perished at the stake, to tell the world—the wrong being now atoned for—how much had perished there, which it had never yet known how to praise" (XIX, 161).

Granted, the above passages may make us smile a little, the first because it is so obviously self-defensive—his "generous sympathy" has been caught looking awkwardly like snooping—and the others because of a certain grandiloquence that seems to claim a purer respect than the jealous minor poet we know is entitled to. For that matter, Zenobia's fine rebuke of Coverdale's presuming to meddle out of "duty" catches up in one last burst all the reasons already shown for regarding his confidence in his "delicate intuitions" as arrogance, hubris: "Oh, this stale excuse of duty!" she whispers in scorn—and we may hear in this too the duty to report the truth in art or anywhere else. What it really signifies is "bigotry; self-conceit; an insolent curiosity; a meddlesome temper; a cold-blooded criticism, founded on a shallow interpretation of half-perceptions; a monstrous scepticism in regard to any conscience or any wisdom except one's own; a most irreverent propensity to thrust Providence aside, and substitute one's self in its awful place" (XX, 170). We recognize how this can be so. But after all, Hawthorne can only have given the artist's role to a narrator whom we come to know in his human limitations *in order* to make us smile at his serious pronouncements. And it should by now be sufficiently clear that when we smile at a speech in this novel, it does not mean we may not be agreeing with it as well. If there is truth in Zenobia's rebuke of Coverdale, is it the whole truth about him? Do those ignoble elements mingling with his better motives—sometimes more, sometimes less— cancel them out altogether? Is not his claim that he judges his friends with sympathy borne out by the facts, above all by the fact of his ambivalence, his inability ever to say "no" alone? It is surely borne out when Zenobia, granting him "a heart and sympathies," is consoled by the sense of herself she finds in his eyes at their farewell. And this is a consolation she has a right to trust—we have seen that the artist's sympathy need not be sentimentality. It belongs only to a God to know human beings wholly, and we may well accept without intellectual dishonor a version of ourselves which, if incomplete, is so on our side, and which leaves our best possibilities open, instead of closing them, as a Westervelt's cynicism would do.

Further, if Coverdale's friends are right to resent his claim to know their inner lives at any particular moment (a living reality is too rich and too much in motion to be entirely contained in any man's description), this does not invalidate his intuition of the general drift of things, his sense of the forces at work within them, and of the tragedy these are bringing about. Remember, he turns out to be right. That tragedy, which once provoked his despairing "Be it so! Let it all come!" (XVII, 197), comes as he foresees. More important, it does not invalidate the Blithedale romance Hawthorne has subtilized for us out of *his* recollections of Brook Farm. Whatever disavowal its author makes of historical accuracy, the novel sets forth exactly the "morality" which his "long brooding thought" has distilled out of that brave experiment. He has given us a picture of man's recurrent Utopian dream, of the type of reformer who exemplifies the danger in its sacrifice of reality for ideas, and of the varying relationships to this core subject of women and of poets, which does, in fact, unite an unsentimental grasp of their errors with a celebration of their virtues and a sympathy for their pain, and in which he has vividly displayed certain grave, permanent possibilities of human life.

And finally, the novel gives us more. It brings into the open what had all along been the inner meaning of Hawthorne's artistic effects. In the prefaces, the confession of his helplessness to show us the Actual unmixed with the Imaginary had looked like modesty, the same modesty that seemed always to characterize his hesitant, wavering thought. But in *The Blithedale Romance,* he was not being modest. On the contrary, he anticipated precisely the audacious enterprise of André Gide in *The Counterfeiters.* He wrote a novel to expose what the art of fiction usually conceals. That is, he wrote a novel which deliberately undermined its own pretensions to truth—which showed why all our visions of the Actual, including his own, must be haunted by doubt, and all our reports on it, including his own, must be partly invention. Moreover, like those many others, this "no" too—to the art he practiced—was accompanied by a "yes." His "equivocation" was revealed as that awareness of life's inexhaustible wealth of aspects and relationships which distinguishes the wise from the merely knowing. And the Hawthorne romance could now be seen as his way of dramatizing a perfectly realistic insight: that a mixture of the perceived and the imagined makes up the world, not only of our fictions, but of our daily lives.

George Eliot's
Daniel Deronda

> In dealing with the types of narration the critic must always limp
> behind [the actual work of novelists], referring constantly to the
> varied practice which alone can correct his temptation to over-
> generalize.... We need more painstaking specific accounts of
> how great tales are told.
>
> Wayne Booth, *The Rhetoric of Fiction*

It is a commonplace of George Eliot criticism, persuasively argued by
Henry James and F. R. Leavis, that *Daniel Deronda* (published in 1876)
is half a great success and half a failure. It's true that James, in his
brilliant dialogue on the novel, expresses three views of it—con, pro,
and that of a judicious mediator between them, but the last clearly
represents the author, and he inclines, if less absolutely, to the Leavis
view. The great half Leavis found quite detachable from the rest,
though the operation might leave a few rough spots: he called it *Gwendolen Harleth*. The other was all the Jewish part, the story of Daniel
Deronda and the characters who belong to it, Deronda himself only the
most extreme example of its "astonishing badness."[1]

I think this opinion is wrong, and wrong not only as a judgment of
the quality of the novel, which seems to me, in spite of the variations
here and there in degree or kind of success to be found in all big
novels, gripping, wise, and beautiful from beginning to end. It is wrong
in a way that shuts out of view the novel's real subject: each part
requires the other, and one doesn't fully grasp the story of Gwendolen
if one ignores the relevance to both its drama and its meaning of that
of Deronda. ("I meant everything in the book to be related to everything else," Eliot wrote, impatient with "readers who cut the book into
scraps and talk of nothing in it but Gwendolen,"[2] and what she meant
to do she did.) Even worse, it shuts out of view the vision of human life

which unites this last of her novels with all her others, for the Deronda story dramatizes precisely that "parent idea" of her whole career and does so with a grandeur of scope appropriate to a final statement.

I realize that, according to certain critical axioms we still share with James and Leavis, that would be just the source of the trouble. James said that in the Deronda story, "invention" preponderated excessively over "observation"; this is a version of Leavis's point that Deronda "was conceived in terms of general specifications," since Eliot would have "invented" to embody her general ideas. And of course, we do tend to assume that for a character and a story to embody general ideas is a danger to their reality. Moreover, her idea in creating Deronda was one of "nobility, generosity, and moral idealism," which for Leavis are here "modes of self-indulgence" and make Deronda "decidedly a woman's creation." He clearly implies—it is the reason for his reservations about Dorothea in *Middlemarch,* and it is certainly another axiom to many—that human excellence, the "ideal," has to be sentimental and unconvincing if presented without irony. The same weakness is ascribed to the portrait of Mordecai, whose vision of a rebirth of nationhood for the Jewish people gives Deronda his great life-task. Mordecai "is merely a license for the author to abound copiously in such exaltations and fervors as the Dorothea in her craves"—a clinching proof of his unreality being the fact that he preaches a "religion of race and heredity" which "is not, as a generalizable solution of the problem [i.e., of Gwendolen's problem] one that George Eliot herself . . . could have stood by." Finally, the Deronda section has also been objected to by some as a "romance," full of storybook coincidence and melodrama through which the self-indulgent woman brought about what she wanted, rather than what life permits.

Now, the facts those judgments rest on must, in the main, be granted. But this simply adds another reason (to that of its greatness) for going back to *Daniel Deronda.* The novel will remind us of something which always needs to be learned afresh, that our critical axioms may be fashions imposed by the success of particular writers and that different writers, combining art's multiplicity of elements in other ways, may give us pleasure and wisdom entitled to be respected too—and to be judged by other rules. Thus, it is true that Deronda and Mordecai are, to a certain degree, "invented" to express ideas and to embody virtues dear to their author, and this does make a difference in their part of the novel, makes it less rich in the concrete particulars of observed experience. But the dazzling success of the observing in one part need not preclude another kind of success for the inventing—to embody ideas—in the other. For that matter, when we look close, the opposition implied begins to seem too crude. Not only are observation and ideas inextricably mingled in each (this James grants is always the case), but, since the two parts are after all products of the same mind, each reflects the same grasp of human reality—in the characters and developments that matter most. And finally, there is an even more important correction the novel offers to our current narrowness. It reminds us that to place life and the wisdom that serves life above art, to care about them too much for irony, may be a source, not of sentimental simplification, but of reality and power. We see this in the way the frequent general comments of the author—so subtle, complex, and humane in their insight—enrich the story's total effect. And a remark in a letter of Eliot's confessing openly that now unfashionable interest in the wisdom that helps us live will suggest how such an interest can lead toward the actualities that give power to fiction, rather than away from them.

> My writing is simply a set of experiments in life—an endeavour to see what our thoughts and emotions may be capable of—what stores of motive, actual or hinted as possible, give promise of a better after which we may strive—what gains from past revelations and disciplines we must strive to keep hold of as something more than shifting theory. I become more and more timid—with less daring to adopt any formula which does not get itself clothed for me in some human figure and individual experience, and perhaps that is a sign that if I help others to see at all, it must be through the medium of art.[3]

In fact, the ideas—and equally the "exaltations and fervors"—of the Jewish part of the novel belong to its greatness, as well as to its unity.

Daniel Deronda is the only novel by George Eliot set in her own present, the 1870s. Its characters are not her familiar middle- or lower-class provincials of a generation or so earlier, tied down, as it were, to occupations, a community, and a close family group, but the titled and the wealthy, whose freedom from such limitations enables them to experience fully what England has become. What it has become is essentially our modern world. And it is the function of Gwendolen Harleth and her fate to exemplify the change.

Gwendolen is presented as a "spoiled child"[4]—this is the title of Book One—affluent, beautiful, assuming preeminence both at home, where she rules over a doting widowed mother and two nondescript younger stepsisters, and in society, where her half-educated cleverness and her spoiled child's self-assurance intensify her charm. The brilliant opening of the novel shows at once the dangerous core of what she is in a scene that expands in meaning as the story goes on. We find her in a German gambling casino—"hell is the only right name for such places,"[5] Eliot wrote just before beginning the novel—exulting in the "sweetness of winning much and seeing others lose," until her sense of being watched with irritating disapproval by the still unknown Deronda shakes her confidence and spoils her luck. To win while others lose—some such phrase will recur like a leitmotif because it is the formula for the moral life in which she has been nurtured. And every episode of her tragic story, for all its immediate realism, will serve to unfold that formula's life-implications.

There is, for instance, her reason for being on the Continent—what she has fled from at home, and then the capitulation that follows her return. She has rushed away on the eve of a proposal by Henleigh Grandcourt, a man who is the exact fulfillment of her wishes, that is, of the wishes of ordinary greed and vanity, and whose case is backed with enthusiasm by all the authorities of her world. He is rich, he is of high birth, and the seal is set on his attractiveness by his impeccably aristocratic manners. They are, in fact, the manners of a man profoundly "bored" by the "brutes" who make up most of the human race, and by what matters to them, and to whom nothing is interesting but the power to impose his will. But the humanity he lacks is not a quality her world or her character has taught her to value. Though she had fled from Grandcourt's proposal after meeting his abandoned mistress and their children and promising the woman, who still hoped for marriage, to get out of their way, her automatic righteousness was more pride than moral sensitivity and was easy because its cost wasn't yet painful. So, when the sudden loss of her family's fortune calls her home to poverty and the stinging humiliation of job-seeking, we get the great scene of her yielding to Grandcourt's coolly renewed courtship. It is a yielding never quite intended, but the powerful seduction and the equally powerful proprieties of the world Gwendolen shares with him bring it about as if independently of her will. Her "no" delays, delays, until at last it becomes impossible to withhold the fateful "yes," she gains what another loses, and the trap which her spoiled child's life has been preparing for her is sprung. The guilt awakened by the betrayed mistress's terrible letter, received on her wedding night and naming her crime with lacerating precision; the hatred of her husband which, from that moment, grows maddeningly, but which she dare not utter or act on; the husband's icy manipulation of her guilt and weakness, forcing her to maintain her splendid facade as his wife—all this is among the great achievements of nineteenth-century fiction. But, as I say, Gwendolen's crime and punishment have a meaning: they dramatize the moral condition of the modern world.

This becomes clear immediately after the scene of gambling, during the flashback intended to show how that ominous eagerness to win while others lose became, by default, the guiding principle of her life. The paragraph with which the flashback begins gives us the key, not only to Gwendolen's story, but to Deronda's and Mordecai's—it is that "parent idea" of Eliot's entire *oeuvre*.

> Pity that Offendene was not the home of Miss Harleth's child-hood, or endeared to her by family memories! A human life, I think, should be well rooted in some spot of native land, where it may get the love of tender kinship for the face of the earth, for the labours men go forth to, for the sounds and accents that haunt it, for whatever will give that earlier home a familiar unmistakable difference amidst the future widening of knowledge; a spot where the definiteness of early memories may be inwrought with affection, and kindly acquaintance with all neighbors, even to the dogs and donkeys, may spread not by sentimental reflection, but as a sweet habit of the blood. At five years old, mortals are not prepared to be citizens of the world, to be stimulated by abstract nouns, to soar above preference into impartiality; and that prejudice in favor of the milk with which we blindly begin, is a type of the way body and soul must get nourished at least for a time. The best introduction to astronomy is to think of the nightly heavens as a little lot of stars belonging to one's own homestead.

Instead of that "blessed persistence in which affection can take root," her childhood has been a "roving from one foreign watering place or Parisian apartment to another, always feeling new antipathies to new suites of hired furniture, and meeting new people under conditions which made her appear of little importance."

Compare this with the world of Eliot's earlier novels. That world always recreated in detail with more than love, with insistent nostalgia, was "a spot of native land" crowded with kin and neighbors, not to mention animals, and providing, as Maggie saw it in *The Mill on the Floss*, "the motives that sanctify our lives," and "the ties that [give] meaning to duty," without which one is "an outlawed soul with no guide but the wayward choice of . . . [one's] own passion." Moreover, instead of the Evangelical Dinah of *Adam Bede*, teaching with contagious emotion the human meaning of Christ, or Dr. Kenn of *The Mill*, teaching the same thing with a more sober intensity, or even Dr. Irvine of *Adam Bede* or Dr. Farebrother of *Middlemarch*, offering a secular wisdom and humaneness rooted in affection for kin and neighbors, we have now, as moral and religious guide, Gwendolen's uncle Mr. Gascoigne. He is a minister, gifted in "administration," his religion "what he would have called sound English, free from nonsense, such as became a man who looked at a national religion by daylight and saw its relation to other things," of whom, though "it could not be proved that he forsook the less fortunate, it was not to be denied that the friendships he cultivated were of a kind likely to be useful to the father of six sons and two daughters." It belongs to the truth as well as the moral significance of this portrait that he is not at all a bad man. On the contrary, it is out of genuine concern for Gwendolen's happiness that, overlooking Grandcourt's past as "wild oats" to which men of wealth and birth are entitled, he urges her to accept him.

But a mere exposé of the modern wasteland is not what this Eliot is after. In aim, as well as in achievement, she belongs with the great Russians, who, Chekhov once said, are always leading us somewhere— unlike the smaller ones like himself, who can only show what they see. Gwendolen's story is to be, in Deronda's words, that of a "painful letting in of light," which is to say, of a woman who has it in her to undergo that hard awakening. She is therefore richer in human stuff, and in fact more "real," than a list of her defects would suggest. She has what Eliot calls "iridescence . . . the play of various, nay, contrary, tendencies." She has a "root of conscience" in her. If she kills her sister's canary when its singing interrupts her own, she buys her a white mouse in retribution. She can be genuinely sorry when her self-absorption wounds the feelings of her weak, helplessly loving mother. And there are even traces in her of a vulnerability to those dark messages from the universe which underlie all religions.

Though she had "always disliked whatever was presented to her under the name of religion in the same way that some people dislike arithmetic and accounts," she had "a liability . . . to fits of spiritual dread." We see this in the episode of the painted skull, which she shudderingly orders to be locked away when she finds it on exploring her new home and which, when a sister's mischief uncovers it during a party, gives her a shock far in excess of its apparent cause. In immediate association with this shock, we are told of her "tremor" when alone at "some rapid change in the light" or "in any wide scene" at the "undefined feeling of immeasurable existence aloof from her, in the midst of which she was helplessly incapable of asserting herself." Death and the infinite space around us—these are precisely the great Terrors that, mocking all human pride (let alone the small conceit of a Gwendolen), drive us to religion and all its substitutes.

To begin with, however, they intensify the need that binds us together and the preciousness of what we can do for each other. And it is this persistent Eliot idea of the importance of human fellowship— how it works and how far that work extends—that the "experiment in life" which is the story of Daniel Deronda was "invented" to explore.

Moreover, it is not only in its meaning that his story is relevant to Gwendolen's: their drama too is one. The "painful letting in of light" which is Gwendolen's story is precisely the story of her relationship with Deronda. Here is how that relationship is described during one of its climactic moments:

> Would her remorse have maintained its power within her, or would she have felt absolved by secrecy, if it had not been for that outer conscience which was made for her by Deronda? It is hard to say how much we could forgive ourselves if we were secure from judgment by another whose opinion is the breathing medium of all our joy—who brings to us with close pressure and immediate sequence that judgment of the Invisible and Universal which self-flattery and the world's tolerance would easily melt and disperse.

Deronda, then, is to be the kind of man who would be drawn into that "lay-confessor" role to a woman like Gwendolen, who would feel all its inevitable difficulties and all the inevitable inner shrinkings (a lay-confessor who couldn't feel them would be too simpleminded for the job) and yet be unable not to carry it out—in short, a highly gifted man, exceptional in intelligence, in psychological insight, in irresistible sympathy, in power of feeling. And yet, as we will see, the fact that he thus obviously serves her story's need for an "ideal" does not prevent him from acquiring a sufficient reality. "An idea being born and breathing," Mordecai says once, "draws the elements toward it, and is fed and grows." In spite of occasional passages in which we detect, more than we should, the author's will at work, signs of her labor to flesh out what came first as an idea, Deronda, and Mordecai too, grow as characters overwhelmingly out of Eliot's wisdom and her psychological insight; they "draw" to themselves a constant stream, not only of general ideas that have a reality-creating power in fiction because of their sheer truth, but also of minute particulars born of observation. In fact, there are many touches in both Deronda and Mordecai—touches showing, with the first, the *experience* of understanding, of sympathizing, of struggling (without confidence) to say what will help, and, with the second, the *experience* of inspired genius—that seem clearly taken from a felt reality she had very close at hand, to wit, herself.

It is true enough that Deronda's story, in comparison with Gwendolen's, is a kind of romance. He has been brought up by the rich and wellborn Sir Hugo Mallinger in ignorance of his parents, though he shares the general suspicion that he is Sir Hugo's bastard son. Since he is also rich enough to be free from the need to work, that vagueness as to his origins results in a drifting detachment, a dilettantish toying with vocations, and a growing hunger for a family and a past that would give him unarguable duties and direction. And lo!—what he needs enters his idle, English gentleman's life from outside its "realistic" possibilities in a series of storybook adventures. There is his rescue from suicide of the despairing and beautiful Mirah, a Jewish girl who is indeed more simply good than life permits, though she serves the story well enough;[7] his search for the mother and elder brother from whom her rascally father stole her away as a child; his discovery that her brother is an eloquent man of genius and a prophet of Jewish nationhood, dying of consumption, who has been waiting for just such a person as Deronda—rich, healthy, English, but also a Jew—to take, as it were, from his dying hands the great Jewish cause. And finally, when Deronda has fallen in love with both Mirah and her brother's dream and begun to regret that he has no right to embrace either, the call to meet his mother at last—and the all-transforming discovery that he is a perfectly legitimate Jew. It perhaps belongs to the melodrama too that on her father's death long ago, Deronda's mother had asked Sir Hugo, a passionate admirer, to bring him up, not only because she wanted freedom for the career of an actress-singer, but because she wanted her son free from what she felt to be the hateful burden of Jewishness, and that this turns out to be just the sort of burden he has spent his life seeking. Add to all that the fact that he is beautiful without as well as within, and you have a story that does indeed sound "romantic."

But Eliot obviously knows this and reminds us herself of the sort of truth which romance can have. "If you like," she says, describing his growing attraction to Mordecai's wild dream for him, "he was romantic. That young energy and spirit of adventure which have helped to create the world-wide legends of youthful heroes going to seek the hidden tokens of their birth and its inheritance of tasks gave him a certain quivering interest in the bare possibility that he was entering on a like task." A plot about the "strange" adventures of exceptionally gifted people may be an appropriate embodiment, just as the old legends were, of genuine life-possibilities, the kind which lie outside our ordinary experience. Moreover, each storybook contrivance in this one justifies itself also because it assists in the unfolding of perfectly real developments. As with the bold coincidences of that other great realist, Dostoevsky, what enables us to suspend disbelief much more than just willingly is the rich and urgent truth of what leads up to and grows out of such contrivance.

It is the felt truth of Deronda, of course—of his gifts of mind and feeling—on which our belief in his story will depend.[8] And these gifts are not simply and sentimentally asserted. The pages describing his youth, for instance, are full of Eliot's characteristically precise psychological detail, by which we are reminded of what such gifts actually consist in and how they work. Here are three examples:

> He had his flashes of fierceness, and could hit out upon occasion, but the occasions were not always what might have been expected. For in what related to himself his resentful impulses had been early checked by a mastering affectionateness. Love has a habit of saying "Never mind" to angry self, who, sitting down for the nonce in the lower place by-and-by gets used to it. So it was that as Deronda approached manhood his feeling for Sir Hugo, while it was getting more and more mixed with criticism, was gaining in that sort of allowance which reconciles criticism with tenderness.

> Certainly Deronda's ambition, even in his spring time, lay exceptionally aloof from conspicuous, vulgar triumph, and from other ugly forms of boyish energy; perhaps because he was early impassioned by ideas, and burned his fire on those heights. One may spend a good deal of energy in disliking and resisting what others pursue, and a boy who is fond of somebody else's pencil-case may not be more energetic than another who is fond of giving his pencil case away.

> The impression he made at Cambridge corresponded to his position at Eton. Everyone interested in him agreed that he might have taken a high place if his motives had been of a more pushing sort, and if he had not, instead of regarding his studies as instruments of success, hampered himself with the notion that they were to feed motive and opinion—a notion which set him criticising methods and arguing against his freight and harness when he should have been using all his might to pull.

Such observations do indeed lack the convincingness and the charm that come from irony. But they convince another way, by their intelligence. And being intelligent, they have another kind of charm than that of amusing deflation—to some a charm more poignant—that of sketching for us the lineaments, neither simple nor sentimental, of actual human goodness. Deronda is, in fact, an attempt to body forth as it develops, lives, and moves, a moral intelligence like Eliot's own, her own wisdom. And that he sometimes fails to sparkle is insignificant when measured against the way he mainly succeeds. Those quoted observations, for instance, certainly express with precision human realities that build a character we must recognize. So, when it turns out that Gwendolen's "hidden helplessness gave fresh force to the hold Deronda had from the first taken on her mind, as one who had an unknown standard by which he judged her" and perhaps "some way of looking at things which might be a new footing for her—an inward safeguard against possible events which she dreaded as stored-up retribution"—we are quite prepared for what follows. It is clearly the dramatic action of that character that he understands at once the anguished appeal for help in her hesitant remarks and gestures and has no choice but to respond. True, what he offers in response can sometimes be called "commonplace." But the question she is driven to is how she is to go on living when she is tormented by remorse for having "thrust out others . . . made my gain out of their loss" and yet is unable "to make amends" as he first advises because "I must go on. I can't alter it." That is, the help she wants is nothing less than an answer to the blackness of vision that comes with despair. And the answer he gives her, as she awkwardly seeks him out at social gatherings and—rarely, briefly—alone, is commonplace only because it gives to that familiar life-blackness the equally familiar response of wisdom. For it is not original ideas that we need amid the great crises, but only to be enabled to feel afresh the hard old truths we "know." What is always overlooked by critics who quote Deronda out of context with a sneer—and who call his talk priggish as well as commonplace—is that *in* its appropriate context, that of the desperate need of one and the desperate groping of another to answer that need, such commonplace regains, exactly as it might in life, all its freshness, its force, and its delicate humanity. But to see this we must examine a few of their encounters in some detail.

Though "his feeling for those who had been thrust out sanctioned her remorse," he tells her one's own wrongdoing, accepted "as one must submit to a maiming" can be "made a reason for more effort toward a good that may do something to counterbalance the evil. Feeling what it is to have spoiled one life may well make us long to save other lives from being spoiled." Gwendolen admits she has been selfish—unconcerned with the feelings of others ("except my mother's"), but is helpless to change because the world has become a "confusion" to her and life itself worthless. To this familiar result of self-disgust, Deronda replies by urging her "with a touch of indignant severity which he was inclined to encourage as his own safeguard," to look "beyond the small drama of personal desires. It is the curse of your life—forgive me—of so many lives, that all passion is spent in that narrow round for want of ideas and sympathies to make a larger home for it." And we are told a moment later:

> The half indignant remonstrance that vibrated in Deronda's voice came as often happens from the habit of inward argument with himself, rather than from severity toward Gwendolen; but

it had a more beneficent effect on her than any soothings. . . . For the moment she felt like a shaken child—shaken out of its wailings into awe, and she said humbly—"I will try, I will think." They both stood silent for a minute, as if some third presence had arrested them—for Deronda too was under that sense of pressure which is apt to come when our own winged words seem to be hovering around us.

Later, when she says she knows what he means, but waves "her small gloved hand in deprecation of the notion that [his advice] was easy to obey" and foresees a rising hatred and rage that may grow uncontrollable,

> the expression she saw on his face pierced her with an entirely new feeling. He was under the baffling difficulty of discerning that what he was urging on her was thrown into the pallid distance of mere thought before the outburst of her habitual emotion. It was as if he saw her drowning while his limbs were bound. The pained compassion which was spread over his features as he watched her affected her with a compunction unlike any she had felt before, and in a changed, imploring tone, she said—
>
> "I am grieving you. I am ungrateful. You *can* help me. I will think of everything. I will try. Tell me—it will not be a pain to you that I have dared to speak of my trouble to you? You began it, you know, when you rebuked me . . . "
>
> "Not if it does anything to save you from an evil to come," said Deronda with a strong emphasis; "otherwise it will be a lasting pain."

This—can one not call it passionate?—relationship between them reaches a high point in Gwendolen's time of terror that she has not been saved from the worst evil, that she is responsible for the drowning of her husband because she willed it and may have delayed the fatal extra moment in throwing him a rope. But though Deronda's struggles to find amid the tangle of her motives and circumstances what will lift her out of crippling guilt intensifies her need of him, and his compulsion to answer her need, his mother's great disclosure dooms them to the separation which ends their story. During one of their last meetings, she is shocked to see him rise to go, clearly drawn to other concerns than hers. And as she rises too, "her proud secrecy disenthroned," unable to check tears, Deronda feels "a crushing pain." Her rock-bottom question then is the occasion of a sort of rock-bottom conclusion, the essential word he finds to say to one whom life has utterly humbled and who is now taking the first blind steps upward. Though she means to be kind hereafter to her mother and sisters, she asks, "Is that the best I can do?"

> "I think so. It is a duty that cannot be doubtful," said Deronda. He paused a little between his sentences, feeling a weight of anxiety on all his words. "Other duties will spring from it. Looking at your life as a debt may seem the dreariest view of things at a distance, but it cannot really be so. . . . You will find your life growing like a plant."

And when he tells her "her sorrow can be as a preparation," and "you can, you will, be among the best of women, such as make others glad that they were born," the words "were like the touch of a miraculous hand to Gwendolen."

This climax of their strange intimacy prepares another even more intense. It is the time when Deronda must tell her of Mirah and of his imminent departure for the "East" to begin a task that not only dwarfs her own trouble, but must separate them for good, and "the world seemed to be getting larger around poor Gwendolen, and she the more solitary and helpless in the midst." And Eliot now makes explicit the meaning of that "tremor" of long ago of which these words remind us. At such a moment "it is as if the Invisible Power . . . became visible. . . . Then it is that the submission of the soul to the Highest is tested . . . and a religion shows itself which is something else than a private consolation." Of course, this "Power," this "Highest," being Eliot's, is reality, which doesn't always give out presents for obedience; and it is Gwendolen's tragic triumph that she has come at last open-eyed into its presence.

Deronda has thus both enacted and uttered what for Eliot is the saving truth of human life. His role in the novel is, in fact, a version of the supreme task one human being can perform for another, that task of parent or friend or teacher which is, as it were, the initial building block of the human community, by which we are helped out of chaos into order, out of despair and impotence into fruitful activity. And the function of Mordecai's vision of the Jewish community which provides the hope and fruitful action of his own life is precisely to show the widest implications of that saving truth.

As I have said, Mordecai is just as little *merely* an ideal as Deronda: he too embodies Eliot's experience as well as her thought. We know from Professor Haight's biography that the chief facts of Mordecai's life—his poverty, his illness, his learning, and his dream—were based on the actual Jewish scholar Emmanuel Deutsch, from whom Eliot learned Hebrew, as well as Jewish history and hopes. But it seems to me that in the reaching out and the utterance which are Mordecai's main actions in the novel, Eliot has dramatized the deepest experience of her own life, that of genius possessed by a genuinely great vision. However "romantic" the story by which the teacher and the disciple are brought together, we are shown with that same precision of psychological detail what it is like to be the bearer of such a vision, what are the difficulties inner and outer that attend it, the hunger for the Other who will understand and the joy of finding him, and the thrilled peace that follows utterance.

Granted, it's a bit hard to swallow that Mordecai's intuition of Deronda as that Other should become a certainty when he happens to see him from a Thames bridge and under a golden afternoon light because these conditions have figured in his meditations and dreams. But the romance of George Eliot is not only revealed sooner or later as a version of reality; often, the more romantic the event, the more bold a realistic insight it will dramatize. Thus, though the meeting under dreamed conditions may require to be accepted as a coincidence, that Mordecai should hold fast to his intuition—and be proved right to have done so—is clearly offered as an example of the responsiveness to data too subtle to be "explained" and the firmness to trust it against "reason" which may be strength and wisdom. It is exactly so that he defends himself from Deronda's skepticism.

> "I could silence the beliefs which are the mother-tongue of my soul and speak with the rote-learned language of a system that gives you the spelling of all things, sure of its alphabet covering them. . . . May not a man silence his awe and love and take to finding reasons which others demand? But if his love lies deeper than reasons to be found? Man finds his pathways; at first they were foot-tracks, as those of the beast in the wilderness: now they are swift and invisible . . . has he found all the pathways yet?"

In Mordecai, then, we have a mind at once passionate and powerful, and his drama is that of such a mind under the pressure of coming death and the fear that it will "stifle" the "life" (of his thoughts) he wants to save, overleaping the pedantries of "reason" in the excitement of feeling his great rescue suddenly at hand. (A word about his eloquence. It has been regarded as self-evidently less realistic than the foreign-sounding speech of the novel's other Jewish genius, the musician Klesmer, who belongs, indeed, among the triumphs of "observation" in Gwendolen's story. But we must remember Mordecai's claim: "English is my mother-tongue, English is the native land of this body." If his "dialect," tone, and manners lack the flavorsome individuality of

Klesmer's, which come from the "world," they have a legitimacy of their own. They are those of a scholar and dreamer whose world is the great texts of his subject.) And when, soon after that romantic coincidence of setting and disciple, "the two men, with as intense a consciousness as if they had been two undeclared lovers, felt themselves alone in the small gas-lit book shop and turned face to face," the "fervors and exaltations" of one, as well as the response of the other, are given fictional reality by the constant play, in them and around them, of that sheer desentimentalizing intelligence I have already referred to. Thus:

> [Deronda] felt nothing that could be called belief in the validity of Mordecai's impression concerning him or in the probability of any greatly effective issue; what he felt was a profound sensibility to a cry from the depths of another soul; and accompanying that, a summons to be receptive instead of superciliously prejudging. Receptiveness is a rare and massive power, like fortitude; and this state of mind gave Deronda's face its utmost expression of calm benignant force—an expression which nourished Mordecai's confidence and made an open way before him.

Then later we are told that Deronda is fully aware, not only of the absurdity to common sense of Mordecai's claim on him, but of the other absurdity of seeing *that* as somehow a merit, of forgetting that passionate enthusiasm and even martyrdom have also accompanied "error and folly." Moreover, just as Deronda's response is made convincing by its sanity, both of reserve and receptiveness, Mordecai, telling how he came by his ideas—of his varied experiences and studies and his struggles with the skeptical—shows an awareness of the world and of the mocking smiles of "common sense" that keep his intensities too sane and real.

His climactic utterance to Deronda begins as an answer to the up-to-date Jew Gideon at the "Philosopher's Club," the only place in London to which he can take Deronda for serious talk. (This is a club of workingmen in love with ideas and argument, and their discussion, a clash of ideas which is also a clash of characters, is not only convincing, but delightful.) The conversation that night, after touching "on the causes of social change" and the datedness of "the feeling of nationality," has landed on the subject of Jewish nationalism. Gideon thinks Jews ought to "melt gradually into the populations they live among," looks for "prejudice to die out," and wants "our expectations rational." To this Mordecai replies:

> "I too claim to be a rational Jew. But what is it to be rational . . . ? It is to see more and more of the hidden bonds that

consecrate change as a dependent growth—yea, consecrate it
with kinship; the past becomes my parent and the future
stretches toward me the appealing arms of children. Is it rational
to drain away the sap of kindred that makes the families of man
rich in interchanged wealth, and various as the forests are various with the glory of the cedar and the palm?"

Now it is easy to see how the prophetic vision which occupies the
rest of the chapter might spoil it as a fiction. But in my view, this does
not happen—the chapter remains alive and absorbing—for several reasons. To begin with, Mordecai's outburst belongs to the *story*, both
because it is interrupted and spurred on by real argument, and because
it is actually an excited appeal to the listening Deronda on behalf of a
people and a task that for Mordecai is, and for Deronda may be, his
own. Then, it dramatizes character: it is, as I have said, a picture of
genius in its moment of full utterance—how it sounds, how it affects
others, and how it is itself affected. And finally, it has an interest that
we can admit to be extraliterary without, I hope, having to apologize. I
have already observed that in Eliot extraliterary concerns are a source
of literary power. The novel shows us too that what they bring into
fiction may simply be interesting in itself. As we have been reminded
by more than one sensible critic, fiction is not lyric poetry, and whether
purists approve or not, novels—especially great novels—do betray and
appeal to an interest in the world outside them without fatal injury to
their integrity. What this novel tells about the Jewish people is for
many of us today quite fascinating. Not only does it show a surprisingly
intimate understanding of the life-implications of Judaism, as well as of
the various and conflicting attitudes of Jews to their own Jewishness.
Even more amazing is her imaginative grasp, years before Herzl, of
what was to be called Zionism, of the sources of that dream of restored
nationhood in ancient and recent history, of the steps needed and
possible to realize it, and of what a national homeland in Palestine
would mean for Jews, for that region, and for the world. In what
follows, then, I will do as my writer has done and, by quoting Mordecai
in some detail, borrow that extraliterary interest for literary criticism.

Mordecai speaks with scorn of the Jew who hears his child recite
the speeches of ancient Greeks, but thinks he has himself "no memories
that bind him to action," and believes "his business in all things is to be
even as the rich Gentile." He grants that—

"Each nation has its own work and is a member of the world
enriched by the work of each. But it is true, as Jehuda-ha-Levi
first said, that Israel is the heart of mankind, if we mean by
heart the core of affection which binds a race and its families in

dutiful love, and the reverence for the human body which lifts the needs of our animal life into religion, and the tenderness which is merciful to the poor and weak and to the dumb creatures that wear the yoke for us."

He reminds them that the unique contribution of the Jews, that "their religion and law and moral life . . . made one growth," was a "spiritual store" they had "kept and enlarged" even while being hunted like animals; that after struggling "to keep their place among nations like heroes" and losing it, they said, " 'The spirit is alive, let us make it a lasting habitation—lasting because movable—so that . . . our sons unborn may be rich in the things that have been, and possess a hope built on an unchangeable foundation' "; and that if multitudes of Jews are now "ignorant, narrow, superstitious," their religious observances but as "nameless relics," the same is true of the gentiles. "Revive the organic center: let the unity of Israel, which has made the growth and form of its religion, be an outward reality. Looking toward a land and a polity, our dispersed people in all the ends of the earth may share the dignity of a national life which has a voice among the peoples of the East and the West—which will plant the wisdom and skill of our race so that it may be, as of old, a medium of transmission and understanding." And in reply to the rational Gideon's doubt that "literal restoration" is possible, Mordecai goes on to describe how the Jews of the world can pool their wealth, knowledge, and skills to make the dream a reality.

> "There is store of wisdom among us to found a new Jewish polity, grand, simple, just, like the old—a republic where there is equality of protection, an equality which shone like a star on the forehead of our ancient community, and gave it more than the brightness of Western freedom amid the despotisms of the East. Then our race shall have an organic center, a heart and brain to watch and guide and execute; the outraged Jew shall have a defense in the court of nations, as the outraged Englishman or American. And the world will gain as Israel gains. For there will be a community in the van of the East which carries the culture and the sympathies of every great nation in its bosom . . . What is needed is the seed of fire. . . . Let the torch of visible community be lit! Let the reason of Israel disclose itself in a great outward deed, and let there be another great migration, another choosing of Israel to be a nationality whose members may still stretch to the ends of the earth, even as sons of England and Germany, whom enterprise carries afar, but who still have a national hearth and a tribunal of national opinion."

America too, he says, was founded by people who "needed a polity" and who formed it out of "memories of Europe, corrected by the vision of a better."[9] And as a final reply to the skeptics, he asserts the human power to choose, a power relevant not only to the future of the Jewish people, but to that which faces Gwendolen and Deronda as the novel ends.

> "I say that the strongest principle of growth lies in human choice. The Messianic time is the time when Israel shall will the planting of the national ensign. . . . Shall man whose soul is set in the royalty of discernment and resolve, deny his rank and say, I am an onlooker, ask no choice or purpose of me? That is the blasphemy of the time. The divine principle of our race is action, choice, resolved memory. Let us contradict the blasphemers and help to will our own better future and the better future of the world—not renounce our higher gift and say, 'Let us be as if we were not among the populations,' but choose our full heritage, claim the brotherhood of our nation and carry into it a new brotherhood with the nations of the Gentiles. The vision is there; it will be fulfilled."

What follows that conclusion will show both the accuracies of feeling by which such passionate vision is given fictional reality and how this reality can remind us of the author in her own moments of deepest fulfillment.

> With the last sentence, which was no more than a loud whisper, Mordecai let his chin sink on his breast and his eyelids fall. No one spoke. It was not the first time that he had insisted on the same ideas, but he was seen tonight in a new phase. The quiet tenacity of his ordinary self differed as much from his present exaltation of mood as a man in private talk, giving reasons for a revolution of which no sign is discernible, differs from one who feels himself an agent in a revolution begun. The dawn of fulfillment brought to his hope by Deronda's presence had wrought Mordecai's conception into a state of impassioned conviction, and he had found strength in his excitement to pour forth the unlocked floods of emotive argument, with a sense of haste as at a crisis that must be seized. But now there had come with the quiescence of fatigue a sort of thankful wonder that he had spoken—a contemplation of his life as a journey which had come at last to this bourne. After a great excitement, the ebbing strength of impulse is apt to leave us in this aloofness from our active self. And in the moments after Mordecai had sunk his

head, his mind was wandering along the paths of his youth, and all the hopes which had ended in bringing him hither.

Everyone felt that the talk was ended, and the tone of phlegmatic discussion made unseasonable by Mordecai's high-pitched solemnity. It was as if they had come together to hear the blowing of the *shophar*, and had nothing to do now but to disperse.

I have said little of the crowd of lesser characters who help make this novel, like *Middlemarch*, a richly peopled world. But one, Deronda's mother, may serve as a final example of the kind of success attained by the "romantic," "invented," Jewish half of the novel, as well as the way "everything in the book . . . [is] related to everything else." It is true that what takes place in the splendid Genoa hotel room might be a scene of melodrama out of grand opera: Deronda finds there a cold, striking-looking woman—a Russian princess, no less!—dying and forced by reawakened memories to pass on to her son the papers and the Jewish identity intended for him by her father, and yet hating this renewal of an old subjection—and this Jewishness—she had rebelled against all her life. But if it is Eliot's operatic—that is, old-fashioned, theatrical—boldness of plotting that is responsible for these scenes, and their momentous consequences, they are also operatic in better ways. Deronda's terrible suspense as he awaits her revelation, the passion with which she defends the "robbery," as he calls it, of his Jewish past and identity, the conflict in him of baffled yearning, anger, and at last a sympathy he cannot withhold (to say nothing of the different sort of suspense we share with him later when he brings his tremendous news to Mirah and Mordecai)—in all this we have opera's emotional power, even its grandeur, and we may well be grateful to Eliot for restoring to our adulthood the reading excitement of youth. But she can do so, as I have said, because the romance is a vehicle for reality. Deronda's mother at least, however briefly we see her, ranks among the novel's triumphs of characterization.

In her that part of Eliot's own experience dramatized by Maggie in *The Mill on the Floss* reappears as the protest of a great artist. "You can never imagine," she tells her son, "what it is to have a man's force of genius in you, and yet to suffer the slavery of being a girl. . . . A woman's heart must be of such a size and no larger, else it must be pressed small, like Chinese feet." Moreover, when she unrepentantly asserts the claims of her own ego against the moral-religious obligations which for Maggie—and Eliot—oppose it ("I wanted to live out the life that was in me, and not be hampered by other lives" and "I was not like a brute, obliged to go with my own herd"), the claim has this time a surprising impressiveness. We hear in it a pride that belongs to her genius. Indeed, it is precisely as an actress that she comes alive. Eliot finely describes the theatrical quality of her speech:

> [It] was in fact a piece of what may be called sincere acting: this woman's nature was one in which all feeling—and all the more when it was tragic as well as real—immediately became matter of conscious representation: experience immediately passed into drama, and she acted her own emotions. . . . It would not be true to say that she felt less because of this double consciousness: she felt—that is, her mind went through—all the more, but with a difference: each nucleus of pain or pleasure had a deep atmosphere of the excitement or spiritual intoxication which at once exalts and deadens.

But we know that her rejection of "other lives" meant a rejection not only of her father and the Jews, but of her own son. The fateful "robbery" committed against him is therefore an extreme example of that eagerness to win though others lose which underlies the story of Gwendolen. And here is how Deronda—half "entreating," half "indignant"—explains the defeat of his mother's long rebellion, a defeat represented by his own glad acceptance of her father's legacy. "The effects prepared by generations are likely to triumph over a contrivance which would bend them all to the satisfaction of self. Your will is strong, but my grandfather's trust—which you accepted and did not fulfil—is the expression of something stronger, with deeper, farther-spreading roots, knit into the foundations of sacredness for all men."

For all men. Mordecai's "religion," far from being "a religion of race and heredity which was not, as a generalizable solution . . . something Eliot could have stood by," is, in fact, a grand example from world history of Eliot's own "religion," and of that "parent idea" of this novel and of her whole career. For what it celebrates are "the hidden bonds that consecrate change as a dependent growth . . . consecrate it with kinship," the "core of affection which binds a race and its families in dutiful love," a connectedness that stretches over time as well as space ("the past becomes my parent and the future stretches toward me the appealing arms of children"). Surely all this is not Jewish alone. These are conditions supplied by any culture in which community is alive, and it is the source of Gwendolen's tragic errors that they have disappeared out of hers. The Jewish "separateness" Mordecai defends is only that "cherishing of one's spot of native land" we must all begin with in order to learn by feeling, rather than through "abstract nouns," what it is to be a human being. "The best introduction to astronomy is to think of the heavens as a little lot of stars belonging to one's own homestead." That Deronda "found an added soul in finding his ancestry" is an example of how every life may be saved from chaos and sterility. For he found that soul because "his judgment [was] no longer wandering in the mazes of impartial sympathy, but choosing . . . with the closer fellowship that makes sympathy practical." As he once observed to Gwendolen—it is a condensed statement of that Eliot religion—"affection is the broadest basis of good in life."

But of course, the universal principle can come into existence only in some particular form. For Deronda, its particular form was Jewish. The task he found was Mordecai's great cause, "to bind our race together in spite of heresy," and to restore the Jewish nation. And though Eliot left its details unspecified, as part of the future that lies beyond her story's ending, that task will not seem to us, as it did to Henry James, a mere occasion for talk. We who have seen the "seed of fire" and the "great migration" will be ready enough to believe that he had real work to do.

The Novels of
William Hale White
(Mark Rutherford)

"The man who digs up unnecessary authors, histories, biographies is a public nuisance," William Hale White remarked in his "Black Notebook." "He adds to our burdens, already too heavy to be borne."[1] In now digging up Hale White himself, I'm aware that I risk appearing to be such a nuisance. When an author is so little read, the suspicion is not unlikely that he deserves no better, that he is, in fact, unnecessary. The suspicion would here be mistaken: the human problems dealt with in Hale White's work and the ideas and attitudes brought to their investigation are far more congenial to contemporary readers than its rural, Puritan, "Victorian" surface might suggest; and its quality, as writing, is remarkable. But considering that risk, it may be prudent to begin with a brief appeal to several authorities whose opinions will carry weight.

First, however, a bit of identification. He was born in Bedford, England, in 1831, and was, like his parents, a devout Dissenter—that is, he belonged to a church which did not conform to the established Church of England—for his first twenty years. After two years of study for the ministry, he was expelled from his seminary for heretical ideas on biblical inspiration and from then on gradually ceased to attend any religious services or to accept literally any religious dogma. He spent most of his adult life as a civil servant, supplementing his income for a time by writing newspaper columns, and he died in 1913.

Hale White did not begin to write books until the age of fifty, and he has left us, not counting works of technical scholarship, eleven small volumes. The first two, *The Autobiography of Mark Rutherford* (1881) and *Mark Rutherford's Deliverance* (1885), are largely an account of his own most important experiences in the guise of fiction. They pretend to be the posthumous autobiography of a poor London clerk and former minister edited by a friend called Reuben Shapcott. The "friend" speaks of having reason to suppose that other manuscripts are lying about among the belongings of the late Rutherford, and sure enough, there followed four novels: *The Revolution in Tanner's Lane* (1887), *Miriam's Schooling* (1890), *Catherine Furze* (1893), and *Clara Hopgood* (1896), and three volumes called *Pages from a Journal* (1900), *More Pages from a Journal* (1910), and *Last Pages from a Journal* (1915). These, the third coming out after Hale White's death, contain short stories, essays, and aphoristic "notes" (as he calls them) extracted from two unpublished notebooks, the "Black" and "White" notebooks. The double pseudonym was a disguise sincerely intended, and Hale White's identity did not for a long time become generally known. Among his last books appeared a short defense of Wordsworth against the charge of apostasy from the supposed political and intellectual radicalism of his youth (1898) and a critical work on John Bunyan (1904). He was also the author of translations of Spinoza's *Ethic* (1883) and his *Emendations of the Intellect* (1895), and it is interesting to find in the preface to the Modern Library edition of Spinoza that "it was desirable to use White's translation because it is the most accurate and elegant extant,"[2] a remark unaccompanied by any hint that he had other claims to distinction as well. Finally, he wrote for his children the short account of his early years which was issued in 1913 as *The Early Life of Mark Rutherford (W. Hale White) by Himself;* and in 1924 appeared two more books of great interest to admirers of Hale White: a volume of correspondence called *Letters to Three Friends* and *The Groombridge Diary*, in which his second wife gives a detailed record, full of his talk and his letters to her, of his last seven years.

In spite of Hale White's obscurity, others, as I say, have shared my view of his merit. The fact is, since 1880, when his books began to come out, his admirers, though they have not been many, have been choice. What is more, there has often crept into their writings on him a note almost of indignation at a neglect they have found it hard to understand. Of the first two books, William Dean Howells declared that they "may yet mark a new era in fiction . . . they carry so deep a sense of truthfulness to the reader, they are so far in temper from any sort of mere artistry, they are so simply and nobly serious. . . . We could not give too strong an impression of this incomparable sincerity." Matthew Arnold and Swinburne and later Joseph Conrad and Stephen Crane admired his work.[3] Edmund Gosse called him a genius and complained, "It appears to us that no author of anything like his rank has in our time been so continuously neglected by responsible criticism."[4] H. W. Massingham considered him the "one imaginative genius of the highest order" produced by English Puritanism since Bunyan. Arnold Bennett called *The Revolution* "the finest example of modern English prose," and D. H. Lawrence remarked of our author, "I *do* think he is jolly good—so thorough, so sound and so beautiful."[5] J. M. Murry has noted that his style, "very near perfection," took its character from "a mistrust of words, a sense of responsibility to personal truth," and the "heavy obligation [placed by Hale White] on the written word of sincerity to deep personal feeling." This critic's grasp of his subject's literary character merits further quotation. That the following is not mere praise but an exact description of a certain kind of writer will, I hope, become clear. Murry speaks of "the manifest oneness of Mark Rutherford. His letters, his novels, his journals are radiations from a simple living centre, function—to use a mathematical term—of one unchanging soul. . . . " His work is "secure against decay because it was moulded by a true man in his own image. He digged down to bedrock in his soul and his work rests unshakeable on that firm foundation."[6]

There are others, but I will close the list with the comments of André Gide, who created a vogue for Hale White in France which, slight as it was, was yet the most marked anywhere in our time. This too must be quoted at length for it will be the text for much of what follows. Coming, moreover, from a mind peculiarly "modern"—in its freedom and complexity—it will help to confirm my view of the relevance of Hale White's work to our own culture and its problems. The comments are all from his *Journal.*

> October 8, 1915: Wonderful integrity of the book [*The Autobiography*]. I do not know any work that is more specifically Protestant. . . . The exquisite qualities of Hale White's style . . . are the very ones I would like to have.[7]

> January 24, 1916: I read in Rutherford . . . a passage about the devil and hell that just happens to back up my thoughts wonderfully. "The shallowest of mortals is able now to laugh at the notion of a personal devil. No doubt there is no such thing existent; but the horror at evil which could find no other expression than in the creation of a devil is no subject for laughter, and if it [does] not in some shape or other survive, the race itself will not survive."[8]

May not this entry be a clue to the devil which dominates *The Counterfeiters,* already at this date being considered?

And, finally, of *Catherine Furze:*

> March 8, 1936: I do not think this book can find many readers in France; less and less: palates spoiled by too many spices can no longer taste what is pure. . . . I find in *Catherine Furze* the so specifically Protestant qualities and virtues which

awakened such profound echoes in me, when, for the first time, I read his two little volumes: *Autobiography* and *Deliverance*. Here honesty and integrity become poetic virtues, beside which everything seems camouflaged, inauthentic, and overloaded. The human soul may be compared to palimpsests: here is read the original writing, so difficult to make out through the accumulation of retouchings and additions. The very style of William Hale White (Mark Rutherford) is exquisitely transparent, scintillatingly pure. He develops to perfection qualities that I wish were mine. His art is made of the renunciation of all false riches. He is apolitical, because there is no politics without fraud.[9]

So admired, then, Hale White may well be thought to deserve more attention than he has received. He deserves it for various reasons: because of his value as the historian of a segment of English culture not elsewhere, except to some degree by George Eliot, so understandingly or so vividly preserved; because of a dramatization of the problems of moral freedom as subtle—and almost, for his time, as daring—as that to be found in the work of André Gide, with whom he has, in fact, a startling affinity; and because of the beauty of his art, in its style and its dramatic clarity and power. A word or two must be said about such matters by way of proper introduction. And yet it is not in these that his most striking quality, the ground of a unique and peculiarly poignant appeal, is to be discovered. They are, as it were, the literary by-products of something that is not in its originating impulse or final effect literary at all. Just so might we find various literary and intellectual merits in a sermon—I mean the passionate sharing of his insight by a spiritual leader who has suffered much and understood much and wishes rather to help others than to demonstrate his abilities; just so might we find them in the talk of one who has met his dearest friend after a long absence and at last, in private and free from the need to show cleverness or to hide weakness, utters what has lain close to his heart; and yet in neither case would it seem better than frivolous to regard them as most important. We will therefore postpone our consideration of the above characteristics, the kind he shares with many good novelists, until after we have tried to understand what he shares with almost no one at all.

The comments I quoted recurred often to the word "sincerity" or to some equivalent. There is, of course, a sense in which any serious writer is sincere—honesty is a basic condition of his profession and some kind of truth its necessary raw material—but we are rarely impelled, except perhaps in mitigation of the charge of failure, to place that word in the center of a critical portrait. With Hale White, however, it must, in fact, go in the center: it is the chief distinction of his work and the source of his finest effects. What it helps us express in his case is the feeling he gives of an especially intimate relationship between the man and his writing. In order to understand the unique qualities of the writing, we must for this reason start with the man himself.

And the first thing we must note about him is that by the age of fifty, when he began to write, he had experienced so much unhappiness that life had come to mean for him chiefly the endurance of suffering. "As we get older," he wrote to a son, "we find that endurance is the exact synonym for life."[10] This is sometimes uttered as a commonplace: for him it was the most immediate of realities. He had been poor and for nearly twenty years had had to work from the time of rising to the time of sleeping to support his wife and four children. No one has described better than he the anguish—an ignoble anguish—of having to give up one's life to a boring and degrading job while all higher gifts rust unused or become mere sources of pain. Worse than this was the fact that while she was still in her twenties, his wife became ill with a progressive paralysis, now called multiple sclerosis, that did not kill her for thirty years but that gradually crippled and blinded her. Most of those thirty years she spent in wheelchairs or in bed. And though amid her sufferings she preserved a courage that could shame her husband, he was never able to forget for an instant the terrible visitation. That he should have been oppressed by it is natural enough, perhaps, but there was a special reason for his vulnerability to misfortune. He had a trial that multiplied the difficulties of every other, and that, indeed, required little support from circumstances to steep his life in gloom. From his early manhood Hale White was afflicted with a tendency to what he called "hypochondria," that is, depression, which was not the occasional bad mood we all know, but an attack of horror and panic that lasted for long periods at a time and that, when not actually upon him, was being, as it were, consciously held at bay. It is interesting that the state recurs so often in his fiction, sometimes named, sometimes not—and even in his criticism, where it is seen to be involved in the work of favorite writers—that we are reminded of the sexual abnormality in Proust which ends by turning up everywhere. Of course, it was a sickness. He spent much money on doctors (though in vain), and he does not fail to point out the questionable validity of the ideas about life, produced by it, suggesting that they ought not to be regarded as "mere logical inferences," but rather as symptoms which must disappear with returning health. Nevertheless, it was impossible not to regard this "hypochondria" most often as the opening of a window on a terrible and undeniable reality, on a vision not less true because the usual pleasures and preoccupations of health (that "divine narcotic"[11]) mercifully conceal it. The terror of it affected nearly everything he said and did, and those who get to know hm well can see its influence in the most unlikely places in his work. It made more precious the simplest pleasures of life, and his serious reflections not only derived from it a kind of desperate urgency but were, by it, forever challenged for their true helpfulness to the soul which struggled and suffered.

It is this which accounts for the chief demand he made on the works of the mind—in art, philosophy, even religion: Do they help men to live? Exclusive preoccupation with the separate disciplines themselves tended to make him impatient all his life. "Poetry, if it is to be good for anything, must help us to live," he remarks in his *Pages from a Journal*. "It is to this we come at last in our criticism, and if it does not help us to live it may as well disappear, no matter what its fine qualities may be."[12] As a rule, we are right to reject such a demand that art, or any other intellectual pursuit, be primarily useful, because it is often made by those with too narrow a notion of what men need or of the manifold ways in which they can be served. But not only was the demand made in his case by one well aware of the peculiar sanctions and seductions of the intellectual life; it was also made by one who sought help for problems of the utmost complexity, for problems, indeed, which are often insoluble. What he sought above all was help to endure uncrushed life's unavoidable pain, and for this it is not things or society that must be changed—the usual notion of those who demand art as "a weapon"—but only, if possible, oneself, one's ideas. It is the help ideally offered by religion. And, in fact, his abnormal need intensified all the influences in his education which had made religious thinking natural to him. For it is an important characteristic of religion that while it deals in ideas which link the individual to mankind and to the universe, these ideas are related directly to the emotional life. They are attempts (whatever else they also are) to help him understand and endure his inevitable sorrows. This is the reason Hale White never lost his reverence for true faith, his nostalgia for a time when his own could have been perfect, and his sense of the special value of those many religious insights that do not depend on the acceptance of systems of dogma, but are clearly the insights of men grappling directly with the eternal problems. And this is why the Bible became for him the most precious of all books, forever read and reread, though he did not get to know it rightly, he tells us, until after he was expelled from his seminary for questioning its unique inspiration.

If religion had been ideally the source of this help, the nineteenth century had, for men like him, destroyed its perfect sufficiency, and such men now sought its consolations also in philosophy and literature. It is significant that the philosopher who meant most to Hale White was Spinoza. Spinoza attempted to reconcile the great helpful ideas of religion—its identification of virtue with inner peace; its lesson of self-forgetfulness, or rather self-discovery, in the higher, the greater, the whole; its lesson of the necessary and healing acceptance of reality (or God's will)—with the demands of the rational intelligence and the facts of nature, and thereby to provide the grounds for "a joy continuous and supreme to all eternity."[13] This was exactly the problem of Hale White, who liked to emphasize that admitted human motive for Spinoza's philosophic quest. And though Spinoza aimed at joy, it was not a joy available to the weak; he led us toward a love of God which does not demand, as the celebrated proposition has it, that God love us in return. One can understand how a man whose life had taught him that inner peace was not, in fact, going to be made easy by a God of prompt rewards might be struck by such an idea.

In other intellectual fields too he sought—religion, one is tempted to say, but, at any rate, this same help to live. In his essays, which range among the works of scientists and at least one polar explorer, as well as of poets and novelists, he is quick to notice the sense of trouble—sometimes, as with Bradley, the eighteenth-century explorer, it takes the form of physical danger—and the medicine used against it: so often, and not only with Bradley, courage. This gives even to his literary criticism, even, indeed, to his most rigorous philosophic reflection, an amazing note of repressed personal feeling. Not that literature as pleasure, using the word in its widest sense, was beneath his notice. On the contrary, like all pleasure it was thrice precious to one whose life so desperately needed sweetening. There is clear personal gratitude in his remarks on Scott, for instance, whose wonderful tales he had read aloud to his wife and children. (So insistent a "practical" emphasis may after all engender a doubt as to whether he was aware of what the art of literature is in itself. Let me not move on without at least a hint that he was. To a friend who told him she did not "understand" poetry because she was interested in "what is said," not in "the way it is said," he wrote that the distinction was a fallacy.

> The noblest office of genius is *realization*, the making *ex*-plicit the world in which we live, and form, therefore, is emphatically reality. . . . There is a passage in Milton—indeed, there are many in the poems of this miraculous master, in which accent alone is tremendous fact.

"Grasping ten thousand thunders, which he sent
Before him, such as in their souls infix'd
Plagues."

He deserts the ordinary rhythm of heroic blank verse in the last eight syllables; they are all slow and their slowness is a great definite creative act.[14]

This statement is one of many which show how his ultimate choices were never made simple by inability to see and feel what "opposed" them.)

One thing more must be understood about the man if we are to understand the reason for his special qualities as a writer. It is the abnormal intensity of his longing for a friend with whom he could share what in youth he called his "heartfelt thinkings." "It is not those who have the least, but those who have the most to give who most want sympathy,"[15] he said, and he speaks in *The Autobiography*, after explaining that the reserve often charged against him was due to a longing for self-revelation which had generally been rebuffed, of "a dream which I had . . . of a perfect friendship."

I always felt [he goes on] that talk with whom I would, I left something unsaid which was precisely what I most wished to say. I wanted a friend who would sacrifice himself to me utterly, and to whom I might offer a similar sacrifice. I found companions for whom I cared, and who professed to care for me; but I was thirsting for deeper draughts of love than any which they had to offer; and I said to myself that if I were to die, not one of them would remember me for more than a week. This was not selfishness, for I longed to prove my devotion as well as to receive that of another. How this ideal haunted me! It made me restless and anxious at the sight of every new face, wondering whether at last I had found that for which I searched as if for the kingdom of heaven. It is superfluous to say that a friend of the kind I wanted never appeared.[16]

As it happens, such a friend did finally appear. And though he was old and she was young, mutual recognition was instantaneous and she became his second wife. Her diary of the seven years they had together at Groombridge, Kent, before he died, tells the story of a union of minds as perfect as any in the history of literature—this in spite of painful troubles due to the difference in age and circumstances or to his unfortunate temperament. And to this woman when she came he said a strange thing: "If I had been given you when I was thirty I would never have let the public hear a syllable from me."[17] The inference is clear that when at the age of fifty he sat down, not at first to the comparative frivolity of storytelling, but to share in secret the history of his own inner struggles and the modest "deliverance" he was able to find, he had chosen the anonymous reader for his perfect friend. It is a fact that the voice—the style—we hear in this work is that of a man alone with such a friend and uttering at last what he had never been able to tell a living soul. And when he offers a reason for making public a tale so "commonplace" and so sad, it is something as distinct from the usual motives for a literary career as this:

> I have observed that the mere knowing that other people have been tried as we have been tried is a consolation to us, and that we are relieved by the assurance that our sufferings are not special and peculiar, but common to us with many others. Death has always been a terror to me, and at times, nay generally, religion and philosophy have been altogether unavailing to mitigate the terror in any way. But it has always been a comfort to me to reflect that whatever death may be, it is the inheritance of the whole human race; that I am not singled out, but shall merely have to pass through what the weakest have had to pass through before me. In the worst of maladies, worst at least to me, those which are hypochondriacal, the healing effect which is produced by the visit of a friend who can simply say, "I have endured all that," is most marked. So it is not impossible that some few whose experience has been like mine may, by my example, be freed from that sense of solitude which they find so depressing.[18]

We are now in a position to understand that "sincerity" which so many readers have found peculiarly characteristic of his work. It comes from this: that he writes at the impulse of such strong personal feeling, out of so pressing a sense of the gravity of man's condition and the urgency of his need, that all considerations of mere craft seem to become subordinate, or else to disappear. And it is because he was able to divest himself of pride as few men have ever been, and to confess (though in disguise) the existence within him of one who suffered and struggled, and who did so not as a hero, but as an ordinary man, that he makes so powerful an appeal to that same unheroic self hidden in all of us, exciting responses more intimate and more moved than are common in literature.

This—so to speak—nonliterary character of his work accounts for its chief literary qualities. It accounts for the remarkable style, which is a simple communication, undistorted by the slightest striving for effect and absolutely faithful to what has been intensely felt and clearly seen. "If the truth is of serious importance to us we dare not obstruct it by phrasemaking," he wrote. "We are compelled to be as direct as our inherited feebleness will permit. The cannon ball's path is near to a straight line in proportion to its velocity. 'My boy,' my father once said to me, 'if you write anything you consider particularly fine, strike it out.' " The beauty that results is impossible to imitate because one of its main characteristics is an unparalleled purity and naturalness of English: there is no self-assertive twisting of the idiom to take hold of. It comes to seem merely a beauty of personality. But though the naturalness, purity, and simplicity of his writing are most often noticed, these alone would be nothing without the emotion which is equally pervasive. One finds in Hale White's work many explicit demands for the right to express intensity, lest moderateness of expression tell its own kind of lie. "There is more insincerity," he remarks in *The Revolution,* "in purposely lowering the expression beneath the thought, and denying the thought thereby than in a little exaggeration."[19] The restraint of his style, like his self-discipline in general, is a visible conquest, and sometimes his short definite sentences resemble nothing so much as the speech of a man who must speak coldly between clenched teeth lest he be overmastered by emotion. This could, of course, become oppressive, but in his case it has not because the conquest has been achieved; the man who speaks so is also a man of mind, aware of more than one perspective on his own experience and capable of irony directed at himself and of humor. When *his* voice vibrates, we are at a point safely beyond sentimentality or a self-pity that is not justified. In fact, while his expressions are always simple and modest, they are clearly meant by an extremely conscious mind in their widest possible signification. This sets up a tension which is one of his chief effects and which can thrill, like understatement.

The art of his novels too takes much of its character from this unusual seriousness and intensity. He has described this art himself, unintentionally, in the following remarks to a son:

> Art is art in proportion to its distinctness. Noble art is distinguished from base art by the perfect clearness of the conception which it aims to embody. I do not assert that there are not other contrasts, but this is perhaps the most striking. The vehicle may be obscure, but in the writer or painter the intention is definite and vivid. Otherwise what burden lies on him to speak or paint? Only because he sees or thinks with intensity and consequently with a definition superior to that of ordinary mortals does he become great.... The sum and substance, to put it in other words, is *realization.* Whatever we have to speak, let it be bounded by a precise limiting line, so that the thing spoken is

marked off from the vague, from chaos, from all other things
with absolute precision. . . . Perhaps I could have concluded all I
had to say in one word. Our actual *experience*, not what we can
invent or dream: and no step a hair's breadth beyond what is
real and solid for us, proved and again proved. This should be
the character of all our speech.[20]

Exactly such clarity of definition—proceeding from just such warmth
of response—appears in his characterization, though this can be of the
utmost subtlety, in his development out of it of dramatic clash and
climax, and in the underlying conception of the meaning of it all which
determines the form of a work. Though Hale White writes in the
discursive tradition of George Eliot, which permits him to interrupt
and comment at will, his novels have the speed and economy of those
of Turgenev, whom, indeed, he admired. His comments, for that matter, tend rather to increase than to dilute intensity, for he hardly ever
interrupts unless he must: he seems driven by emotion to utter his
larger thought. The reader may have noticed how sometimes, even
before one knows what is to be said, the mere fact that a writer is being
thus driven to generalize can in itself be moving.

The intimate relation between his writing and his character accounts, finally, for the peculiar unity of his work noticed by Murry.
Never the professional fulfilling merely some literary purpose, he
brought to every utterance nothing less than his whole self. This is why,
as has been suggested, his highest flights of philosophic reflection are
charged throughout with the emotion which was their human origin
and are often, oddly, as poignant as his accounts of love or pain. And
this is why he can pass directly from such heights to the most humbly
practical concerns—the pathos of the workman's fleeting Sunday, or
how to break the habit of drink—without the slightest air of incongru-
ity. Such concerns, being for him the true basis of all the rest, are seen
naturally in a larger perspective that exposes their furthest meaning
and unites them with what is highest. As he wrote of a character, "his
passion was informed with intellect, and his intellect glowed with passion. There was nothing in him merely animal or merely rational."[21]
For those to whom the novels fully reveal themselves, therefore, it is
likely that the writer will at last be overshadowed by the man. They will
be moved again and again to a response that is more than aesthetic,
more than intellectual, and drawn first perhaps by the quiet triumphs
of his art, they may find that the slightest essays or notes, the letters,
and not least the lovely *Groombridge Diary* of his second wife, so full of
his wise and passionate conversation, grow as precious to them as the
ripened works themselves.

All that I have so far tried to make clear can be summed up by a passage from one of his late stories. The passage concerns a certain friend of the narrator called Robert, who has chosen to give up the woman he loves in order to be true to a spiritual vocation which must bar her from his life forever. Though we are shown his particular trouble, however, the significant thing for us now is its intensity and its result.

> What made the separation especially terrible, both to Veronica and Robert, it is hard to say. Here are a couple of lines from one of Robert's letters to me which may partly explain: "There is something in this trouble which I cannot put into words. It is the complete unfolding, the making real to myself, all that is hidden in that word *Never*." Is it possible to express by speech a white handkerchief waved from the window of the railway train, or the deserted platform where ten minutes before a certain woman stood, where her image still lingers? There is something in this which is not mere sorrow. It is rather the disclosure of that dread Abyss which underlies the life of man. One consequence of this experience was the purest sincerity. All insincerity, every-thing unsound, everything which could not stand the severest test, was by this trial crushed out of him. His words uniformly stood for facts. Perhaps it was his sincerity which gave him a power over me such as no other man ever possessed.[22]

This is the power of Hale White.

But it is not, this power, by any means the whole story. The reader may even be relieved to know that Hale White did not look exclusively into his own heart, but that, like most novelists of importance, he also recreated a solid world inhabited by people other than himself. He did this with such vivid and subtle accuracy, indeed, that his work has marked value as history.

His world is chiefly that of the Dissenting lower middle class in the East Midlands of England. He grew up in this region—in Bunyan's own town of Bedford and in the Calvinist sect of Independents—and his stories rarely stray far from this center of his most lively memories. He writes, therefore, of a people whose relation to a religious tradition is one of the most important facts about them. He was among them, moreover, at a time of greater and more disturbing changes in belief than had been seen for generations. The Higher Criticism—that study of Biblical texts which suggested that they were the work of fallible men rather than the infallible word of God—the advance of geology, which cast doubt on the Biblical history of the earth, and the new conditions of life introduced by the Industrial Revolution were terrible blows to religious fundamentalism. It is the results of these blows on character and social relationships in the world of Dissent which furnished Hale White with the materials for his stories.

He shows us that there were roughly three ways to respond. There were those who closed their minds entirely to new ideas, as in self-protection, and this produced the rigid mechanical dogmatism, sometimes sincere, sometimes hypocritical, which has been the target of so much criticism. (Remember Dickens's Mr. Chadband, or Gosse's *Father and Son,* or the attack of Matthew Arnold in his *St. Paul and Protestantism.*) There were others who rejected their religious heritage just as absolutely for a "free-thinking" that could, of course, be extremely intelligent and adequate to many of life's problems but that could also be thinking of the shallowest, easiest, and, what is worse, most blindly complacent kind. And there were still others who could not reject what seemed true knowledge and true ideas, but who found it painful and at last unnecessary to give up their religion altogether. These, to adapt the words of Hale White, committed the heresy of seeking the meaning of dogma, that is, of regarding their religion as a language of symbols, a mode of expressing wisdom eternally applicable to human life, that required only to be properly translated. And if this seemed to put their religion on a par with any of the historic accumulations of wisdom, whether in religion, philosophy or literature, a very plausible case could be built to show that the Judeo-Christian insights went deepest, covered more, and were more helpful than all others. It was to this category, as we shall see, that Hale White himself belonged, so that in spite of his expulsion from the Dissenting college, his work can constitute for a secular generation an introduction to the profound meaningfulness of religious formulations and ways of thought. There was also a fourth kind of relationship to religion, and this was the perfect faith of those wholly untouched by the new ideas because ignorant of them or uninterested. In other words, it had been possible, and was still so here and there though skeptics might deny it, to find in one's religion all the room needed for a rich and intelligent life, to find that it gave life a meaning which included all that was important. There were many such believers whom Hale White honored, some by whom he was, indeed, deeply influenced. It is a special interest of his fiction that he shows with the most delicate inwardness what beauty, wisdom, and peace such faith can sometimes make possible.

Religion, moreover, has never been an isolated matter, but involved, often inextricably, with social status and attitudes and political convictions. The period to which Hale White's fiction is chiefly devoted begins in his father's time, around 1815. The Industrial Revolution and the just-ended war with Napoleon had brought about a severe economic depression: violent uprisings were not uncommon. And yet it was also a time of such intense political reaction that the radical was treated as practically a traitor or an agent of defeated France. Workers' political clubs had to go underground, and they were hounded by government spies and *agents provocateurs*. Most prominent among the radicals, or the mere wild protestors, were the Dissenters. The Manchester weavers who gathered to petition George IV for political and economic relief and were shot down by the militia at "Peterloo" were Dissenters, and intensely devout. Even the pulpits of their ministers were then not too lofty a sphere, as they later became, for the expression of political opinion. The drama of this state of affairs is preserved in all its excitement in the pages of Hale White, who goes on to show us how for many the coming of better times meant also a blunting of political consciousness, a growing snobbery, for they could now hope to rise in status, and the gradual transformation of their religion into a social form which made the Higher—the Anglican—Church increasingly seductive.

The Dissenting community in the period he describes was therefore a much richer mine of human material than the familiar caricature of it would lead one to expect: rich in external conflicts, as those with different relations to the common traditions came together, and rich too in the more interesting and painful internal ones, as men for whom vital matters were at stake in their development changed and grew. It is Hale White's value for us as a social historian that he suffered these conflicts himself or watched the suffering of those he loved, and being gifted with great psychological penetration, could present them to us from the inside in all their variety and intensity. Because of him that vanished society need not be peopled for us exclusively by bigots and hypocrites, but also by recognizable and complex human beings.

The reader will by now have recognized his similarity to George Eliot. The resemblance between their work is often striking. But if the greater quantity of life which Eliot so masterfully recreates and organizes entitles her to superior rank as a novelist pure and simple, she is not the greater writer. Partly because of the peculiar nonprofessional relationship to writing already described, Hale White's scope was deliberately narrowed to those things alone which in fact or in imagination he had intensely experienced. And the result has been not only limitation, but a psychological subtlety, a wisdom, a force and precision of language, and a dramatic power she never matched. [So I thought when I wrote those words some years ago, and I leave them to show

how deeply Hale White moved me. But since then, though his stature has not diminished in my mind, that of Eliot has risen. It now seems to me absurd to place him above her in such qualities—as he would have agreed, for he revered both her mind and her art.]

Even more than by the society he recreates, however, the reader of today is likely to be interested by Hale White's thought. And here it will help us to be aware of that other affinity, which, as I have said, suggests a peculiarly modern complexity, his affinity with André Gide. Though the *milieux* in which the two writers discover and embody their meanings could hardly be more different, these meanings themselves are surprisingly alike, finding expression often in almost identical formulations. Here are several passages from the work of Hale White which will at once demonstrate the resemblance, and provide the basis for a definition of Hale White's central ideas. For readers of Gide they will hardly require comment.

> Each person's belief or proposed course of action is part of himself, and if he be diverted from it and takes up with that which is not himself, the unity of his nature is impaired, and he loses himself.
>
> The symbolism of an act varies much, and what may be mere sport in one is sin in another.
>
> The universe is so complex that nothing is true save a word fitted to a particular occasion.
>
> There is no human truth which is altogether true.
>
> The curse of every truth is that a counterfeit of it always waits on it and is its greatest enemy.
>
> We are compounded of sincerity and insincerity in every thought: the laughter of the brightest, the prayer of the most devout, is tainted with insincerity, not because we have not the will, but because we have not the strength to be otherwise.[23]

Remember the aged La Perouse in *The Counterfeiters*, who suggests that no matter how hard we try to hear the voice of God, it is only the devil we can succeed in hearing, that is, only our selfishness, whatever the noble profession in which it comes disguised. But if Hale White mistrusts the self, he also defends it:

> It is impossible totally to exclude the "I" in our most unselfish acts. We ought not to torment ourselves because we cannot

exclude it. We must not set pleasure so sharply over against unselfishness.

The practice of self-denial is good; it may be learnt. More difficult than self-denial is enjoyment, rejoicing in that which ought to delight us. This perhaps may be partly learnt, but not without the severest self-discipline.[24]

Was it not in just this "puritanical" manner, on reasoned and moral grounds, that Gide forced himself toward the delight an older morality had taught him to shun? "It has long seemed to me," we read in *Fruits of the Earth,* "that joy is rarer, more difficult and lovelier than sadness . . . [and] not only a natural need . . . but also, indeed, a moral obligation."[25]

Perhaps life is too large for any code we can as yet frame, and the dissolution of all codes, the fluid, unstable condition of which we complain, may be a necessary antecedent of new and more lasting combinations. One thing is certain, that there is not a single code now in existence which is not false; that the graduation of the vices and virtues is wrong, and that in the future it will be altered. We must not hand ourselves over to a despotism with no Divine right, even if there be a risk of anarchy.[26]

There is one statement, finally, in which the resemblance between the two writers is most vividly shown, and in which Hale White's thought—the conflict which drives it forward, and the way this conflict is resolved—is most clearly expressed. It comes from an essay called "Principles."

What we have once *heard,* really heard in our best moments, by that let us abide. There are multitudes of moments in which intelligent conviction in the truth of principles disappears, and we are able to do nothing more than fall back on mere determinate resolution to go on; not to give up what we have found to be true. This power of determinate resolution which acts independently of enthusiasm is a precious possession. . . . One would like to have a record of all that passed through the soul of Ulysses when he was rowed past the Sirens. In what intellectually subtle forms did not the desire to stay clothe itself to that intellectually subtle soul? But he had bound himself beforehand, and he reached Ithaca and Penelope at last. . . . After six months [at a long and difficult task] I began to flag, and my greatest hindrance was, not the confessed desire for rest, but all kinds of the most fascinating principles or pseudo principles, which flattered what was best and not what was worst in me. I was narrowing my intellect, preventing the proper enjoyment of life, neglecting the sunshine, &c., &c. But I thought to myself "Now the serpent was more subtile than any beast of the field," and his temptation specially was that "your eyes shall be opened, and ye shall be as gods." I was enabled to persevere, oftentimes through no other motive than that aforesaid divine doggedness, and presently I was rewarded.[27]

The reader may remember Vincent in *The Counterfeiters*, for whom the devil had to provide an ethic to "legitimize" his behavior, because Vincent "continues to be a moral being and the devil will only get the better of him by furnishing him with reasons for self-approval."[28] But the passage bears an even more marked resemblance to the labyrinth chapter of Gide's *Theseus*, which, like the above essay, is one of its author's most complete and significant utterances. Gide's labyrinth is that of self-indulgence, in which each of us can lose himself if he risks it without a thread that will link him, as Theseus is linked to Ariadne, to the past, to duty, to his own best resolves—to something, in short, held above his immediate desires. For the place is difficult to escape from because it is filled with vapors which "not only act on the will and put it to sleep; they induce a delicious intoxication rich in flattering delusions. . . . Each [victim] is led on by the complexities implicit in his own mind to lose himself . . . in a labyrinth of his own devising."[29] Thus even our highest powers can be put in the service of the Sirens, proliferating marvelous reasons for a self-indulgence that will destroy us. It is interesting that Hale White ends here too with the devil—the serpent—so dear to both writers as a symbol of the self, with its subtlety and its temptation of pride. But if each requires the self to be thus held in check, it is not by a chain fashioned by others, not by a principle heard from without. It is by a principle inwardly heard, and by a thread of which the *spool* remains in the hero's own hands.

The source of the affinity between Hale White and Gide has perhaps already been made plain. It is the Protestantism in which, as it happens, both were strictly nurtured. Though each cast off early the orthodoxy in which he began, each retained what was capable of a life outside the orthodox forms. In brief, they retained the two great ideas which Protestantism, though it often distorted or even contradicted them, has made important in our culture. (These ideas are also human, needless to say, and others have found them elsewhere.)

The first idea is that of the primary importance of the moral problem. How should I live? is the question signalizing Bernard's emergence into manhood, which is thus shown to mean also into an awareness of moral responsibility. He wants at last not simply to be free and to enjoy himself, but to live right and to use his freedom for an upward progress. Bernard's question is at the bottom of most of what our two authors have written, and it is the tendency of each—for the moralist tends to become a generalizer—to formulate his answers into guiding principles. At the same time, however, beside this need to seek the right and be in it, each has kept with him from his Protestant heritage another element equally crucial. This is the idea of "the priesthood of all believers," the idea that no *other* priest, but only himself, only an "inner voice," can be the proper judge of the individual's moral rectitude. Of course, as our writers show us, these two ideas must often stand opposed. For the general principles which each is forever deducing from experience must forever be tested against fresh experience, lest some vital difference has arisen in self or situation, or lest what led one man upward lead the next man down. The conflict between these two movements of the mind, the perpetual criticism passing back and forth between principles and changing particular contexts, has been for both Gide and Hale White the motor, as it were, for an ever deeper and more audacious exploration of the moral life. It has made that life eminently adventurous for them, made it one for which, if freedom of conscience is necessary, that same freedom creates endless dangers and difficulties. But it has also enabled them to avoid the two typical extremes, so prevalent today. For, on the one hand, it sets them apart from those who live by principles they have placed once for all beyond question, and who would suffer reality to be distorted or simplified rather than that a principle be doubted. And on the other, it sets them apart from those who cynically reject principles altogether and give themselves up instead to the immediate cues of every new context or of personal appetite.

Now there are certain modes of attack on both these attitudes. The preoccupation with moral questions, for instance, is supposed to be narrowing, and, in literature, anti-aesthetic. Thus, E. M. Forster speaks in his *Aspects of the Novel* of "that tiresome little receptacle, a conscience, which is so often a nuisance in serious writers and so contracts their effects—the conscience of Hawthorne or of Mark Rutherford."[30] But this is rather like complaining that the requirements of literary form are a nuisance and contract a writer's effects. In fact, the moral conscience, like form, like many rules and regulations, is what makes effects possible, because it gives definition to the mere chaos of experience. If nothing were right or wrong, good or evil, if there were no *ought*, then all would be one and nothing would make any difference. It is the lack of a conscience that is the real literary handicap, because it means the lack of a mode of discrimination—and even of a motive for discrimination, that is, of interest in life. (Forster himself, I need hardly say, had a conscience of particular firmness and delicacy.) Of course, any complaint about too narrow or simpleminded a morality, which means too narrow or simpleminded a view of human experience, would be entirely legitimate. But it should be remembered—Gide is the great example, but Hale White is another—that for the subtle mind a conscience is precisely a goad toward further subtlety.

Far more serious has been the attack on the other idea, that of the "priesthood" of each man for himself; after World War I there was a steady decline in the prestige of the free conscience, and not only in the comparatively unintelligent realm of politics. In a famous and influential essay, T.S. Eliot, for instance, seemed to see the Protestant "inner voice" as *necessarily* in conflict with principles—which were presumed to be *necessarily* derived from some outer authority—never itself, in its "best moments," the author of them. It is the voice, he told us, which "breathes the eternal message of vanity, fear, and lust.[31] Yet the self-exaltation of Protestantism was never at its best either pride of self or lust for self-gratification. The self was exalted not as an object of worship, but as an instrument for use, the only reliable instrument in matters as complex and changing as those of the soul. The purpose for which it was used remained precisely a search for the altar on which it might not vainly be given up, the soil in which the grain of corn might "die" and bear fruit. It has always, in fact, been a development peculiarly characteristic of the Protestant tradition that to a God personally descried and freely chosen the self should be utterly abandoned.

The price for this assumption of personal responsibility has not been small. It accounts for the introspective gloom which marks so much of Protestant culture and the sounds of anguish that frequently issue from it. (The progress of Bunyan's Pilgrim would have been less agonizing, as well as less thrilling, if it had led at the outset to a center of authority where the burden of decision could be shifted to others.) It accounts too for the frequent eccentricities which rise to make a mock of human freedom. But the reward is at least commensurate with the price, for it is nothing less than the liberty to maintain a personal relationship with the Highest, with reality, justice, and truth. Thus Hale White, in his freedom, sometimes pined for the certainty and security it denied him, and Gide has perhaps been led by his into eccentricity. But, in return, each has been enabled to stay honest, to explore deeply the new paths his new experience has opened for him, and, most important for us today, to learn and show that freedom is not incompatible with morality, or with a *self*-discipline which can keep it moving "upward."

In spite of their profound affinity, however, a word must be said in conclusion of their differences, which are also great and interesting. They flow, chiefly, from this: that Hale White explores the moral life with his eye on human suffering, from which it is his main concern to seek deliverance; Gide, acquainted though he is with suffering, tends to regard it as failure: it is his pride to concentrate rather on his goal of happiness, and to seek it happily. The result is that Gide seems to write for human strength, inspiring courage and leading to joy; Hale White for inevitable human weakness, mitigating terror and assuaging pain. Though their insight into the nature of moral problems is remarkably alike, Gide uses his to open the way before us, and Hale White seeks instead to show us where we can legitimately rest, what amid the dangers of the way can support us when we fall. What he finds, like the discoveries of Gide and for the same reasons, can never be offered as absolutely sure. There are extremities, moreover, in which no tool or weapon of the mind has ever availed, and since he will not lie, he can only counsel us in these to remember that others have passed through them and to endure. But testimony exists to the admittedly peculiar fact that his books have done more than delight and liberate; they have consoled. Earlier in time and different in temperament, Hale White does not carry us so far nor in so many directions as Gide, who is the greater of the two, as he is surely one of the greatest forces for intellectual and moral liberation among the writers of our period. But if the French writer is the more dazzling and instructs us more widely, it is the English writer whom we can love.

The Novels of Mary McCarthy

The following discussion originally covered McCarthy's work up to 1968. To this has been added a section dealing with *Birds of America*.

Though Mary McCarthy's novels are not all equally successful, each has so much life and truth, and is written in a prose so spare, vigorous, and natural, and yet at the same time so witty, graceful, and, in a certain way, poetic, that it becomes a matter for wonder that she is not generally named among the finest American novelists of her period. She is much admired, of course, and has achieved a best seller, but that is not the same thing. The reason, I think, is that she is a sort of neoclassicist in a country of romantics. The sprightliness and detachment of her prose, her preference for sense over sensibility, her satirical eye for the hidden ego in our intellectual pretensions are qualities we are not comfortable with in this country. They may amuse, but they also antagonize. And they don't, among all our "heaven-storming Titans," seem Important. At any rate, whatever the reasons, the qualities and meanings that lie beneath her sparkling surface tend, even by admiring critics, to be misconceived. Her novels have been called "essayistic," for instance—designed to persuade us of ideas rather than to present living characters and felt experiences. And their subject is often supposed to be a supercilious, zestfully destructive view of people she dislikes, a view unredeemed by any examples of the humanly admirable—except in the heroines who represent herself. These charges are so common, in fact, that it may be useful to begin with a preliminary answer to each.

As to the first, though she has written mainly about her own class of American intellectuals, people who try to live by ideas or to give the appearance of doing so, and has, therefore, naturally admitted the play of ideas into her stories, her chief concerns have always been psychological, emotional, and, above all, moral, the concerns of the novelist. Whenever her characters express ideas, something of more urgent human interest is also going on, whether they know it or not. And though her novels, like most of those which are nowadays taken seriously, are meaningfully organized, it is no simple polemical formula that turns out to be their meaning. It is rather the kind of vision, precisely the novelist's, which moves us, which enlarges our sympathies, and which brings us closer to a complex reality. The fact is, if one remembers her novels freshly at all, it is surely characters and not ideas which their titles bring first to mind—the man in the Brooks Brothers shirt, Macdougal Macdermott, Will Taub, Henry Mulcahy, Domna Rejnev, Miles Murphy, Warren Coe, the girls in "the group" and certain of their men and their parents. In novels these days, McCarthy has complained, "there are hardly any people," only "sensibility" and "sensation," but her own have been an exception. Moreover, though she is, of course, right in noting the enormous difference between her art and that of the novelist she says she would most like to resemble, Tolstoy, yet her admiration for the godlike realist is reflected at least in the way her intentions are always buried deep inside a flesh of vividly rendered particulars. The concrete world of her people, their tics of behavior, their ways of talking—a precise notation of these gives her work throughout the special authority of the visible and the audible. Indeed, her eye for the particular qualities of things makes half the charm of her style, where it adds to the more sober virtues deriving from her intelligence and honesty a flashing witty poetry of metaphor.

As for that other notion, that she is a heartless satirist whose chief interest is to demonstrate her own superiority to the silliness of her victims—this is just as mistaken. While she does make characters out of people she regards as morally weak or ugly or dangerous, and makes them with a bold thrust toward grotesque extremes that recalls another writer she admires, Dickens, the norms of sense or decency which such people violate are equally vivid in her novels. We see these norms both in the passionate indignation between her lines and in the large number of her characters who cannot live without struggling toward them or becoming their champions. In fact, it is precisely one of her distinctions that she has succeeded in creating good people— even out of twentieth-century intellectuals!—who are at once convincing and attractive. (Her Domna Rejnev is a delightful young woman.) It should be added, however, that the characters she values are not necessarily intellectuals. On the contrary, they may be, like Warren Coe, the kind of people at whom her clever, learned heroines tend to smile. And we must add also, what is equally unnoticed by the run of her critics, that the heroine who represents herself is often, for all her cleverness, the character most roughly treated by the ironical author. If she ends by coming out all right, it is with a rightness reached after much agonizing error, and itself riddled with imperfections sadly accepted.

Amid the currently fashionable criticism of fiction, a kind which concentrates so hard on technique or symbols that it often bypasses what technique and symbols are intended to serve, McCarthy's ideas on the subject can be liberatingly sensible. Here (from "Settling the Colonel's Hash" in *On the Contrary*) is a remark that may be taken as an introduction to the present study:

> It is now considered very old-fashioned and tasteless to speak of an author's "philosophy of life" as something that can be harvested from his work. Actually, most of the great authors did have a "philosophy of life" which they were eager to communicate to the public; this was one of their motives for writing. And to disentangle a moral philosophy from a work that evidently contains one is far less damaging to the author's purpose and the integrity of his art than to violate his imagery by symbol-hunting, as though reading a novel were a sort of paper-chase.
>
> The images of a novel or a story belong, as it were, to a family, very closely knit and inseparable from each other; the parent "idea" of a story or a novel generates events and images all bearing a strong family resemblance. And to understand a story or a novel, you must look for the parent "idea," which is usually in plain view, if you read quite carefully and literally what the author says.

The same thing is surely true of the serious writer's total *oeuvre:* all his works will, for the same reason, show this family resemblance. Since McCarthy, in spite of the abundant social reality in her novels, is as autobiographical a novelist as Fitzgerald or Hemingway, we can best approach the "parent idea" underlying her career by beginning with her life. And the first point to make is that it has been a life blessed— and cursed—with an unusual amount of freedom. Orphaned at six, she was taken care of for years by coldly cruel guardians and later by grandparents who were kind but detached. Doris Grumbach tells us that a former Vassar classmate, now a psychiatrist, remembers that at college Mary McCarthy was " 'aloof, independent, irrelevant . . . lonely,' seemingly rootless because she, unlike most of the others, had no real family she had to please. 'She appeared to be much freer than we were and this fascinated and frightened us.' " Such freedom resembles, it is true, the freedom to think and do as they wish that many clever young people of our time claim as a right, but for the orphaned Mary McCarthy, it was a condition more serious than a bright student's pose. She was really free, and had to experience what this meant in her deepest nature. And the kind of freedom that comes from having no family to please—is it not a freedom from those pressures, loyalties, urgencies of feeling that, though they hamper us, also give us a sense of who we are, of what is real, of what is right? To lack such direction can mean one is at the mercy of merely plausible ideas on such matters, ideas which decent people hope to choose according to their truth, of course, but which, amid the multiple "truths" life offers, even the best of us are in danger of choosing with our vanity, or our fear, or our lust. To be directed by external authority has its own dangers; these are the dangers of freedom.

Her work is about the painful mixed blessing of freedom for her kind of people—for intellectuals—and in particular, about how hard it has been for intellectuals in our time to behave decently and humanly. For to be free and clever has often meant only to be able to escape from difficult, limiting reality into the realm of flattering abstractions. And yet—for I have said that to speak of what she dislikes is to speak of only half her subject—if she shows what makes her kind go wrong, she shows just as vividly what makes them go right. She shows that some-times, even in intellectuals free to please themselves, there arises a love for reality that is greater than love of self. This development, because it means that the self must be willing to suffer for something it values more than its own ease, can be one of the moving and beautiful events of a human life—it can be heroic. At any rate, the conflict between these two tendencies of the mind is at the center of all McCarthy's novels. Because this conflict is her own, her reports on it have the variety, complexity, and intensity of personal experience. But because the freedom to live by ideas, ideas which may lead away from the real as well as toward it, is what distinguishes the whole class of twentieth-century intellectuals, her tales of the troubled Mary McCarthy heroine have developed naturally into social satire.

The exquisitely written *Memories of a Catholic Girlhood* (1957) re-veals how deeply rooted McCarthy's stories are in her own life. She tells us that she was born in Seattle in 1912 to a Protestant mother, whose own mother was Jewish and who accepted her husband's religion, and a Catholic father. The mother was beautiful. The father was a partial invalid, irresponsible as a breadwinner, but handsome, charming, a delight to his children with his stories and presents. When she was six, both parents died in one week from flu. The rich McCarthy grandpar-ents, whose Catholicism was a "sour and baleful doctrine in which old hates and rancors had been stewing for generations, with ignorance proudly stirring the pot," placed her and her three brothers in a house as poor as their own was luxurious and under the guardianship of a couple of Dickensian monsters, a great-aunt and a German-American husband. The theme of the first chapters of *Memories* is injustice, and McCarthy describes the needless poverty, the ugliness, the sadistic, self-righteous beatings with an unaccustomed, if controlled, intensity of rage and pity.

At the age of eleven, she was rescued and taken to Seattle by her other grandfather, who was a model of the Protestant virtues. To cite qualities she later found he shared with Julius Caesar, Grandfather Preston was "just, laconic, severe, magnanimous, detached." She was no longer wretched, but she remained an outsider—in her new home, whose moral standards were oppressively high; in the Catholic convent school she went to first, where she lost her faith; later in a public school, among the school "hearties"; finally in an Episcopal boarding school, where she was set apart by her "brilliance" and her independence. And here, at sixteen, she underwent experiences which, as described in the chapter of *Memories* called "The Figures in the Clock," clearly foreshadow the characteristic moral vision, and even the organizing "conflicts," of the fiction to come.

In this chapter the conflict is between the wicked conspirator Catiline and Julius Caesar. Acting the part of Catiline in a play written by her Latin teacher, she made a sensation by reading her lines so as to *vindicate* the rebel, to champion his self-willed brilliance—and thereby her own—against mere dull law and order. Shortly after this, however, a strange thing happened. Under the guidance of Miss Gowrie (the fictitious name she gives her teacher), the girl fell in love with Julius Caesar! "The sensation was utterly confounding. All my previous crushes had been products of my will, constructs of my personal convention, or projections of myself, the way Catiline was. This came from without and seized me . . . the first piercing contact with an impersonal reality happened to me through Caesar." She and her teacher loved that mind "immersed in practical life as in some ingenious detective novel, that wished always to show you how anything was done and under what disadvantages . . . the spirit of justice and scientific inquiry that reigned over the *Commentaries*." "Justice, good will, moderation, and *uncommon fidelity*," why, she asks, quoting Caesar's praise of a conquered Gaul loyal to himself, "should these substantives of virtue have stirred the Seminary's Catiline? At the time I was sublimely unaware that my fortifications had been breached, that the forces of law and order were pacifying the city while the rebel standard still waved on the ramparts."

What she loved in Caesar hints not only at the moral values in the novels to come, but at their art—their way with details and their way with sentences. But we are not done with the meaning of this rich chapter. Another insight alternates with the first "like the two little wooden weather figures in a German clock, one of which steps out as the other swings back into the works, in response to atmospheric pressures." The "good Gaul" whose loyalty to Caesar she and Miss Gowrie admired was after all a "quisling," traitorously loyal to his people's conqueror. Later, when "bad Gauls" merged in her mind with those who resisted Hitler, she was angry with her Latin teacher for having steered her wrong. But then, later still, it came to her that it had been Miss Gowrie who had seen to it that her Catiline costume was especially gorgeous—she has at last "an eerie sense that Miss Gowrie, unsuspected by me, was my co-conspirator." It appears that for her teacher too that preference for Caesar, for "impersonal reality" and law and order over the lawless ego, was haunted by the contradictory possibility that the ego can have a self-justifying beauty, or that law and order, with changes in "atmospheric pressure," that is, in the context, may serve error, and the self-asserting individual be in the right. And in her note to the chapter, McCarthy tells us that this conflict is rooted in her inheritance. "Caesar, of course, was my [Preston] grandfather . . . Catiline was my McCarthy ancestors. . . . To my surprise, I chose Caesar and the rule of law. This does not mean that the seesaw between these two opposed forces terminated; one might say, in fact, that it only began during my last years in the Seminary when I recognized the beauty of an ablative absolute and of a rigorous code of conduct."

A word about her life after the Seminary. For a summer, she studied acting; then, from 1929 to 1933, she attended Vassar College. In 1933, she married the actor and unsuccessful playwright Harold Johnsrud, and began to write reviews for the *New Republic* and the *Nation*. Her essay "My Confession" tells how at this time she was drawn into political controversy by her indignation at the smug dishonesty of American Communists and especially by their defense of the "Moscow trials," in which the exiled Trotsky was being discredited by an elaborate structure of lies. In 1936, her marriage dissolved, she lived in Greenwich Village, wrote reviews, and worked for an art dealer. A year later she began to write a monthly "Theater Chronicle" for the recently revived *Partisan Review*. In these essays there was much good sense and some affected and excessive rigidity of principle, as she herself admits in a preface to the book *Sights and Spectacles* (1956), in which they were later collected. In 1938, she married the critic Edmund Wilson. The marriage ended after seven years, but he was the father of her only child, Reuel, and it was at Wilson's suggestion that she began to write fiction. Her first story, "Cruel and Barbarous Treatment," became the opening chapter of *The Company She Keeps*. For a while she was a college teacher—at Bard in 1945–46 and at Sarah Lawrence for one term in 1949—and her history since then, aside from her marriage to Bowden

Broadwater, which lasted from 1946 to 1961, and to James West in 1961, is mainly the history of her books.

In 1956, along with *Sights and Spectacles,* she published the first of two works on Italian cities, *Venice Observed,* and in 1959, the second, *The Stones of Florence.* Each book is an account of the city's history, architecture, art, and people. The first is the slighter, the more personal and anecdotal, the second the more sober and scholarly, and at the same time, the more passionate: the art and architecture of Florence moved her intensely. In fact, her book about Florence is surprisingly readable for so scholarly a work, and the reason is only in part the lively, taut, and elegant style. Even more important is her clear concern throughout with the "human interest" of the history and the art.

In 1962, the essays she had been writing since 1946 on a variety of subjects were collected in the volume *On the Contrary.* These differ in quality. Most valuable are her contributions to the political debates of the time—on the Moscow trials, on McCarthyism, on Communists in the schools—and her essays on fiction and drama, "Settling the Colonel's Hash," "The Fact in Fiction," "Characters in Fiction," and "The American Realist Playwrights." Of the latter group it is enough to say here that they constitute, by implication, a defense of the kind of art she herself has practiced. This is a realistic art, which gives us what might usefully be called *samples* of reality rather than *symbols* of it. (She herself speaks of "natural symbolism.") For the reader to do justice to such work, he needs to be alert rather to human matters—the psychological or moral meaning of actions or tones—than to literary allusions and strategies.

We are now ready for the novels, on which her permanent reputation will surely rest. The first of these, *The Company She Keeps* (1942), consists of six chapters published originally as stories in magazines. In a very interesting and useful *Paris Review* interview, McCarthy has said that though she had originally intended them as separate stories, "about halfway through I began to think of them as a kind of unified story. The same character kept reappearing, and so on. I decided finally to call it a novel in that it does in a sense tell a story, one story." The reappearing character is Margaret Sargent, of whom we learn at the end that she was the daughter of a tolerant, intelligent Protestant father and a beautiful Catholic mother, and was brought up as a Catholic, after her mother's early death, by a vulgar and bigoted Catholic aunt. Not only has McCarthy given her heroine a background substantially like her own; she has told us herself that the stories are all autobiographical except one, "Portrait of the Intellectual as a Yale Man." In fact, the book is remarkable for the honesty of its self-exposure, an exposure which dares to include the ignoble and the humiliating and which shows a kind of reckless passion for the truth that is to remain an important element of her talent.

This passion for the truth not only provides the motive power behind the self-exposure in these tales. It turns out to be their underlying subject as well. The author has suggested, and it has been repeated by many critics, that the "one story" of the book is that of the heroine's vain search, amid her many identities, for some real identity underlying them all. But this search seems actually to be less important than her moral development, a development of which the ultimate goal is not to know what she is, but to behave as an adult should. What we mainly watch as her story unfolds is Miss Sargent's increasingly desperate struggle, against all the temptations to falsehood in the intellectual life of her time, to stop lying and to live by the truth.

She begins far enough from any truth. In the first chapter, "Cruel and Barbarous Treatment," which is not so much a story as a witty satire on nameless generalized types and their typical behavior, she is a married "Woman with a Secret" delighting in an affair with a "Young Man" chiefly because it "was an opportunity, unparalleled in her experience, for exercising feelings of superiority over others." Playacting irresponsibly with life's realities, she reduces them to fashionable clichés that minister to her vanity. The second chapter, "Rogue's Gallery," in which Miss Sargent works for a rogue who runs an art gallery and appears as a naïve, good-natured foil for her colorful con man of a boss, seems a mere exercise in the Dickensian picturesque. But in the third the book's deeper story continues: the heroine's playacting is complicated by an opposing impulse. "The Man in the Brooks Brothers Shirt" is an account of how Miss Sargent, now seen in the role of poised, sophisticated New York intellectual, is drawn into an affair with a businessman on a cross-country train trip because she enjoys playing that role before such an audience. And yet, showing off an advance copy of a new book, she wonders uneasily "if her whole way of life had been assumed for purposes of ostentation." When the man speaks shrewdly about her past, she leans forward. "Perhaps at last she had found him, the one she kept looking for, the one who could tell her what she was really like. . . . If she once knew, she had no doubt that she could behave perfectly." Then there is her horrified shame, when she awakens in his compartment, at the drunken sex of the night before which she gradually remembers. (This is the first of those cool "shocking" notations of the unattractive particulars of "romantic" episodes for which McCarthy has won a certain notoriety, though far from being exploitations of sex, they seem expressions of a puritanical disgust.) Finally, she becomes aware of a reluctance to leave the man, who, falling in love with her, had changed in her eyes from the vulgar-businessman type to an actual and attractive person; and at this "a pang of joy went through her as she examined her own sorrow and found it to be real." The affair dies away after the trip, and the story ends with both falling back into the stereotypes from which they had briefly emerged, but Margaret Sargent has acquired substance as a character with the disclosure that she is divided, like the rest of us, and that the hunger of her intellectual's vanity is opposed by a hunger for reality.

In "The Genial Host," we see this new Miss Sargent again. She is now the dinner guest of one Pflaumen, who is shown as having repressed both his natural tendency to fat and hairiness and his natural personality of a Jewish paterfamilias to become the elegant familiar and host of clever, fashionable, successful people. Moreover, this reality-avoider collects his guests for their "allegorical possibilities," that is, for the chic intellectual positions to which they have sacrificed their own reality. Thus, Margaret, hotly defending Trotsky against the party's Stalinist, and delighted at the effect she is making, is horrified to note that Pflaumen is beaming at her for performing as expected, while the party's one honest man, a poor young Jewish lawyer, is applauding ironically. The story ends in another capitulation: she dare not yet rebel against Pflaumen and the falsenesses by which she sings for her suppers, she is still too "poor, loverless, lonely." But in the next, "Portrait of the Intellectual as a Yale Man," though she is still in need, she has ceased to capitulate.

This story is mainly about the Yale Man, who, though naïve and second-rate, has been welcomed onto the Stalinist-dominated weekly magazine the *Liberal* because he comes as a healthy, happy, clean-cut, average American, a type rare among them. This was a time—the thirties—when out of loyalty to the ideal of communism a large proportion of the intellectual establishment had accepted so many of the lies and brutalities of the Stalin dictatorship that they had lost the sense of the relevance to politics, and even to life, of the ordinary decencies. Such people lied in defense of the Communist party's shifts in policy or vilified the opposition rather than debate with it, and did both with a sincere feeling of virtue. Jim Barnett, the Yale Man, is not one of these; he tries to be honest, but he is able to make a living as a radical political commentator only because his shallowness is precisely suited to the intellectual climate of this milieu, from which the Stalinists have largely excluded reality.

Margaret Sargent was put into this story, says McCarthy, "because she had to be in it," that is, for the sake of the unity of the book to come, but her role turns out to be crucial, for she is there as an eruption of integrity into that world of blur and lies. Now when she defends Trotsky, it is among Stalinist editors who can fire her from the magazine job she needs. "You had to admire her courage," Jim thinks, "for undertaking something that cost her so much." Even her way of taking Jim for a lover is significantly different from her past behavior. She submits to this married man's sudden overpowering lust—and perhaps to her own as well—with a "disconsolate smile"—no playacting here. Jim quits his job indignantly when she is fired, and in this time of proud excitement, he gets an idea for an important book. But the effort to write the book and to live on that moral peak is beyond his means. He gives up both, gets a handsome job on the conservative magazine *Destiny,* and though he continues to send checks to the American Civil Liberties Union, he grows increasingly impatient with opinionated unsuccessful left-wing intellectuals. And for Margaret he comes to feel a kind of hatred. Pathetic though she is in her "too tense" clinging to her truth, in her unsuccess, she is somehow triumphant. In the story's beautifully written last pages, she haunts him as a reminder of the dead illusion of his youth, the illusion that he could be free of "the cage of his own nature" and better than himself.

In the last story, "Ghostly Father, I Confess," after five years of an unhappy second marriage to an architect apparently congenial but authoritarian and unimaginative, Margaret is spending an hour on a psychoanalyst's couch. She has been sent by her husband, who is fed up with the way she uses her "wonderful scruples as an excuse for acting like a bitch." And now, though she disapproves of psychoanalysis, whose conclusions can never be proved wrong since all disagreement is mere resistance, and considers her doctor a limited man, she finds herself drawn into an agonizing search for the cause of her misery and bad behavior, for it is also a search for the "meaning" that will redeem her life from "gibberish." The story is crammed with the upwelling, emotion-charged facts of her life—from the childhood passed between her father's rationalism and her aunt's vulgarities to the second marriage, in which she feels herself suffocating amid such stylish middle-class culture-objects as "her white pots of ivy, her Venetian blinds, her open copy of a novel by Kafka . . . each in its own patina of social anxiety." McCarthy seems to have thrown boldly into the story the confusion of her own life. Yet it moves with a nightmarish coherence amid the chaos, and, in fact, what she understands at the end makes the story a unity and a fitting conclusion to the book's whole development.

The story is about the pressure on Margaret Sargent to accept the life of the intellectually sophisticated middle class which she detests. And for that life she is now to be made fit by a mode of "therapy" which is presented as the most insidious of all its ways of avoiding reality. The object of the therapy is to perform a "perfectly simple little operation." First, the consciousness is put to sleep by "the sweet, opti-

mistic laughing-gas of science (you are not bad, you are merely unhappy . . . poor Hitler is a paranoiac, and that dirty fornication in a
hotel room, why, that, dear Miss Sargent, is a 'relationship')." Then the
doctor cuts out "the festering conscience, which was of no use to you at
all, and was only making you suffer." But to have a conscience is to
remain aware of what is outside one's wishes, and to prefer the truth,
however painful, over lies, however gratifying. Under the pressure of
the idea that she is unhappy merely because she is ill, "her own sense of
truth was weakening. This and her wonderful scruples were all she had
in the world, and they were slipping away." And it is this that makes
her most miserable. She can't behave as she should, but not to know
when she does evil, and not to mind, is to lose her grip on reality and to
shrink from a healthy adult into an invalid or a child.

The story ends with an apparent inconclusiveness that is really, as I
have said, a sufficient conclusion, both to the story and the book. She is
almost persuaded by her doctor that she can be good and free and
strong inside her marriage, which is to say, that all can yet be well at no
painful cost, when she remembers a dream she had begun to tell him
earlier. In this dream, she had enabled herself to accept the embraces
of a Nazi type by pretending that he was rather Byronic. As she walks
away from the doctor's office, feeling the hateful expected tug of an
attraction to him, she suddenly understands the dream. It has told her
that all will *not* be well, that unable to love herself except through the
love of men, she will again seek a new love to rescue her from past
failures and will again snatch at it blindly and perhaps unscrupulously.
But though in the dream she pretended the Nazi was a Byron, "she
could still detect her own frauds. At the end of the dream, her eyes
were closed, but the inner eye had remained alert. . . . 'Oh my God,'
she said . . . 'do not let them take this away from me. If the flesh must
be blind, let the spirit see. Preserve me in disunity.' "

Thus is completed the "one story" of Margaret Sargent. Beginning
as a manipulator and falsifier of reality, she is now its true lover, who
would rather suffer than pretend and whose suffering, because it
means the clarity of mind to see the truth and the courage to face it, is
the measure of a new dignity.

It is no doubt true, as Elizabeth Hardwick has suggested, that all
such "frank" confession is in part self-exculpation. But McCarthy's
frankness in confessing weakness and error in this book seems to earn
her the right to move on, for a completer truth indeed, to the virtues of
her defects. At any rate, the portrait of Margaret Sargent carries conviction, and her struggle toward honesty has a permanent relevance to
our experience.

Certain themes in the first book are repeated in *Cast a Cold Eye*

(1950), a collection of four stories and three early versions of chapters of her *Memories*. In "The Weeds" is treated somberly, and in "The Friend of the Family" with bitter humor, the sort of marriage seen in "Ghostly Father." It is the marriage that destroys the individual's integrity, his troublesome loyalty to the truth of his own nature. "The Old Men"—spare, swift, witty, and perfectly told—shows how a young man who has long been uncertain of his own identity comes to feel that the self is no more than a "*point du départ*" for "impersonations," and that reality, the actual, is "pornography" and to be avoided. At this,"blithe and ready to live, selfishly and inconsiderately," he sings out the Yeats epitaph which gives the book its title, and shortly afterward, as if for want of any reason to live, he abruptly dies. The story is full of life and life's terrors and richly suggestive, but what it means as a whole I've decided I don't yet know.

McCarthy has defended *The Oasis* (1949) from the charge that it is not a novel by insisting that it was not intended to be, that it is a *conte philosophique*. This explains its lack of action, for instead of plot we have slight episodes explored for their large meanings and characters revealed less by what they do than in long satirical descriptions. But it cannot eliminate the sense that the tale's developments, which ought after all to arise by an inner necessity, are sometimes arbitrarily asserted, as if to get things moving. And yet the reminder of an elegant eighteenth-century prose form does point to qualities that will keep the tale, in spite of its imperfections, interesting for a long time. The satirical descriptions do not merely imitate but genuinely duplicate the qualities of eighteenth-century prose masters—the psychological insight, the general wisdom, the witty, epigrammatic, gracefully balanced sentences.

The Oasis is the story of a group of New York intellectuals—based apparently on well-known friends of the author, but to the rest of us recognizable as contemporary types—who, shortly after World War II, form a colony called Utopia in the Taconic Mountains of New York State. The colonists fall mainly into two factions. The "purists" hope the colony will illustrate "certain notions of justice, freedom, and sociability" derived from their Founder, a saintly Italian anarchist lost in "a darkened city of Europe." This group is led by Macdougal Macdermott, a man who rightly senses that he does not naturally belong to "that world of the spirit" which he yearns to enter, but who, "ten years before . . . had made the leap into faith and sacrificed $20,000 a year and a secure career as a paid journalist for the intangible values that eluded his empirical grasp. He had moved down town into Bohemia, painted his walls indigo, dropped the use of capital letters and the practice of wearing a vest" and become the editor of a "libertarian magazine." The "realists," on the other hand, have come only for a holiday from the pressures of real life. They look upon "conspicuous goodness" like the Founder's as a "form of simple-mindedness on a par with vegetarianism, and would have refused admission to Heaven on the ground that it was full of greenhorns and cranks." Moreover, they find absurd the assumption of "human freedom" which underlies all that the purists believe, for they are inheritors of Marxian "scientific socialism," and though they had discarded the dialectic and repudiated the Russian Revolution, "the right of a human being to *think* that he could resist history, environment, class structure, psychic conditioning was something they denied him with all the ferocity of their own pent-up natures and disappointed hopes." And since "ideological supremacy" has become "essential to their existence," they look forward with pleasure to the colony's failure. They do, however, wish it to fail convincingly, of its own foolishness, and this seduces them into unusually good behavior. Soon Will Taub, their leader, finds that he participates "in the forms of equity with increasing confidence, and though of course he did not take any of it *seriously,* his heavy and rather lowering nature performed the unaccustomed libertarian movements with a feeling of real sprightliness and wondering self-admiration, as if he had been learning to dance."

In Will Taub we have the first full-fledged example of the enemy in McCarthy's world, the Other to all that she values. He is one who is at home only in the realm of ideas, who is flat-footed in his behavior with children, women—in all nonintellectual relations—who feels pain at the very word "Jew" because "his Jewishness [was] a thing about himself which he was powerless to alter and which seemed to reduce him therefore to a curious dependency on the given." And this rejection of the "given," the real, on behalf of a world of ideas where he can reign supreme involves too a rejection of moral responsibility. It is for the realists a felt oddity in Utopia that "here they were answerable for their deeds to someone and not simply to an historical process." And Taub is even capable, like the later Henry Mulcahy, of beginning to believe his own lie (that an embarrassingly cowardly reaction of his is due to former police persecution) in order to maintain his cherished supremacy.

These two characters, and Joe Lockman, the go-getting businessman who comes to Utopia determined to get more spiritual profit out of it than anyone else, are the tale's most vivid portraits. But it is a fourth, Katy Norell, to whom its chief events tend to happen and out of whose responses its meanings emerge. Katy, a teacher of Greek, suffers from "a strong will and a weak character," an awkward compulsion to tell the truth even when it aggravates her problems, and a readiness to feel guilty when things go wrong. Though it was her "instinctive opinion . . . that the past could be altered and actions, like words, 'taken back,'" her husband's disgust with her, on one occasion when it seems serious, gives her a frightening glimpse of life "as a black chain of consequence, in which nothing was lost, forgot, forgiven, redeemed, in which the past was permanent and the present slipping away from her." This character, weak but scrupulous, who wishes life were easy but can't shut out the perception that it is hard, is, of course, a sister of Margaret Sargent as well as of the later Martha Sinnott, though, unlike the others, she pays for representing her author's inner life by being one of the less vivid characters in her book. But it is out of her inner contradictions that the book's closing insights come. These insights are initiated by the last of several challenges to the colony's "sociability"— the stealing of their strawberries by some rough interlopers, whom Katy herself, frightened when her pleading is answered with threatening gestures, demands be ejected by force. Taub taunts her with her contradiction, her yielding to "human nature," and at this, lulled or liberated by the dinner wine, she begins to understand. They did wrong, she thinks, to cling to the strawberries without needing them— it was only the idea of the strawberries they cared about. They had let "mental images" possess them as the idea of sex dominates the mind in pornography. But the mind should stick to its own objects, "love, formal beauty, virtue"; they should not have tried to make real things dance to the mind's tune. And this is only a small example of their fundamental error. As the tale draws to an end, she realizes that Utopia is going to fail because of their wish to "*embody* virtue." If they had been content to manufacture, not virtue, but furniture, it might have survived.

It is a rueful, if not tragic, conclusion. To replace the stubborn complexity of people and society with ideas is the mistake of both parties in Utopia. The cynics who insist that our behavior is determined by history and the "idealists" who believe that man can be what he wishes to be are shown to be equally removed from the life we actually live. And yet those like Katy Norell, who see how both are wrong, who feel and suffer life up close, are better off, if at all, only because it is better to understand. For their superiority consists mainly in desiring a virtue they know they can never attain.

"And search for truth amid the groves of academe"—this quotation from Horace prefaces McCarthy's next novel. The search for truth, and the human defects that hinder it, we have seen to be her permanent subject. Now again the private concern becomes a way of understanding the large public matters that her life has brought before her: this time the political liberalism of the "witch-hunting" era of

Joseph McCarthy (the 1950s) when the reactionary right, not the Communist left, frightened or confused intellectuals into self-betrayal; and progressive education, with its own less obvious hindrances to the search for truth. But *The Groves of Academe* (1952) is her first real or completely successful novel because now, for the first time, she has found a setting, characters, and a plot that dramatize both her private and her public subjects in one lively story. With this novel, moreover, her resemblance to Jane Austen, already evident in the irony, sanity, and grace of her prose, and the combination of moral concern and tough intelligence in her approach to people, grows even more striking. She gives us now, in that same prose, a group of characters vividly and comically idiosyncratic, with a wonderful comic villain in the center. She gives us a plot which evolves with perfect illuminating logic from the moral qualities of the characters. And she gives us the peculiarly Austenish pleasure of watching good, intelligent, and articulate people work their way through much painful error to the relief of shared understanding.

The plot is an ingenious stroke of wit. Its humor is based on the fact that where in the outside, nonintellectual world it had become dangerous in this period to have once been a Communist, in the world of liberal intellectuals a man persecuted for a Communist past had become almost a holy martyr and entitled to defense. McCarthy's joke is that when the incompetent, irresponsible (though learned and brilliant) Henry Mulcahy is about to be let go by the liberal president of Jocelyn College, he is able to win the support of his colleagues by pretending to have *been* a Communist. The joke reaches its climax when an old anarchist acquaintance of Mulcahy's is interrogated by President Hoar and a faculty committee about whether their colleague really had this claim on their respect and protection, and the anarchist, who "sings," betrays the shocking secret that Mulcahy's Communist past had been a lie. Upon which, in an explosion of topsy-turvyness, Mulcahy comes raging to Hoar like the righteous victim of a witch-hunt, and using the secret investigation as evidence that the president has betrayed his liberal principles, forces *him* to resign.

It is a pity to tell the punch line of such a story, but the fault is less grave than it might be because the fun here lies in the characters and in the fine detail by which they and their world are kept always very much alive. Most of all, the story belongs to the magnificently repulsive Henry Mulcahy, in whom the kind of intellectual dishonor which we have already begun to recognize as McCarthy's chief target is carried to breathtaking extremes. It is moreover a special triumph of the book that she has shown us this comic monster from the inside (she calls the technique "ventriloquism," as George Henry Lewes once wrote of Jane

Austen's "dramatic ventriloquism"), mimicking his mode of thought so fully and felicitously that it is impossible, for all his excesses, not to recognize him as real.

In Henry Mulcahy, a pear-shaped, soft-bellied father of four, Ph.D., contributor to serious magazines, Guggenheim Fellow, etc., the intellectual's besetting sins—his lust for supremacy and his preference for flattering ideas over mere facts—undergo a marvelous efflorescence. He not only identifies himself with Joyce, Kafka, and other "sacred untouchables of the modern martyrology"; he comes to regard disloyalty to himself as "apostasy," and the dismayed Domna Rejnev discovers that "behind Joyce . . . is the identification with Christ." At the same time, his great lie is to him the work of an artist, who creates out of life's raw material "a figurative truth more true than the data of reality." (Remembering vaguely that he had once heard the phrase "heart murmur" used of someone in his family, he is soon exclaiming to himself—sincerely!—that he holds Hoar "personally responsible for the life of his wife and/or son.") And, when the defeated president finally asks him, "Are you a conscious liar or a self-deluded hypocrite?" Mulcahy replies, "A Cretan says, all Cretans are liars." Having thus put in question the very possibility of finding truth, he frankly declares, "I'm not concerned with truth. . . . I'm concerned with justice."

The faculty for whom Mulcahy has thus set a special problem in truth-seeking are all sharply realized, but those who share the center of the stage with Mulcahy are two teachers who are most different from him, and who bring what Miss McCarthy honors as effectively to life as he recreates what she despises. Domna Rejnev and John Bentkoop are also intellectuals but to them the truth matters more than their own success and comfort. In Miss Rejnev, beautiful twenty-three-year-old daughter of Russian émigrés, whose "finely cut, mobile nostrils quivered during a banal conversation as though, literally, seeking air," and who, in a crisis, asks herself "What would Tolstoy say?" this intellectual passion is endearingly childlike in its ardor and even in its vanity. The ardor we see when she hears of Mulcahy's "persecution": "Her strange, intent eyes were shining; she tossed her head angrily and the dark, clean hair bobbed; she clicked her pocket-lighter and drew in on a cigarette. 'This cannot be permitted to happen,' she declared quickly, amid puffs of smoke. 'One simply refuses it and tells Maynard Hoar so.' She jumped up, knocking a book off the desk, and seized her polo coat from the coatrack. 'I shall do it myself at once to set an example.' "

And we see the vanity when she warmly praises Mulcahy's learning to silent colleagues out of her pleasure in honoring excellence. "She rather enjoyed the idea that she was sufficiently spendthrift (that is, sufficiently rich in resources)." But this pride is so far from the smug confidence of the self-worshipers that a colleague lets her pour out a passionate argument without interrupting "because he knew her to be honest and presumed that therefore, before she had finished, a doubt would suddenly dart out of her like a mouse from its hole." Sure enough, it is her agonizing recognition not only that she had been wrong about Mulcahy, but that she had been seduced into pretending not to know defects in him which she did know, into a sort of lying, that is to be her climactic experience in the book.

The deep, the metaphysical opposition between Mulcahy's kind and hers emerges during a painful dinner at the Mulcahy home when Domna suddenly learns she has been defending a liar. Uneasy, he tries to recoup by suggesting that, being handsome, she is a "monist," but that unattractive people like himself "know that appearances are fickle. We look to somebody else to discover our imperishable essense." And he asks her if she could love a leper, meaning, as she understands, himself. "If you mean a moral leper, no," she says. "Fair without and foul within has no charm for me. Nor the reverse, for that matter. . . . People whose inside contradicts their outside . . . have neither essence nor existence." Mulcahy, in short, can feel virtuous when he does evil and entitled to loyalty even by those whom he betrays because he believes instinctively in a sort of dualism according to which the concrete world, where actions have consequences and entail responsibilities, can be regarded as mere "appearance"—of secondary importance beside those abstractions (Norine Schmittlapp of *The Group* will call them "intangibles") which his ego can manipulate. The others are like Domna—or like Virginia Bentkoop, who, in a charming touch, though "she had met Domna only once, at a college lecture . . . divined correctly that her feet were wet." They are people who notice and respect the actualities of the world.

This, however, is a progressive college, and these are liberals of the fifties, and the combination has guaranteed Mulcahy's triumph. For, as the novel has also been suggesting, and as one teacher puts it at the end, progressive education means a concern with "faith and individual salvation"—that is, the student's inner quality is considered to be more important than his demonstrated mastery, through hard work, of real subject matter. This has a sinister resemblance to Mulcahy's self-defense that "appearance"—the mere concrete facts of what one is and does—is somehow less important than one's invisible "essence." And it is a view that is plainly akin to the tendency of many liberals of the era to separate "justice," in the words of Mulcahy again, from "truth," to consider scruples that interfered with work for a "good cause" mere ivory tower pedantry. Not that McCarthy fails to make clear that the progressive college and its liberal faculty are right and attractive in many ways, and create a world in which good things can grow as well as bad. But her story makes it even clearer that there is no safety in good intentions when their pursuit requires us to ignore the truth.

Because *The Groves of Academe* is about college teachers, much of its drama comes to us in the clash of explicit ideas amid explicit descriptions of the college world and its intellectual character. For some readers this may sometimes clog or confuse the otherwise lively story. There can be no such objection to *A Charmed Life* (1955), for though this novel is equally rich in meaning, its meaning is more centrally human and expressed more completely by the rushing story alone. And the style, having to argue and explain less, having only to serve the urgent events and emotions, seems lighter, swifter, and richer in McCarthy's characteristic poetry.

Perhaps too the novel is her best so far, the most poignant and powerful under the usual ironic control, because she has here found a subject which dramatizes the conflict among her own most cherished values—that "seesaw" between the demands of the self and those of "impersonal reality"—and which, therefore, taps her own strongest feelings. This conflict is foreshadowed in a new twist given to her familiar heroine. Martha Sinnott is another woman of mind, another lover of that "impersonal reality," but an element in the type hitherto regarded as only a source of difficulty is now permitted to present fully its own case. For this very clever and learned young playwright is also a woman, as her husband tells us, with "an obstinate childish heart," one to whom reality speaks a "little language" and who cannot bear that it ever utter, in her marriage, what is not true and beautiful and good. She not only insists that life conform to her dream, but, to make it conform, she dares to act as if, in the words of Katy Norell in her weakness, "the past could be altered and actions, like words, 'taken back.' " McCarthy herself tells us that the novel is about "doubt," and it is true that the doubt which, among contemporary intellectuals, automatically dogs every dream and every piety is important in the story. But even more important is the "obstinate childish heart" by which the doubt is opposed. It is her heroine's "romanticism" that is now this "neoclassic" novelist's subject, and it is that romanticism's tormenting ambiguity which gives the story its wealth of meaning and its almost desperate intensity.

The romantic demand which Martha Sinnott (her last name suggests the McCarthy heroine's usual vain wish) makes upon life acquires a special urgency as the story opens because she has, to finish a play, come back with her second husband to the same Cape Cod town where she had once lived with her first—that is, to a place where her new love and new hope are in danger. New Leeds is dangerous for two reasons. First, because it is a contemporary Bohemia, full of artists and intellectuals who live in a state of freedom from tradition, convention, morality, and regular work. These are people who are always divorcing and remarrying, sinking into alcoholism or fighting it, falling down flights of stairs or into wells, and who yet seem to bear a charmed life—nothing seems to hurt them. The reason for this grows clear when Martha, in a moment of near hysteria, cries out that though the New Leedsian will never "admit to knowing anything, until it's been proved," and though he is always setting himself free to do as he pleases by demanding, "Explain to me why not. Give me one reason why not," the fact is, "you don't really doubt. You just ask questions, like a machine. . . . Nobody is really curious because nobody cares what the truth is." The New Leedsian's life is charmed into unreality by his moral indifference. Nothing matters to him and so nothing can hurt him. And that she is right to fear this moral casualness emerges when her husband goes out of town for a night and she is brought together by a friend—for the fun of it—with her ex-husband, Miles Murphy.

Miles is the second danger she fears. He is not quite a typical New Leedsian, since he is capable of disciplined study and work (he is a writer and a psychologist). But he shares with the others their moral qualities. He is unscrupulous, and can cheat not only an insurance company, but also a friend. And he is brutally self-regarding and self-assertive: Martha has never been able to resist his utter inability to doubt himself.

The promise in all this is fulfilled when Miles takes her home from the party. After a struggle in which she yields partly to force but even more to the pressure of Miles's conviction that it isn't worth fighting—there is no "reason why not"—she lets him have her. One reason soon appears. Shortly afterward, she finds herself pregnant. And though for the ordinary New Leedsian this would not have mattered, since her husband need never know what happened, for Martha it matters to the point of anguish. She cannot bear to have a child of whose paternity she must always be in doubt, or who might give the awful Miles a claim on her, and she cannot bear to base her life with John upon a lie. She decides to have an abortion. And it is in her struggle to determine whether this is right or wrong that we come upon that ambiguity already mentioned.

Such a way of making everything beautiful again has, to begin with, an unsettling resemblance to the ordinary New Leedsian's tendency to evade the consequences of his mistakes, to shirk responsibility. And yet the romantic dream need not always be self-indulgent fantasy. It may be the faith—the religion—which directs and ennobles our lives.

In fact, Martha's inner struggle is sometimes described in religious terms. During one terrible night she is besieged and tempted by the devil himself, and at her blackest hour she finds rising to her lips the cry, "Father, let this cup pass from me." Her devil, of course, is a New Leedsian. "The medieval temptations, with all the allures of gluttony and concupiscence could not, Martha thought, have been half so trying as the sheer dentist-drill boredom of listening to the arguments of the devil as a modern quasi-intellectual." He utters now all the bright ideas of contemporary sophistication, and his object is to convince her that her vision of the good cannot stand up under rational cross-examination. (In the voice of the psychologist Miles the devil whispers that she doesn't want a baby and is merely seizing this pretext to get rid of it.)

Her dream is thus opposed by the devil because it is a dream of living for what is right and not for what is merely pleasant. Indeed, among her weapons, as she struggles, is a sense of how the right makes itself known that would have won the approval of the author of *Pilgrim's Progress*. It is worth quoting for its bold recapitulation of an unfashionable morality, as well as for its prose.

> Yet all the while the moral part of Martha knew that she would have to have an abortion because all her inclinations were the other way. The hardest course was the right one; in her experience, this was an almost invariable law. If her nature shrank from the task, if it hid and cried piteously for mercy, that was a sign that she was in the presence of the ethical. She knew this also from the fact that she felt no need to seek advice; what anyone else would do under the circumstances had no bearing. The moral part of her seemed to square its shoulders, dissociating itself from the mass of weakness that remained. It was almost a social question, she observed with wan interest: the moral part of her would stop speaking if she did not do what it commanded. But how, she cried out, weeping. How am I to do it, all by myself? There was no answer. The rest of her, the low part, apparently, was supposed to devise the methods. The lawgiver was impractical, a real lady, disdaining to soil its hands, leaving the details to its servants. Martha could have laughed aloud, except for the pride and awe she felt in the acquaintance. She would not have guessed she had so much integrity. In the midst of her squirming and anguish, there was a sensation of pleased surprise.

Thus the past-canceling abortion, which might well have seemed a New Leedsian act, takes on the character of an act of moral heroism, of faith.

Having won the inner battle, she gets the external help she needs from the artist Warren Coe. Warren, a beautifully realized comic character, who listens with enormous respect to the "deep" talk of people like Martha and seems created to be her butt, turns out to be her very counterpart in what matters most. What he is and what the others are and, indeed, what the whole story is about is suggested in a delightful discussion of Racine's *Bérénice,* which is read aloud at that fateful New Leeds party. This play, in which the newly crowned emperor Titus must renounce forever his beloved Hebrew queen because a Roman emperor may not marry a foreign monarch, is a tragedy about the conflict between love and duty. And though Miles and Martha came together at first like brilliant equals among ordinary people, it soon appears that it is Warren and not Miles whose ideas she shares. Miles thinks "love is for boys and women," at which Martha raises her brows and Warren, hearing his wife blandly agree, declares, "I could eat that *rug.*" When Warren wants to give a hypothetical man who likes to murder old women a reason not to, Martha sympathizes with his wish for universal principles superior to the self, but Miles thinks we do what we can get away with. "The electric chair . . . that's the reason we give him," he tells Warren, and than adds a remark for which one is tempted to forgive him all his crimes: "For you, it's an academic question. If you don't want to murder old women, let it go at that. Don't worry about the other fellow. Live selfishly." The play itself illuminates Martha's position by contrast. It is Racine's view that one can't live the moral life and have one's heart's desire as well. But Martha wants honor *and* she wants her love, she wants both together again as if her one lapse had never occurred; and in the world of Mary McCarthy, as well as of Racine, such a wish has to be vain.

As Martha is driving home from the Coes' with Warren's loan for the abortion in her pocketbook, her husband, who thinks her recent preoccupation has been due to her worry about buying him a proper Christmas present, leaves a note in her typewriter: "Martha, I love you, but life is serious. You must not spend any money on Christmas." And in this moving touch we are surely intended to see that John is not as mistaken in the nature of her errand as he appears on the surface. She does want to buy him a present, and she is buying him something only an "obstinate childish heart," impatient of adult seriousness, would dare to fix on. Moreover, she turns out to be childishly extravagant too—she pays with her life. She is killed in a head-on collision with another car. This death has been called arbitrary, but it is, with a sort of playfulness, given roots in the tale. The other car is driven by a woman who significantly resembles Martha, a woman with a past, a writer, an intellectual, and a "cautionary example of everything Martha was trying not to be," and she is driving—of course—on the wrong side of the road. It is clearly because Martha has been such a woman that she is now at the woman's mercy. With this death, the real, with its chain of ineluctable consequences, asserts its dominion over her romantic dream.

And yet—is Martha only another New Leedsian after all? Obviously, she is not—she bears no charmed life. The saving difference is that she cares, "cares about the truth," and cares enough—McCarthy tells us this in the *Paris Review*—to "put up a real stake." We read near the end, "The past *could* be undone, in certain conditions. It could be bought back, paid for by suffering. That is, it could be redeemed." In fact, what makes her happy in her last moments is the conviction that she is earning back, by means of her suffering, the right to her husband's trust, that whether or not she later tells him what she has done, her ordeal would restore "truth between them again," and "it would be all right." It is apparently thus, and thus alone, that the romantic's "obstinate childish heart" can be reconciled, in the world of Mary McCarthy, with her implacable devotion to "impersonal reality."

The Group (1963) was McCarthy's first best seller, but to many critics it was an embarrassing failure. There were two objections to the book. The first was that it exhibited a descent, surprising in so "intellectual" a writer, to the preoccupations and the language of women's magazines. The second was that its characters were "dummies," all alike and all created merely to be "humiliated." Now it is true that the success of the book is not uniform throughout, but to speak of that kind of "descent" was possible only to those who took literally what was intended as irony, who ascribed to the author preoccupations and language of which the whole point is that they testify to the limitations of the characters. (McCarthy herself has said that the novel is "as far as I can go in ventriloquism," and that almost all of it is enclosed in "invisible quotation marks.") And that same inattention to significant detail probably accounts for the failure to notice that the novel's many characters are, in fact, sharply distinct from each other. The truth is, *The Group* differs from her early work chiefly in its scope. Where each previous novel had been about some problem of a commited intellectual (though her heroines did, indeed, yearn toward the more centrally human), *The Group* is about the characteristic attitudes and life patterns of a whole social class, as shown in the loves, jobs, marriages, and housekeeping, as well as the clichés of thought and language, of a group of more or less ordinary girls.

To this one must immediately add, however, that the girls in her group *are* upper-middle-class college graduates of the thirties, which is to say they belong to a species one of whose main characteristics is a pride in keeping up with advanced ideas. In fact, these girls are a suitable subject for their author because their chief problem is another version of McCarthy's permanent problem: the danger to the emotional and moral life, when the guidance of family ties and traditions has disappeared, of the freedom to live by ideas. McCarthy has said the novel is about "the loss of faith in progress." This must refer to the author's own loss of such faith, since the characters who have it keep it to the end; it might be more exact to say that the novel shows the poisonous effects of that faith—of the confidence of most of these ordinary girls that they know better how to manage their lives than people ever knew before. In general, their troubles result from the fact that they are cut off by their advanced ideas from the realities of life and their own nature; less up-to-date, they might well have been better and happier people.

The novel consists of chapters written from the viewpoint and in the language of the chief members of a group of Vassar friends (class of 1933) and what unifies their varied, interweaving histories is the story of one of them, Kay Strong. It is at Kay's marriage to Harald Petersen in 1933 that we first meet them, at her funeral seven years later that we see them together for the last time, and it is mainly because of her, her parties, and her often grotesquely pitiful troubles, that the girls keep coming together during the years between. A sketch of what the girls are like and of what they represent should make clear both the qualities and the meaning of the novel.

Kay seems at times an oddly confused conception. McCarthy apparently began by thinking of her as another "sister" to Margaret Sargent; at least, her college personality and her life seem clearly autobiographical. An attractive girl, she came to Vassar from out West, dominated her college friends with her crushing analytical cleverness, was interested in the theater, married a would-be playwright whose bullying made her miserable, longed to be admired and was often awkwardly honest. But the girl whose troubles we now follow—this later Kay quite convincing and alive—lacks any kind of intellectual distinction or even interests and could not conceivably dominate anyone. In fact, her tragedy is precisely that she is a childlike creature, "a stranger and a sojourner" in this time and place, and pathetically driven by a snobbish longing for "nice" things, who depends for her ideas and for her prospects of acquiring identity, self-respect, admiration on a husband who totally fails her. This husband is another of McCarthy's fine monsters of egoism. A second-rate talent whose ambition is due mainly to jealousy of the rich and the successful and whose cheap brilliance is used for self-display, self-exculpation, or the sadistic pleasure of exercising his power over his vulnerable wife, he is shaped to be the perfect frustration of her needs. He denies, for instance, with his ill-bred, outsider's contempt for all tradition, Kay's need for traditional elegance in the home and at the table. Some funny and horrible moments come from their warring ideas of a proper meal.

Priss and Libby are simpler, less interesting types. The first is mousy and stammering, loves neatness and order, and is easily mastered by tidy theories and confident men. Seeing a stain on a friend's dress, she mentally applies Energine ("her neat little soul scrubbed away"), and it is she who is the book's ardent New Deal Democrat, eager to make society to conform to an ideal of the reasonable. (Her pediatrician husband is an anti-Roosevelt Republican, but he is infatuated with his own new deal in the form of up-to-date theories of infant care, theories he forces on his screaming baby and equally suffering wife with inhuman rigidity.) Libby, on the other hand, is not interested in bettering the world, but in rising in it, her need to be the envied herione of every encounter so frantic that she is incapable of even thinking the truth, and her chattering mouth seems to Polly like a "running wound."

With Dottie, we come to a more original creation. Dottie is a shy, humorless, literal-minded girl, who is most at home in cozy chats with "Mother" and whose shyness conceals a great power of love, sexual and emotional. Her story is a tragicomedy in which a girl clearly made to be happy with old-fashioned romance and marriage but ready to behave as the new epoch thinks right is coolly and efficiently deflowered and then sent to be fitted for a pessary by a lover who doesn't even kiss her, let alone pretend that the "affair" has anything to do with love. (Docile little student of the Zeitgeist though she is, that omitted kiss does bother her.) Later, in one of the novel's wittiest and most touching scenes it is her *mother* who, with a timidly "bold" respect for love which is already out of date, presses Dottie to seek out that first lover. Dottie, scorning those old attitudes (and her own emotions), insists on going through with a practical marriage.

In Norine Schmittlapp Blake, occasional mistress of Kay's husband, McCarthy gives us another example of that perversion of the life of the mind to which clever people are liable—this time as it appears among ordinary college graduates. Her mind and her talk are wholly given up to advanced ideas—her very apartment, painted black as Macdermott's was painted indigo, is a "dogmatic lair," all its furnishings "pontificating . . . articles of belief." She is so quick to display her superior progressiveness that it is she who announces near the end the change from one epoch and style of intellectual cliché to another by declaring that of course "no first-rate mind can accept the concept of progress any more." As before in McCarthy's work, the reason for such a love of "ideas" is an inability to see, let alone to value, real things, an inability that is almost literally a blindness. This was foreshadowed in college, where she declared that a Cézanne still life (which the coldly knowing Lakey called "the formal arrangement of shapes") presented "the spirit of the apples." That phrase, with its implied scorn for the concrete, becomes her leitmotif, and we find her later feeling pleasantly superior to people like the sensible Helena, who seems to shrink from "imponderables" and "intangibles." (It is part of the same indictment that her husband, Putnam, is a fund raiser and publicist for labor organizations—that is, not a real laborer at anything, but a manipulator of notions and "images" for causes that entitle him to feel virtuous even if he lies—and that he is impotent.) Not only is Norine's apartment so filthy that poor Helena experiences an awkward block when she goes to her bathroom; her preference for lofty "intangibles" over mere realities enables her to feel superior in virtue while she is up to her neck in moral nastiness. This is carried to a comic climax when Helena asks her pointedly where Kay had been while Norine and Kay's husband were, as Norine put it, with her fine intellectual disdain for middle-class euphemisms, "fornicating" on her couch. " 'Kay [a Macy's employee] was working,' said Norine. 'The stores don't observe Lincoln's Birthday. They cash in on the fact that the other wage slaves get the day off. It's a big white-collar shopping spree. When do you think a forty-eight-hour-week stenographer gets a chance to buy herself a dress? Unless she goes without her lunch? Probably you've never thought.' "

This extreme example of the mode of life and thought McCarthy detests evokes, in one of the novel's best scenes, a wonderful explosion of the other mode by which she has always opposed it. It is Helena who explodes, the rich girl to whose parents McCarthy gave her own Protestant grandfather's passion for education, and whose encyclopedic knowledge and many accomplishments have left her wry, unassertive, good-natured—passionate about nothing but the truth. The simple concreteness of what she says when at last she can stomach Norine's falseness and ugliness no more, though it is intended literally, is also intended as samples of larger things, and her outburst is worth quoting at length because it is so funny and true and because it can be taken as implying the fundamental McCarthy creed.

> "If I were a socialist, I would try to be a good person. . . . You say your husband can't sleep with you because you're a 'good woman.' . . . Tell him what you do with Harald. . . . That ought to get his pecker up. And have him take a look at this apartment. And at the ring around your neck. If a man slept with you,

you'd leave a ring around him. Like your bathtub . . . I'd get some toilet paper. There isn't any in the bathroom. And some Clorox for the garbage pail and the toilet bowl. And boil out that dishcloth or get a new one. . . . I'd unchain the dog and take him for a walk. And while I was at it, I'd change his name." "You don't like Nietzsche?" "No," said Helena, dryly. "I'd call him something like Rover." Norine gave her terse laugh. "I get it," she said appreciatively. "God, Helena, you're wonderful! Go on. Should I give him a bath to christen him?" Helena considered. "Not in this weather. He might catch cold. Take a bath yourself, instead. . . . And buy some real food—not in cans. If it's only hamburger and fresh vegetables and oranges." Norine nodded. "Fine. But now tell me something more basic" . . . "I'd paint this room another color." . . . "Is that what you'd call basic?" she demanded. "Certainly," said Helena. "You don't want people to think you're a fascist, do you?" she added, with guile. "God, you're dead right," said Norine. "I guess I'm too close to these things. . . . Next?" "I'd take some real books out of the library." "What do you mean, 'real books'?" said Norine, with a wary glance at her shelves. [Earlier we had been told that these shelves contained "few full-size books, except for Marx's *Capital*, Pareto, Spengler, *Ten Days That Shook the World*, *Axel's Castle*, and Lincoln Steffens," all trademarks, as it were, of the radical intellectuals of the time.] "Literature," retorted Helena. "Jane Austen. George Eliot. Flaubert. Lady Murasaki. Dickens. Shakespeare. Sophocles. Aristophanes. Swift." "But those aren't seminal," said Norine, frowning. "So much the better," said Helena. . . . "Is that all?" said Norine. Helena shook her head. Her eyes met Norine's. "I'd stop seeing Harald," she said.

Two members of the group remain to be mentioned, aside from fat, comfortable Pokey, who is most valuable for bringing into the story her funny parents, absolutely stupefied with their wealth and self-importance, and their even funnier butler, Hatton, whose mastery of his profession entitles him to a self-importance greater, if possible, than that of his employers. These other two rank with Helena among the characters respected by their author, and with them the novel comes to an end.

Helena, Lakey, and Polly have McCarthy's respect because, like other characters she has valued, they are honest, incapable of hurting or using others for their own advantage, and attentive to what is outside themselves—they notice things. But they differ significantly too. In Helena and Lakey, intellectual development has crippled ordinary humanity. Helena is so enormously cultivated, so utterly knowing, that she is incapable of passion—except, as I've said, for the truth. She is cool, virginal, she even looks like a boy rather than a woman—charming to talk to, in short, but not a girl to marry. In Lakey it is her sensibility that has suffered the crippling overdevelopment. She is aware of failures of tact or artistic taste to the point, at times, of torture. It is fitting that she becomes an expatriate, spending years as a rich student and connoisseur of art in Europe, and that, though her exquisite refinement is housed, appropriately enough, in a person of exquisite beauty, she too turns out to be a girl one doesn't marry. She startles her friends by returning from Europe with a woman lover, as if, for the most scrupulous feminine sensibility, the male is too gross. This is not shown as a degradation. She is now obviously attractive as a human being, able to wince at her past snobberies, and so on. But she is also obviously incomplete. Polly Andrews alone is all that a woman ought to be, and this may be why she is referred to several times as a creature out of a fairy tale.

Polly seems, in fact, to be an audacious embodiment of a McCarthy daydream, the author's "ideal," the sort of person the little daughter of her gay invalid father and beautiful mother might have become if her hair were long and golden, if her parents had lived, and if her happy childhood had fulfilled itself, after the inevitable fairy tale trials, in a properly happy ending. For Polly's childhood too was delightful with games and presents. Her father too—one of McCarthy's most successful comic creations—is a gay, fun-dispensing invalid. (He is a manic-depressive.) In her poor apartment house, Polly seems to her first lover "a girl in a story book—a fairy tale. A girl with long fair hair who lives in a special room surrounded by kindly dwarfs." What is this fairy tale creature like? She takes pleasure in the work of the kitchen, and even the laundry, she makes her own Christmas presents, she is happy and generous in love, she has a sense of humor—in short, she has the gift of being able to live enjoyably in the real world. Then, as we have found before, this openness to the real has a moral dimension. She is not only honest and morally conscientious—often to comic and troublesome extremes—she is a nurse: her profession is to help people. When she decides to marry a handsome doctor, her chief praise of him is that he is "good." (An oddly foreign word to people in her world—her mother says, "I suppose you mean he's a bit of an idealist.") And yet—her Jim is a psychiatrist. But no, this turns out to be only a spell put on him by the evil spirits of the Zeitgeist. He took up psychiatry, he explains, under the mistaken impression that it was a science, but he is changing to research. He will study "brain chemistry"—that is, the reader of Mary McCarthy will by now understand, he will give up the delusive freedom of psychiatry, a freedom to deal masterfully in untestable ideas, and work instead with concrete "impersonal" realities. Polly marries this good man, and taking her father to stay with them—to the horror of all their up-to-date friends—they live happily, for all we know, ever after.

As I have said, *The Group* is not perfectly successful. A defect of its method is that characters whose human importance is comparatively trifling (Libby) or who are of mainly sociological interest (Priss) are treated as fully as those who engage the author more deeply; with such characters, though they are often amusing, the narrative urgency slackens. And there are Polly's two lovers, who seem created only to make points with or to serve the plot. Nevertheless, the book is mainly a pleasure to read. The pleasure comes from the characters (most of them), so pathetic and comic, so true, in their struggle to live up to their advanced ideas or to cling to reality amid the general falsenesses; from the continuous vivifying detail of their setting, appearance, tone, and gesture; and from the sheer quantity of people and experiences the story brings to life.

Between 1963, when *The Group* appeared, and 1968, McCarthy published five nonfiction books. One, called *Vietnam* (1967), is a report of her impressions of the war, which, for eight years, the United States had been waging in that country, a war some Americans regarded as a righteous crusade against communism and others as an unwarranted, arrogant, and brutal intervention in another country's internal affairs. The book expresses McCarthy's opposition to the war, and gives for it an appalling and convincing mass of evidence. This is not the place to comment on her position. But what is relevant here is the intensity of her involvement in this great public tragedy, and her insistence that it must be regarded as a moral problem, to be solved by doing not what is "practical" but what is right. "Either it is *morally* wrong for the United States to bomb a small and virtually defenseless country or it is not," she tells us, " and a student picketing the Pentagon is just as great an expert in that realm, to say the least, as Dean Rusk or Joseph Alsop." Reading this sentence—and indeed the whole book—one wonders if it is only Domna Rejnev who asks herself the question "What would Tolstoy say?"

Such undercutting of authoritative theorizing by a return to the human realities which the theories obscure is, we have seen, the primary action of McCarthy's mind. It is in this sense that she is a "realist," and this is why realism, which it is nowadays fashionable to consider a worked-out vein, has shown in her fiction undiminished possibilities of intelligence, feeling, wit, and grace. She herself remarks in the *Paris Review* that she can't help "a sort of distortion, a sort of writing on the bias, seeing things with a swerve and a swoop, a sort of extravagance."

But though, like any serious artist, she selects her own kind of data to serve her own vision, her stories are surely offered as true examples of the experience of our time. That "swerve and swoop" are only the wit, play, and poetry in her manner of reporting what she has seen, and these qualities are not more important in her work than her accuracy. Like the "philosophy of life" it expresses, her art comes from her loyalty to the life we actually live, her pleasure in the concrete particulars of people and the world, her refusal to be seduced away from them by ideas, however fashionable or however flattering. She is, in fact, one of several current novelists and critics—Saul Bellow, with his boisterous insistence on the life of feeling, is one; Lionel Trilling, with his critique of what he calls the second environment, that cozy conformist world of received ideas inhabited by so many "nonconformists," is another—who write out of impatience with their own class of intellectuals. Different though they are in so many ways (Bellow, for instance, is quite as "romantic" as McCarthy is "neoclassic"), they stand together against the intellectual's tendency to value chic ideas more than the human experience or the human ends they are supposed to serve, or, worse still, to conceal from himself, with the help of such ideas, realities he prefers not to see.

As for the contempt thought by many to be her sole motive power, the cutting satire supposed to be her main quality, these, as I have tried to make clear, are by-products of something more fundamental. They come not from an intellectual's superciliousness, but from an intellectual's hunger for the ordinary decencies and delights of life. When she deals a blow, it is precisely at the kind of people who think cleverness is better. What has given McCarthy's work its deepest interest is that, with all her "brilliance," she knows very well how little the mind's accomplishments may be worth in the face of life's agonizing difficulties, and that before the nonintellectual virtues—kindness, honesty, conscientiousness, the ability to take pleasure in people and the world—she lowers willingly her formidable weapons.

Since 1968, McCarthy has published six more books. She continued her exposé of the Vietnam War in *Hanoi* (1968), a report of her visit to the capital of North Vietnam; in *Medina* (1972), about the trial and acquittal of the officer in charge of the 1968 mission into the village of My Lai which resulted in the massacre of unarmed civilians by American soldiers (Captain Calley, who actually led the mission, had already been found guilty); and in *The Seventeenth Degree* (1974), which reprinted her previous Vietnam writing, as well as a long review of a recent best seller on how the war was handled by our presidents and their associates in Washington, D.C., and which is prefaced by an intimate memoir of her experiences while acting and writing against the war. In *The Mask of State: Watergate Portraits* (1974), she reported the televised (Senator) Ervin Committee hearings into the political scandal which ended in the resignation of President Nixon. Those four books are mainly vivid on-the-spot journalism. The other two, *The Writing on the Wall and Literary Essays* (1970) and the novel *Birds of America* (1971), are literature.

These last-named works confirm one's sense that she belongs among those especially interesting writers whose self-exploration becomes more and more a way of understanding the world. For many of the essays, though devoted to other writers, turn out to be about her own deepest preoccupations. And the idea in her previous novels that "freedom for her kind of people—for intellectuals" has often led only to "escape from difficult, limiting reality into the realm of flattering abstraction" has become in both books a frankly gloomy vision of the whole drift of contemporary civilization.

The three most recent essays in *The Writing on the Wall*—on Ivy Compton-Burnett, Orwell, and Nature—are full of what might almost be notes for *Birds of America*. Compton-Burnett is seen to be obsessed by the ambiguities and contradictions in "two insistent words . . . : Nature and Equality." Orwell is shown as a man who felt "obliged to believe in progress," but who loved "some simpler form of life" and "hated the technology he counted on to liberate the majority." And in "One Touch of Nature" she finds that Nature has ceased to determine values, but "has become subject to opinion" and "is no longer the human home." *Birds of America* is, in fact, a rich study of the contradictions within and between those two ideas, Nature and Equality, which we have dreamed we can bring together, and of how Equality, given irresistible power by technology, is destroying the values associated with Nature. The contradictions are brought to life in the relationship of nineteen-year-old Peter Levi and his much divorced artist (harpsichordist) mother, Rosamund Brown, who, though the story and its point of view are his, remains a sort of loved and opposed other self throughout.

Peter and his mother have returned to the New England town of Rocky Port for the 1964 summer holiday preceding his junior year abroad, and the story begins with his memory of their first visit four years earlier, the happiest time of his life. In that earlier period, he was "deeply in love with his mother," and he also loved Nature, which meant then the New England countryside and above all its wild birds. Of his mother, we see chiefly what she can share with Peter—her delight in the pleasures and customs of her childhood and of an earlier, simpler America, and in particular, in cooking real food. Since she is "a hopeless romantic" who "turned everything into a game," she decides to cook only American recipes from an old Fannie Farmer cookbook, and nothing that has been "naturalized" less than a hundred years. The story is in part the funny spectacle of her difficulties as she struggles to follow the old recipes with the proper ingredients and utensils in a town whose shops "get no call" for such things any more, and of Peter's "mature" irony at a childish intensity and lack of logic he really enjoys. But it is also about the pleasure they take in their food, their walks, their games. And above all, it is the story of their love, the love of two people who "notice things" with exceptional sensitivity and hence are always scrupulously just both for and against each other and themselves, and of the playful delicacies by which they express, or conceal, their feelings. When the flashback ends and we return to the 1964 Rocky Port, we find it buried four years deeper under the "improvements" of technology. The mother's struggle for old-time reality in the kitchen has grown a bit frenzied: she wants "fowl" rather than fryers because they're cheaper and "economy is contact with reality. I love reality, Peter. I hope you will too"—but spends gallons of gas hunting for real jelly glasses. Peter, less simply "in love" and more aware of the outside world—civil rights workers vanishing in Mississippi—begins to wonder if she isn't "making too much of the minutiae." He has become, moreover, a devotee of the ethics of Kant, whose categorical imperative—perform no action whose principle you would not accept as a universal law—is his supreme commandment, and so is uneasy about the aristocratic refinement of taste by which his artist-mother instinctively decides what is good and right. The rest of the novel, though its tone stays mostly light or ironic, draws out for Peter the increasingly painful implications of the battle these two fought with Rocky Port, each other, and themselves.

The absurd idea of some reviewers, indicating a kind of tone deafness, that Peter is a "prig," without "passions or contradictions," and Rosamund is an "overcultivated cipher," seems to rest on the assumption that passion must be sexual—or at least noisy—and that characters with intelligence, wit, and learning, especially if their manners are reserved, must be unreal. But "the mightiest of the passions," as Shaw's Jack Tanner declares, is "moral passion." And what chiefly characterizes Peter and his mother, what makes them funny and touching, is the unremitting intensity of their moral concern, their way of seeing moral issues in minutiae. As for contradictions, it is precisely Peter's inner tug-of-war that is the point of his story. And this keeps it alive as fiction even when "story" of the usual kind is, in varying degrees, abandoned.

The adverse reviews say the novel turns into an "essay" and imply that its fictional vitality disappears. Now, it is true that except in these first two chapters, another in the middle, and the last, the book is not a conventional realistic novel: what we are given of characters and their relationships is mainly what can serve a development in ideas, and the wide and witty exploration of the ideas certainly makes for a good deal of the fun. But if "essay" means a kind of writing in which the author merely announces her own worked-out conclusions, then all the chapters, even that of Peter's long philosophic letter to his mother, are clearly something else, and this a something else which retains precisely the reality peculiar to fiction. For fiction restores reality to ideas by giving up the pretense that they exist apart from particular persons in particular situations and that they are static. In *Birds of America* all the ideas emerge from the mental life of *Peter*, whom we have come to know in nonintellectual ways as well; in her mimicry of idiom, tone, and personal style McCarthy is as amusingly accurate with this American boy of the 1960s as she has been with so many other characters. Moreover, his mental life is a constant struggle among ideas that actively contend with each other. In short, the novel gives us ideas in their living state. For, as Gide's Edouard affirms so passionately, ideas "live; they fight; they perish like men." Edouard admits that "ideas exist only because of men; but that's what's so pathetic; they live at their expense."

So Peter's encounter in a train to Paris with some Midwestern American schoolmarms, as kind and neighborly as they are naïve and vulgar, becomes a squirming inner battle between the taste, intellect, and need for privacy he shares with his mother and his American egalitarian sense of justice. So, though his letter to his mother begins by rejecting her ethics of "taste" as those of a "snob," it goes on to tell of a battle he fights to keep clean the public toilet of his Paris lodgings which others leave digustingly filthy, a battle which leads him to a devastating possibility: "Could humanity be divided into people who noticed and people who didn't? If so there was no common world." And later, it is his own reactionary tendencies that are jolted. After smiling at an elderly Italian's old-fashioned faith in the power of American technology to free men from slavery and want, he is reminded that the picturesque European simplicities he prefers are only what slavery and want look like to the comfortable outsider—Mistrust the picturesque, the man says. It stinks.

The climax of this conflict occurs in the next-to-last chapter when Peter argues in the Sistine Chapel with the novel's chief spokesman for contemporary American civilization, his sociologist faculty adviser. This man, named with Dickensian appropriateness Mr. Small, had earlier reduced Peter's complex dissatisfactions to neurotic symptoms easy to "explain" and advise. He now has a foundation grant to study the flight patterns of the new, and mainly American, flying creature, the tourist.

Not only does Small defend against Peter's "elitist" objections both American capitalism and the technology by which, at some temporary cost here and there, it spreads the good things of life more and more widely; he also demonstrates the new "anti-elitist" trend in American education in his belief that the great frescoes are really in essence abstractions—Norine Schmittlapp's "intangibles"—accessible to all with the right feelings. To him, Peter's insistence that they say something in a language which a little education would illuminate is only the old business of shutting out the "disadvantaged." Finally, he tries to share their lunch check equally, though he in fact ate more than Peter, and then, with the "warmth" of the new "with-it" teacher, gives Peter a farewell hug to show their differences don't matter, a neat illustration of that blurring of distinguishing particulars some egalitarians call justice—or love.

The last chapter is again pure—and poignant—fiction. It depicts a series of betrayals. First, Peter finds sleeping on his lodging stairs one cold winter night a stinking, drink-stupefied woman, a *clocharde*, waiting for him "like a big package with his name on it: Peter Levi, Esq., Noted Humanitarian." Taking her to his room for a night's shelter, he experiences all the little self-betrayals generated by moral actions that make one's flesh crawl: if one doesn't act, one feels guilty, but if one does, one feels hypocritical, for no action is ever enough to make up for the irrepressible reservations. Then President Johnson betrays his election promises to keep America out of war by bombing North Vietnam; when Peter goes to the zoo for comfort in his horror and despair, an angry swan wounds the bird-lover with a beak dripping with polluted water; in a hospital afterward, technology almost kills him with penicillin, to which he is allergic; and finally, his mother tells him she will play in Poland for the U.S. State Department because "it's just music." He knows he can reawaken her moral common sense, but the fact that he should need to destroys her authority for him forever—a small sample of the division between the generations in the 1960s. And the book ends with a brief but tellingly described dream visit by Kant, who announces gravely that, not God, Whom men have long managed without, but "Nature is dead."

This bold statement of the book's "message" in its last line, far from flattening the closing emotional effect, oddly intensifies it. We feel an earnestness in the author that drives her to abandon the usual coyness of fiction. The fact is, for Mary McCarthy the death of Nature, in spite of her Kant's disclaimer, is very much like the death of God announced by Nietzsche. Her Nature (as the capital letter suggests) is only the line to which God has lately retreated; both serve, in Arnold's phrase, as that reality not ourselves which makes for righteousness—as well as sanity, health, beauty. And the tragedy at the heart of her novel is not only that Nature is dead, but that it has been murdered by an ideal she also values, the ideal of Equality.

The novel has shown why the fact that these are in conflict is—for Peter and his mother and their enlightened contemporary readers—at once painful to admit and hard to deny. We like to think that nature supports our humanitarian bias, that being the same for all and in all, it teaches that all should be treated alike. But nature is actually the realm of minute particulars, and every real relationship to these must also be minutely particular; that is, it is the realm of differences and inequalities, both in things and in our power to notice, appreciate, and possess them. For this reason, if people are to share in all life's goods, these goods must be stripped of the particulars that limit their accessibility. They must be "processed" into easily reproducible and portable (also inexact and tasteless) approximations of the real thing—and this applies to products of the mind as well as to those of nature. Nor is it only those two kinds of products that make for inequality and call for such processing. There are also the particulars of custom and tradition that have evolved out of the history of nations, neighborhoods, families. These give us our unique childhoods, the sources and objects of our emotional lives, our identities, but they do keep us apart. Equality therefore demands that such uniqueness be replaced by a generalized humanity we can share. In a single sentence, the pursuit of equality is an attempt to live by an idea, and so, however "self-evident," beautiful, and irresistible the idea, a constant flight from reality. Hence the quotation which serves as a motto for the book: "to attempt to embody the Idea in an example, as one might embody the wise man in a novel, is unseemly . . . for our natural limitations, which persistently interfere with the perfection of the Idea, forbid all illusion about such an attempt . . ."

The ego-serving manipulation of reality McCarthy has always detested in intellectuals (including herself) thus turns out to have been only her personal near-at-hand example of the process of technology. Since this process serves the idea of equality, she cannot, of course, reject it, but her novel is a record of what it costs. With the growing power of technology, there is no longer any reality not ourselves. Not only has it replaced Nature, and our "second nature," custom, with life-reducing conveniences and abstractions, but, far worse, by giving man control over what once controlled and educated him, it has put our whole world at the mercy of the ego-driven human will.

A sad conclusion. And though many of us refuse to give up a sort of animal faith in the power of human creativity to save us yet again— even from the human will—the pessimism of this rich and moving novel is certainly an appropriate response to the world we now inhabit.

The Novels of Saul Bellow

The following discussion of Bellow's first six novels was written before the publication of the latest two, which will be discussed at the end of this chapter.

It seems fitting, in an essay on the novels of Saul Bellow, to give up the pretense of impersonal expertise and to admit the feeling out of which the essay comes. My feeling, then, is gratitude. Few novelists have given me so much pleasure. Open his novels anywhere, I am tempted to say, and whatever the eye falls on will probably be at once urgent, moving, profound, lively—and, after the first two novels, funny as well. To a generation of serious readers, who are usually concentrating every nerve and muscle to be in the right, his style brings the message, "Take it easy. You are already more right than you know." And that enjoyable surface is only part of the story. What deepens the pleasure, and the gratitude, is that it is the natural expression of a vision of human life that is itself, and without fatuity, on the side of joy.

This vision is not new. It is that of the English Romantic Movement, the bright affirmative romanticism, rather than the whining or despairing kind of other times and places. In Bellow the thoughts of Wordsworth and Blake are coming back to life. I am thinking of the Wordsworth who spoke of "the bond of union between life and joy" which is formed in infancy; who, as an adult, found salvation from the strain of will and intellectual cleverness by going home to his sister and relaxing into simplicity and naturalness and the "sweet counsels between head and heart"; who had

> a sense sublime
> Of something far more deeply interfused,
> Whose dwelling is the light of setting suns,
> And the round ocean and the living air,
> And the blue sky, and in the mind of man,

who said of man,

> Our destiny, our being's heart and home,
> Is with infinitude, and only there,
> With hope it is, hope that can never die,
> Effort and expectation and desire,
> And something evermore about to be,

who clung with all his might to those "spots of time" which give

> Profoundest knowledge to what point, and how,
> The mind is lord and master—outward sense
> The obedient servant of her will.

I am thinking of the Blake who even more absolutely than Wordsworth affirmed that the world we live in is created by the human mind— "mind-forged manacles," on the one hand, or, on the other, the glories seen and made by the liberated imagination, borne aloft by feeling. All these ideas are fundamental Bellow themes, and "feeling"—their source—is the key word, for them and for him. Bellow's work, like theirs, is a passionate retaliation against the forces in our culture that inhibit or pervert our power to feel, which is our life, and that thereby attempt, in terms as obsessive in Bellow as the word "feeling" itself, to make us "die" and not "live."

Not only is each of the novels, as I will try to show, an account of the adventures of a man of feeling. The very language in which they are written is a language aimed, with increasing boldness and precision, to express feeling. I don't mean to describe it, as, say, D. H. Lawrence tried to do. What Bellow describes, and in torrents of thick detail, is the world of concrete particulars in which feeling takes place, by which it is generated or mocked. But he describes that world in a manner which duplicates the tone, pace, and phrasing of a warmhearted man's actual responses to it. His prose can be read aloud with the same kind of pleasure one gets from the dialogue of a good play.

Nor is it only concrete particulars that his style captures as a man would feel them. Far more original is the way that style gives life to the abstract formulas of culture. For it belongs among Bellow's gifts as a novelist that he is a very intelligent and learned man. Not only do his heroes move about among ideas as easily as among other elements of experience; he has created a number of convincing sages, men of genius more or less grotesquely human, in whom the furthest reaches of his thought could be embodied. He keeps all this intellectual freight alive, in part, by jumbling together the language of erudition—literature, philosophy, sociology, psychology, history—with the idiom of nonintellectual, urban-American, often Jewish-American, speech. There is a shock of freshness. But the words "jumbling together" could be misleading. Such informality, as one might call it, is not merely a literary device, but rises naturally from the fact that Bellow and his heroes turn to the world of culture, not as subtly smiling specialists to a private preserve, but as men of feeling led by the needs of life. ("My personal preference," says Augie March, "was for useful thoughts. I mean thoughts that answered questions that moved you.") They philosophize, grow poetic, reach for grand historical parallels for their ordinary American experience with the spontaneity of a curse or a shout of joy. And the result is not only that Bellow's style (at its best) brings us the great ideas warm again with fresh feeling, but that it shows us the homeliest immediacies of life movingly imbued with large significance.

And this brings up the last thing I want to say by way of preface. Bellow's novels are not so much philosophic novels as religious. In all of them the particulars of the story are designed to bring before us the questions, What is man? How is he related to his fellows and the universe? How should he live? His heroes are all driven to seek and put their lives somehow in harmony with—the will of God, they may sometimes call it, though they don't know what He is or whether He exists. One might call it, instead, reality, or the flow of force which produced the stars and grass and men, or the deepest truth about our nature and its sources of happiness and pain. And if turning from "God" to "reality" seems to make the word "religious" inappropriate, add that it is in feeling rather than in the data of "objective" systems and machines that Bellow finds his clues to that reality, a reality which is therefore for him, as it was for the great romantics, limitless in every direction, mysterious, yet somehow related to and malleable by human desire and imagination.

His first six novels are *Dangling Man* (1944), *The Victim* (1947), *The Adventures of Augie March* (1953), *Seize the Day* (1956), *Henderson the Rain King* (1959), and *Herzog* (1964). Each of these is different from the others, even surprisingly so. It would be a crime for a critic to be so intent on disengaging their deep-lying unity that he blurred that enjoyable uniqueness and, worse still, denied by implication the artist's freedom in each new work to see and say new things. Though his heroes do turn out, like those of Fitzgerald and many other writers, to be brothers—men of feeling all, fighting the same war—their war is covered at different depths, at different cultural locations, from different points of view; sometimes he shows how it is lost, sometimes how it is won; in *Henderson* we see a withdrawal from it into the wilderness leading to a burst of prophetic inspiration; and in *Herzog* it is lost and won at the same time. Such variety having been granted, however—and one must grant more: a steady increase in power and scope—one is free to make the other point. Bellow has also demonstrated a most impressive consistency of vision, impressive because it testifies to his early and continuous grasp of his own truest self. This, oddly enough, makes his first novel grow more interesting as its successors pile up.

Now it is true that this first novel (the journal of a twenty-seven-year-old intellectual waiting to be drafted into World War II, who despises the compromises by which most people live, but whose superior gifts only make him despise himself more and who ends hurrying into the army with the despairing cry, "Long live regimentation!") is, as the author himself has wryly acknowledged, another blow struck for "the lousy—Wasteland outlook" which Bellow was to leave behind. But read it in the light of the later books and there rises clearly to view the Bellow hero in his earliest definition, hungering for something else.

The very first page of the novel announces the whole career to follow:

> This is an era of hardboiled-dom. . . . Do you have feelings? There are correct and incorrect ways of indicating them. Do you have an inner life? It is nobody's business but your own. Do you have emotions? Strangle them. To a degree, everyone obeys this code. And it does admit of a limited kind of candor, a close-mouthed straightforwardness. But on the truest candor, it has an inhibitory effect. Most serious matters are closed to the hard-boiled. . . . If you have difficulties, grapple with them silently, goes one of their commandments. To hell with that! I intend to talk about mine, and if I had as many mouths as Siva has arms and kept them going all the time, I still could not do myself justice.

Further, Joseph is a man who "is greatly concerned with keeping intact and free from encumbrance a sense of his own being, its importance." Though he had been a student of history—the Enlightenment, romanticism—books have been chiefly valuable to him as "guarantors of an extended life, far more precious and necessary than the one I was forced to lead daily." Naturally enough, he is given to "ideal constructions," and, indeed, has tried "to work out everything in accordance with a general plan," a plan which involves his friends, his family, his wife. He finds now that his plans were wrong—he has not allowed sufficiently for human corruption. But he has not therefore sunk into simple pessimism, denial of the possibility of goodness or happiness. (Of pessimists he asks, "Is that all they see, these people?") This is to

Joseph as foolish as the optimism that denies human depravity. To him the world is not good or bad but itself, ineffable, marvelous, strange to the point that one clings to the "nearest passersby." And he continues to believe in the value of "ideal constructions," though he knows they may grow parasitical and destructive.

The present time, however, through Chicago's ugly streets which seem to mock man's great past, through an old communist friend who cuts him dead because his opinions have changed, through his well-to-do brother offering him money and "practical" advice, keeps pressing him to admit that what he values is unimportant, that what matters is the right opinions or money or power. He fights back, but the stubborn shouts of greeting, for instance, by which he forces the communist to acknowledge his existence, are comically bitter and desperate; his retort to his brother comes out in a voice that shakes. And the conflict's ultimate meaning and conclusion are made plain in Joseph's dialogues with The Spirit of Alternatives, also known as Tu As Raison Aussi, an occasional visitor who dramatizes the intellectual's awareness of the mocking other view.

This companion suggests that Joseph might be wise to stop fighting, to stop "preparing yourself for further life. . . . The vastest experience of your time doesn't have much to do with living. Have you thought of preparing yourself for that?" "Dying?" Joseph replies. "What's there to prepare for?" You can't prepare for anything but living. . . . You want me to worship the anti-life. I'm saying that there are no values outside life. There is nothing outside life." "Life" vs. "anti-life"—as immediately grows clear, this polarity is closely related to two warring attitudes to the self, one which naturally accompanies all happy, fulfilling activity, and another which makes such activity impossible and which the modern world, with all its might, keeps dinning into our ears. When Joseph insists that to him the war, though he would not want to be spared this common experience of his time, is only an "incident," that what matters is "the self," which must not be governed by chance or accident, but by ourselves in freedom, what matters is that one follow one's own destiny in spite of such "incidents," the Spirit replies, "Then only one question remains." "What?" "Whether you have a separate destiny. Oh, you're a shrewd wriggler. But I've been waiting for you to cross my corner." Sure enough, Joseph grows pale, refuses to answer, his teeth chatter, the Spirit kindly runs and gets a blanket to cover him with, etc. And soon after, Joseph asks his draft board to take him.

This first novel, then, is indeed the tale of a defeat. Joseph does not have what it takes to maintain, without help from outside, that faith in his "separate destiny" which he needs in order to "live." But he has gone down fighting, and this fight, and the nature of the warring parties, will remain, as I have said, Bellow's permanent subject.

For highest rank as a work of fiction, *Dangling Man* is perhaps too much an actual journal, with no character but Joseph fully developed and no single, intensifying action to dramatize its theme. (It is so beautifully written and so true and alive throughout that this hardly matters.) Bellow's second novel, however, is a masterpiece.

To begin with, *The Victim* is a novel about anti-Semitism. It is, in fact, Bellow's profound accuracy in capturing what is essential in the anti-Semitic situation—what makes for it in the gentile who claims to be the Jew's victim, and in the Jew who thereupon becomes the gentile's, how it operates, what it feels like—which gives this entirely realistic novel an air of Kafka-like nightmare. But though its subject seems more modest in scope than those of the others—a familiar social problem—the modesty is only on the surface. This tale of Jew and gentile ends by being another chapter in Bellow's exploration of what it is to be a human being.

The Jewish victim is Asa Leventhal, who, after a miserable childhood, a lonely youth, a frightening struggle for safety in the world of making-a-living, has at last found a good enough job and a loving wife. But the novel's story is an account of the lapsing of that luck, the return of deeply expected, almost, to Leventhal, normal disaster, in the form of his gentile "victim" Kirby Allbee, an old acquaintance who shows up during a broiling New York summer when Leventhal's wife is away on a visit. As a white Anglo-Saxon Protestant formerly well-to-do New Englander, Allbee has been trained from childhood to think well of himself and to expect the best, the opposite training from Leventhal's. He is now, however, a drifting alcoholic. And since he lost a job years ago shortly after Leventhal (recommended by him to his boss) had, in the boss's office, noisily resented what he thought was insult, Allbee now claims that that "scene" caused him to be fired, that it was maliciously intended to do so because Allbee had once spoken against Jews, and that Leventhal, being reponsible for his ruin, owes it to him to help him back on his feet.

Not only is this charge utterly fantastic to Leventhal when he first hears it. It is accompanied by a steady stream of gentlemanly observations about "you people" which implies that the Jew is naturally outside the human community and its decencies, a community to which this degraded, irresponsible, alcoholic bum of a gentile as naturally belongs. And yet, as Allbee, amid the insults, keeps appealing for sympathy and asking him to be "fair," Leventhal, for all his anger and repulsion, little by little gives him everything he asks for: money to tide him over, a bed in his apartment, help in finding a job.

Bellow evokes beautifully in all this (as any Jew will know) the maddening paradox of anti-Semitism, in which the Jew is forced to be better than others at the same time that he is being called worse, or is accused of betraying human values precisely by those who are inhumanly tormenting him. But most interesting of all—and the core of the book—is his exploration of the Jew's own "guilt" for his victimization; for, as Leventhal admits to an indignant fellow Jew who declares, "He [Allbee] sold you a bill of goods," "I must have wanted to buy." This guilt is not due, as some have said, to an insufficient responsiveness to others, though Leventhal once feels the nightmare is driving him to face up to such a fault. It is due to exactly the opposite: a responsiveness to the feelings, the sufferings, the accusations of others that is far in excess of the demands of ordinary social life. "You want everyone to like you," that same friend complains, and Leventhal once, when the insults let up, even feels a shocking trace of affection for Allbee. A nervous flutter of self-criticism follows in him all the blows of life; his touchy self-defensiveness, against accusations that don't always exist, is precisely an attempt to fight off his own uneasy sense of possible guilt. If Leventhal accuses himself of "indifference," this is only the error of one who feels deficient in virtue because the amount he demands of himself is so inordinate.

The Talmud says, "All Jews are mutually accountable to each other." Sure enough, Leventhal "liked to think human meant accountable." And at the height of his suffering from Allbee, he has a dream of painful frustration from which he awakens to a thought that brings tears of joy, though he knows it will fade in the morning. "Everybody committed offenses, but it was supremely plain to him that everything without exception, took place as if within a single soul or person." As that painful dream might be his life, so this thought is his life's most characteristic fruit. To this quintessential Jew we are all part of one being, sharers in all guilt, all pain—brothers. In his depths, he does feel responsible for Allbee's ruin. And Allbee knows this! He clings to Leventhal, appeals for sympathy and fairness—in situations in which he would surely know most people would laugh in his face—because, for all his half-believed fantasies of the other's inhumanity, he counts on the Jew to be deeply reached by that appeal.

Allbee is, in this respect, exactly the other's opposite: he is the quintessential anti-Semite. Wonderfully subtle in his detection of human evil, he cannot endure to admit that any of that evil is his: it must all be the Jew's. And in this lies the secret relevance of some fascinating conversations Leventhal has with the first of the Bellow sages, a fine old man named Schlossberg. In a cafeteria crowd they talk of Disraeli and Caesar, and Schlossberg finds both distasteful because he prefers the naturally human over what, to *prove* something, aspires above it. People want to become more than human, he says, not to sweat, not to suffer, so maybe they will not have to die. "More than human, can you have any use of life? Less than human you don't either."

Nor is his love for the natural an excuse for a low idea of the human. Schlossberg admits that under the microscope man seems "lousy and cheap." But he insists that to his feelings, which in this matter count as much as anything, "greatness and beauty" are as real as "black and white." "I'm entitled as much as you. And why be measly? Do you have to be? Is somebody holding you by the throat? Have dignity, you understand me? Choose dignity. Nobody knows enough to turn it down."

To be fully human, then, is to accept the burden of defect, guilt, and death that are the human condition, but to do so without hating oneself or others, without lapsing into disgust, cynicism, cold-heartedness. And to shoulder this burden, to do so with love and joy, is here seen to be the Jew's peculiar calling—or, if you like, the natural product of his history of suffering combined with his traditional culture—as it is the secret motive of the anti-Semite to throw the burden off. The nightmare's climax, in which Allbee comes back to Leventhal's apartment (he had at last been thrown out) to kill himself by gas where he would also be killing the sleeping Jew, seems to catch this up in one symbolic act. For to load upon the Jew all the faults of man and to feel that this makes him unworthy to live is to confess that where those faults appear in oneself one is oneself unworthy to live. Allbee's attempted suicide-murder is, in fact, a climactic rejection of his own, as well as the Jew's, humanity.

Moreover, when the two meet again years later, Allbee, wiser, more humble, enabled at last to get along (though still making mechanically the same self-exculpating anti-Semitic remarks) suddenly takes Leventhal's hand and admits that he knew back then that he owed him something. Are we not being told that this Jew, as in the story of the one of Galilee, was a sort of savior of his own persecutor, that by taking on himself the ruined man's burden of weakness and guilt, he had helped him—in spite of that moment of near disaster—to learn some humanity and live?

I must add in conclusion that I have indicated only the main ideas that rise from this novel's unusually cryptic closeness to fact. The book is dazzling in its line-by-line reality—of setting, of character, of dialogue, of emotion, of tone—and this reality means a richness of suggestion, of ambiguity, that must tease forever the sweating critic who seeks to generalize.

In the next novel, however, such concentrated meaningfulness was joyously abandoned.

The Adventures of Augie March was a kind of explosion, though an explosion which only released into full freedom impulses that had appeared in Bellow's work before. His liberating idea would seem to have been that of thumbing his nose at the prevailing clichés of literary and intellectual sophistication (carefulness of language and form, man alienated and doomed) and expressing openly for once his dearest beliefs in a manner appropriately easygoing and heartfelt, the manner of improvisation. So we get that colloquial language previously described ("freestyle," Augie, who tells his own story, calls it, "first to knock, first admitted"). So we get the novel's picaresque form, a flood of adventures in merely chronological order. And so we get in Augie a Bellow hero unbothered by the Spirit of Alternatives, immune to the ironies of worldliness—in short, an unqualified embodiment of Bellow's romanticism.

The story is that of the growing up during the twenties, thirties, and forties of a boy too poor to complete a formal education, but so good-looking, intelligent, and emotionally responsive that people are always being drawn to him, trying to help him or at least to win his support for their life-visions and purposes. The most persistent of those who would "recruit" him to their visions is his elder brother Simon, one of the book's finest creations. Simon, like Joseph's brother Amos, has married money, having been left by gruesome early humiliations absolutely raging to be rich. But though he comes with expensive presents to the poor dirty room where Augie lies reading books he has stolen in order to sell, and, in the face of the opposition he senses from the books on the floor, preaches the wisdom of being practical, he also goes into Augie's toilet to cry, and there flicker in him constant impulses to suicide. Simon is a powerful image of the deathward current of our money culture, one of those for whom, because they seek what is against life, to win is to lose. Others in the long procession of vivid salesmen for their own visions are the crippled Einhorn, who transfigures an ignoble daily life by his greatness of spirit; Thea, a girl Augie loves, who is impatient with human meanness and seeks nobility among animals and birds—she gets Augie to help her train an eagle in falconry as Dahfu will later get Henderson to improve his soul with lions; Robey, the eccentric millionaire who wants Augie's help in writing a book on human happiness, one chapter of which would speak of a time of "joy without sin, love without darkness, gay prosperity," when man would cease to be "drilled like a Prussian by the coarse hollering of sergeant fears"; Bateshaw, the mad genius, in whom Joseph's desire for a "separate destiny" is a wild passion and leads him to believe he has learned to synthesize life. To all of these Augie is sympathetic, but none can seduce him finally from his allegiance to his own nature, and to all he finally says no.

What is this Augie who is the Bellow alternative to the way we live now? The novel in its freedom is strewn with definitions of his temperament, but his mocking and affectionate friend Clem Tambow sums them up well in a conversation which epitomizes the whole book: " 'You are a distinguished personality. You are a man of feeling. Among us poor drips at the human masquerade you come like an angel. . . . You arrive as for a ball, smiling, and beaming. . . . You have a nobility syndrome. . . . You want there should be man with a capital M, with great stature.' " Naturally, an Augie who makes such demands and who, as he puts it, "refuses to live a disappointed life" must run into trouble: his defeats, like those of Candide, are a source of much of the book's drama and comedy. And for Clem the force which brings the trouble is reality. "You know you're going to ruin yourself," Clem says, "ignoring the reality principle. You should accept the data of experience. Why don't you read some psychology?" But, like Joseph, Augie replies, "It can never be right to offer to die, and if that's what the data of experience tell you, then you must get along without them." Nor is this a mere quixotic rejection of reality, for earlier Augie had told someone, "I don't like low opinions, and when you speak them out it commits you, and you become a slave to them. Talk will lead people on until they convince their minds of things they can't feel." Augie believes with Keats in the holiness of the heart's affections. And since facts may be variously interpreted and the world we live in is the world as we interpret it, to call that "real" which mocks man's aspirations and thereby chokes off the flow of his energy and joy—his life—is for Augie, as it was for those earlier romantics, a mere weakness of spirit, a submission not to the facts, but to low opinions.

But it is not only the cynical ideal-denying view of reality which Augie opposes. It is also the opposite excess, a concentration on the ideal that would deny the lowly original self, the earth out of which it grows. He is against "specialists," and when Clem tells him his ambition is too general, he must be "concrete" like Napoleon and Goethe, Augie replies that he doesn't want to "go die in one subdivided role or another, with one or two thoughts, those narrow persistent ideas of your function." He doesn't want to be an expert, despising amateurs and pursuing difficult triumphs. At another time, taking a class at the University of Chicago, he smells the stockyards his lofty professors ignore and decides that formal pursuit of the ideal necessitates too many detours, the bypassing of too much natural life. What he wants is the ideal and the ordinary utterly one, aspects of the same reality. And though he sometimes, even tearfully, admits his ordinary self may not be "good enough" to win without strain to those heights on which life is no longer "disappointed," he wants no promotion in life that does not come out of that self as naturally as fruit from a tree. "Easy or not at all" is his slogan.

And here we come to the climax in our discovery of this Chicago boy's kinship with those early nineteenth-century champions of the responsive heart. It is worth quoting at length, as the fundamental Bellow—dream, if not always his secure belief:

> "I have a feeling about the axial lines of life, with respect to which you must be straight or else your existence is merely clownery, hiding tragedy. I must have had a feeling since I was a kid about these axial lines which made me want to have my existence on them, and so I have said 'no' like a stubborn fellow to all my persuaders, just on the obstinacy of my memory of these lines, never entirely clear. But lately I have felt these thrilling lines again. When striving stops, there they are as a gift. I was lying on the couch here before and they suddenly went quivering right straight through me. Truth, love, peace, bounty, usefulness, harmony! And all noise and grates, distortion, chatter, distraction, effort, superfluity, passed off like something unreal. And I believe that any man at any time can come back to these axial lines, even if an unfortunate bastard, if he will be quiet and wait it out. . . . He will be brought into focus. He will live with true joy. Even his pains will be joy if they are true, even his helplessness will not take away his power, even wandering will not take him away from himself, even the big social jokes and hoaxes need not make him ridiculous, even disappointment after disappointment need not take away his love. Death will not be terrible to him if life is not. The embrace of other true people will take away his dread of fast change and short life. And this is not imaginary stuff, Clem, because I bring my entire life to the test."

Doesn't Wordsworth tell us substantially the same thing—that the original, the true self, the self undistorted by noise and chatter and "the big social jokes and hoaxes," is always available to those who cease from striving and let "the affections gently lead" them on? Come back to that self, the poet also tells us, and we come back to the chief realities of the universe, and, "with an eye made quiet by the power/ Of harmony and the deep power of joy,/ We see into the life of things."

Augie goes on having trouble, but he has many joys too, and we leave him at the end still committed to living by feeling, by love, still finding most true among the data of experience what confirms him in his hope, for himself and others. And if reality seems to laugh at him, he laughs back. "Is the laugh at nature," he asks on the last page,"— including eternity—that it thinks it can win over us and the power of hope? Nah, nah! I think. It never will. But that probably is the joke [he concedes at least so much], on one or the other, and laughing is an enigma that includes both."

I am ready to agree with Bellow and some others that the novel is not perfectly satisfactory. Because its author has given himself up too freely to his own ruling ideas and feelings, the novel's flood of vivid life has more variety on its surface than in its depths, its characters often echoing each other, its episodes sometimes seeming only more of the same. Articulation of form—or more simply, plotting—is after all the best way to ensure steady growth in meaning. Then too, as Bellow remarks in the September, 1964, *Show,* Augie is "too effusive and uncritical," too "ingenuous." He is too uncrushable to serve as a fully convincing test of his own ideas. But all this having been granted, I would say myself that Bellow's gamble on his own spontaneous wealth has paid off. The book is, on the whole, irresistibly enjoyable, more full of the world, of people, of wisdom, of beauty, of fun than any dozen novels by his contemporaries. And if Augie is a dream, he is like many dreams, a vehicle for much reality, and, as a storyteller's voice, an attractive and original creation.

The next novel, however, was another leap in an opposite direction—from a Bellow type whose nature rules out disappointment to a "brother" in whom the same tendencies rule out anything else.

In *Seize the Day* Bellow paused, as though parenthetically, in his celebration of the truly human to acknowledge its agonizing disadvantages. It need not surprise us, however, if in the very process of spiraling horribly (and hilariously) downward to despair, his pitiful slob of a hero begins to seem—a hero, precisely, and ends that spiral, though he is sobbing beside a reminder of man's final defeat (a corpse), with a feeling of "consummation." I say it need not surprise us because if being human has its disadvantages, that good which they are the disadvantages of must have a hand in, may even transfigure, all the pain.

Wilky, or Wilhelm Adler, a man of forty-four, good-looking but too distracted even to keep himself clean, is the kind of person who, "after much thought and hesitation . . . invariably took the course he had rejected innumerable times." He had quit college at the lure of a phony movie scout—again the dream of rising out of the anonymous mass, though here seen in its vulgar American form: sudden, easy stardom. He had married and left a woman who was wrong for him, and is now cut off from beloved sons and unable to marry a girl he loves. He had quit a good job out of indignation at a slight. And on this "day of reckoning" which is the novel, he watches in despair how a Dr. Tamkin, a half-literate stock "expert" who also claims to be a psychologist, loses the last of his savings, which, knowing he shouldn't but in crazy hope, he had given him to invest.

He knows his problem. "It isn't the money," he reflects during one of his desperate attempts to get help from his unsympathetic father, "but only the assistance; not even the assistance, but just the feeling. But he may be trying to teach me that a grown man should be cured of such feelings. Feeling got me in dutch at Rojax. I had the *feeling* that I belonged to the firm, and my *feelings* were hurt when they put Gerber in over me." Augie March once spoke of the "sea of feeling" he was struggling in, and this novel is full of water images for feeling's insidiousness and surging power. ("He found himself flowing into another channel." "Like a ball in the surf, his self-control was going out." He is haunted by the phrase "sunk though he be beneath the watery floor," left over from English I, the only college course that still makes sense.)

Now, to say that he is unduly vulnerable to feeling is to say too that he finds unduly difficult those emotion-curbing disciplines by which we keep ourselves safe, we husband and direct our resources. Sure enough, the Others, the successful ones among whom he flounders, are precisely those who are good at such things, who live sensibly, who give (of money, energy, feelings) only what they must, who calculate and save. Wilky's wife is one example of the type. But the main Other is his father.

The retired Dr. Adler, a highly respected, self-respecting, *clean* old man, has helped Wilky as much as seems reasonable. But he is now losing patience with this discreditable failure and slob of a son, who is not only a drain on his pocketbook and his thoughts, but a reminder, by his youth, of the death Dr. Adler can't bear to think about. In a climactic scene, Dostoyevskian in its emotional power, the finally ruined Wilky comes to his father, who is having his cherished body oiled and massaged at the time, in a last appeal for help. Provoked by this extremity of appeal into his own extremity of response, Dr. Adler cries, "You want to make yourself into my cross. But I am not going to pick up a cross. I'll see you dead, Wilky, by Christ, before I let you do that to me!" Wilky goes out, has a last painful phone conversation with his icy wife, and then, rushing off in pursuit of Tamkin, finds himself drawn into a crowded funeral parlor. Looking down at the dead man a moment later, he thinks first of him and next of himself, and at last he is shaken by sobs so violent that a bystander says he must be the dead man's brother. "They're not alike at all. Night and day," someone answers. And then we get, with a final water image, the tale's beautiful and mysterious last paragraph. "The flowers and lights fused ecstatically in Wilhelm's blind, wet eyes; the heavy sea-like music came up to his ears. It poured into him where he had hidden himself in the center of a crowd by the great and happy oblivion of tears. He heard it and sank deeper than sorrow, through torn sobs and cries toward the consummation of his heart's ultimate need."

"They're not alike at all. Night and day." Indeed not, for Wilky is *alive*. Tamkin has helped us to see this—that great comic creation, a smelly pauper, a half-literate, a cheat, an uneasy self-assertor against his own obvious insignificance, and *also* a man of genius and of prophetic eloquence. Tamkin's medical objective is to "bring people into the here and now. The real universe. That's the present moment. The past is no good to us. The future is full of anxiety. Only the present is real—the here and now. Seize the day." And he writes a hilariously illiterate but profound poem for Wilky that describes the rewards awaiting the man who, eluding the tyrannies of crippling ideas, can give himself up to the living moment. It is called "Mechanism VS Functionalism: Ism vs Hism" and its meaning, he explains, is that if you can avoid "mechanism," which destroys, and "have confidence in nature, you would not have to fear. It would keep you up. Creative is nature. Rapid. Lavish. Inspirational. It shapes leaves. It rolls the waters of the earth. Man is the chief of this. All creations are his just inheritance. You don't know what you got within you. A person either creates or destroys. There is no neutrality." Elsewhere, Tamkin has said that the destroyers are those who have allowed the "pretender soul" whose interest is that of the "society mechanism" to enslave in them the "true soul" that "wants to love, go outward, wants truth." As a result, they are full of murderous or suicidal impulses, the two being really one since all murder is the result of a wish to kill the inner pretender who has cheated us.

Wilky, however, is not one of these. "A man like you" says Tamkin, "has trouble, not wanting . . . to exchange an ounce of soul for a pound of social power." Indeed, the force of love in him (he is even moved at the thought of his cold-hearted father) once leads in the subway to a sudden intoxicating sense, like Leventhal's, that the people around him are his brothers and sisters—he blesses them—and though he knows the vision won't last, he clings to it as possibly his most useful clue, "truth, like." And so Tamkin can promise Wilky, "There's hope for you. You don't really want to destroy yourself. You're trying hard to keep your feelings open."

There is, however, one respect in which even this wisdom is a confidence trick. For Tamkin seems to promise that keeping his feelings open is going to *pay*, and that it will lead Wilky out of his troubles to happiness, maybe even to money. But the tale has been whispering something else. Though Wilky shrinks from his troubles, he somehow feels that to lose them would be worse. And once "he received a suggestion from some remote element in his thoughts that the business of life—the real business—to carry his peculiar burden, to feel shame and impotence, to taste these quelled tears—the only important business, the highest business was being done." Another bit of poetry that haunts him is, "Come then, Sorrow . . . / I thought to leave thee,/ And deceive thee,/ But now of all the world/ I love thee best." It is because his "real business" is to remain emotionally alive—that is, to taste, to know completely, at last to exemplify what it is to be a human being—that he has so little talent, or even wish, for self-protective hardening. And because to stay thus "alive" in a world like ours is almost necessarily to suffer, his troubles are his realest triumphs. This is why that experience at the funeral is "the consummation of his heart's ultimate need." Facing now the ultimate human sorrow, and feeling it with a generous fullness which is precisely the opposite of his father's tight, fearful refusal to look, Wilky may be said to have reached the climax of this "day of reckoning"—to have grown most fully alive to the human condition. Father, let this cup pass from me, he may wish, as another wished before him. But like that other again, he is "somehow" aware that for the deepest fulfillment, he must drink that cup to the bottom. This reference to Jesus is not arbitrary. Bellow finds most useful that great exemplar of the human. For when Dr. Adler refuses to take up a *cross* and advises his son to make the same refusal, it is hard not to conclude that this Wilky, who feels and gives himself and suffers, has almost deliberately taken the opposite road. He has become a man of sorrows to be more completely a son of man.

There is something wrong in thus detaching from its living body—if I have, in fact, done so—the mere general meaning of so brilliant, concrete, funny, and passionate a work of art. Let me close then with the reminder that it is such a work, full of the world, full of people, urgent and true in every single stroke, and marvelously accurate in its language, the language of Wilky and of New York and of the feeling heart.

In *Henderson the Rain King* Bellow again tries something different. This time we get a Bellow hero surprisingly free from minority status, and, as it were, peripheral problems. Henderson is not an intellectual or a Jew or a poor boy or a failure. He is a white Anglo-Saxon Protestant, he is a millionaire, he is immensely big and strong. He has everything—just like America. And the beauty of this is that, since he is also a Bellow hero, he is able to demonstrate, in his misery and need, what is lacking when one has "everything" as America has it. He is able to speak for an America facing the main problem. He tells us so himself—and defines the problem—when he has come to know better why he went to Africa.

> Change must be possible! . . . Americans are supposed to be dumb, but they are willing to go into this. It isn't just me. You have to think about white Protestantism and the Constitution and the Civil War and winning the West. All the major tasks and the big conquests were done before my time. That left the biggest problem of all, which was to encounter death. . . . And it's the destiny of my generation of Americans to go out and try to find the wisdom of life.

The wisdom of life is the wisdom that will conquer, if not physical death, then its terror, and its poison, which is the feeling that life is cheap and meaningless.

After the fact, one can see how this conception—that of combining in a single character the Bellow openness of feeling with the power, wealth, and size of America—might have produced the book's delicious peculiarities. (Of course, it takes an author this full of nerve, of zest for the new, of inventiveness.) Bellow would seem to have been led by it to break free of a pedantic realism into a kind of cartoon-like heightening of all effects, into a tale of fantastic adventure. (Talk of men of feeling—Henderson's feeings are so strong a shouting temper of his kills an old lady in the next house. Or talk of suffering—he "is to suffering what Gary is to smoke. One of the world's biggest operations.") Those, however, who complain of Henderson's unreality seem to be operating too simply "by the book." Don Quixote, Parson Adams, My Uncle Toby are also cartoons. In fact, there is hardly a phrase of the excited American lingo in which Henderson tells us his story, not a spasm of his stormy soul, that isn't the hilarious or moving "excess" of a man we recognize.

The first page sets up the central problem. Henderson, a man of fifty-five, tells us he is suffocating under the accumulating facts of his life, and in spite of elegant forebears, feels like a bum because he acts like a bum. It is true, he once saw in a book, "The forgiveness of sins is perpetual and righteousness first is not required," and this promise of a renewal of life and joy as near as his own heart thrills him so that he spends a whole afternoon looking for the sentence in his father's library. But all that comes out of the books, for his spirit's need, is money! The old man used bills as book marks, and as he looks they keep fluttering to the floor.

Though a bum, however, "In my own way I worked very hard. Violent suffering is labor, and often I was drunk before lunch." Why is he suffering? Chiefly because a voice inside him keeps saying, "I want, I want," but doesn't ever say what it wants.[1] However, it is certainly not what he gets: not his wife, for instance, a cold woman whom he married to please his father (she was of his own class) and who repelled him once and for all by laughing when he confessed that he'd like to go back to school and become a doctor like his idols Sir Wilfred Grenfell and Albert Schweitzer; and not his rich man's life of pleasure and pointless activity. Service in World War II, in which he was wounded, was a relief, but after that, because a Jewish buddy spoke of raising minks, Henderson promptly decided to raise pigs—all over his beautiful estate—"which maybe illustrates what I thought of life in general."

All the details, in short, are significant, as well as vivid, lively, funny—for instance, again, his second wife Lily, as American as he in her bigness, and also in her American woman's tendency to idealize and moralize while the dirt out of sight is conveniently ignored: her underwear and her floors are not clean. But this joke on the American idealist is an affectionate one—*she* doesn't laugh when he mentions his medical dream and she becomes a wife truly loved and loving. Still and all, he'd be interning at sixty-three! So the voice goes on tormenting him, he goes on mocking his life with boorishness and violence, and the climax comes when he joins the sensible respectable Others in forcing his teen-age daughter to give up a Negro foundling she wants to keep. "Sweetheart, your daddy did what any daddy would do" is his treasonous plea. Going home on the train he groans, "There is a curse on this land," and when, soon after, that old lady's death reminds him that "the last little room of dirt is waiting," he has to get out—he joins some friends who are taking a trip to Africa.

Henderson goes to Africa in search of his soul ("If I couldn't have my soul, it would cost the earth a catastrophe!") or—he quotes St. Paul—"to leave the body of this death"—and the exciting adventure story that follows, as fantastic and as real as *Gulliver's Travels,* is an account of how he finds what he wants and silences that inner voice. The adventures take place among two tribes, the Arnewi and Wariri, and here too the details, though apparently pure invention for the sake of vividness and fun, turn out to be meaningful as well.

The Arnewi treat cows like brothers and sisters and are akin to cows in their passive submission to fate: when frogs make their water undrinkable during a drought, they do nothing but cry. (Poor Henderson, however, plunging in with his American energy and know-how, blows the cistern up altogether.) It is fitting that their ruler should be a woman, and that this woman's wisdom, for she is very wise, should be better at sensitively registering what our hero is than at helping him to change. "Grun-tu-molani," she tells him, meaning, "You want to live." And the recognition moves Henderson deeply.

But that can only be a first step, for, as Dahfu, king of the Wariri says, "What could be grun-tu-molani on a background of cows?" It is among the warrior tribe of Wariri, and especially as a disciple of their king, a man educated at colonial schools and a Wariri of genius, that Henderson completes his African education. Instead of cows, it is lions they honor, their king having to establish his claim to the throne by capturing bare-handed a lion in whom his late father is reborn. Their rituals not only reenact dangerously an intimacy with death, but also their belief in man's power to shape his fate. *They,* during the drought, take action: they bring rain by manhandling their gods. It is because now only Henderson is strong enough to lift and carry Mummah—he begs for the chance to do something so great—that he becomes their Rain King. And this initiates his relationship with the king, who thereupon attempts to teach Henderson in full consciousness, as one might put it, what the tribal customs impose on the tribe. (Naturally enough, like many great developers of their cultures' implications, Dahfu is hated—and at last killed—by his people.) He invites Henderson to join a lion in a cage, and to imitate the beast's motions and his roar, and he promises that Henderson will thus be set free from his fear of death and lifted to a lion-like nobility of life. This is fantastic, yet the terrified Henderson goes into the cage because Dahfu shows, with a profundity and eloquence that fill him with rapture, that these shenanigans have a meaning far beyond appearances. (Henderson's response here gives us movingly—and comically—the state of spiritual exaltation, the rush and stammer of inspired thought.) Their meaning is pure Blake, though I don't imply that it is any the less heartfelt Bellow.

Dahfu believes that "nature might be a mentality," and that the mind of the human may associate with the All-Intelligent to perform certain work. By "imagination." It is true that "right now this very valuable possession appears to make him [man] die and not live." But this is because he lets himself become a kind of slave, submitting passively, and with increasing misery, to the endless cycle of "fear and desire." "Any good man will try to break the cycle. There is no issue from that cycle for a man who does not take things into his own hands." How? By casting out inhibiting fears, accepting the cues—in lions, for instance—for noble conceptions, and letting these shape our natures and our lives. For, he says, "The career of our species is evidence that one imagination after another grows literal. . . . Birds flew, harpies flew, angels flew. . . . And see here . . . you flew into Africa. All human accomplishment has this same origin, identically. Imagination is a force of nature. . . . It converts to actual. It sustains, it alters, it redeems!"

Henderson can't really go along with the king's faith in animals. Man must go on, he thinks, from the "creature blessing" to a "second blessing." But basically, he feels the king is right. Toward the end he says to his faithful servant Romilayu, "We're supposed to think that nobility is unreal. But that's just it. The illusion is on the other foot. . . . They say, Think Big. Well, that's baloney, of course, another business slogan. But greatness! That's another thing altogether. . . . I don't mean pride or throwing your weight around. But the universe itself being put into us, it calls out for scope. The eternal is bonded onto us. It calls out for its share. This is why guys can't bear to be so cheap." What is imagined can be real. And the greatness we imagine truly belongs to us because "the blue sky" in Wordsworth's language and "the mind of man" are akin.

And so Henderson comes home full of the joyous intention of entering medical school. He may be interning at sixty-three—he may even be dead—but death in life he need no longer fear. And meeting an orphan boy in the plane who seems to him, in Wordsworth's phrase, to be still "trailing clouds of glory" (though his own, he thinks, got dingy, "I always knew what it was"), he runs around the snowy airport cheering the kid up in his arms—love of life and of his fellow men in one closing image.

Again I must say I have sketched only the main ideas: both Henderson and Dahfu have much more to tell us. It is impossible in this space to do justice to the book's wealth of thought, or the vividness, humor, and intensity with which it is all dramatized.

And now, *Herzog*. Is this novel a success? I'm not sure. It did seem for a while that the actual details of a life—people, events, memories, reflections—are given in it with such abandon that they burst free of any controlling intention, and that the only intention which survives is that of plunging into the life's original chaos to see what can be found. But the neatness-loving Henry James called those Russian novels which are the best we have, "great, fluid puddings," and one must beware of making the same mistake. Certainly, the novel does have a rough shape, and a shape which, being large—the shape of a life's development—might well make legitimate the free recording of all in that life that, however obscurely, was *felt* as important. Moreover, every page is alive with such telling realities, responded to with such passion and such far-ranging intellectual brilliance, and set down in language which enacts this man Herzog's moment-by-moment responses so dramatically and so comically, that it is dangerous to open it to check on a quotation: it will be hard to break away from the narrative's immediate hypnotic power. Finally, like the preceding five novels, this one shows an enviably brave artist leaving behind his achieved triumphs and evolving, to express a new state of his inner life, a kind of novel equally new.

As before, Bellow has sought a way to get at once to the heart of matters and to stay there all the time, and he has never managed this so completely. The story is told by flashbacks, memories, but memories leaped to under pressure of immediate excited thought and feeling, so that they have the force of present happenings. And what dramatizes that pressure is chiefly a stream of letters (never to be mailed) which, in a time of nervous collapse, of loss of control over his blazing mind, Herzog feels compelled to write, letters "to the newspapers, to people in public life, to friends and relatives, and at last to the dead, his own dead and finally the famous dead." The letters, and the thoughts which accompany and interrupt them (all centering chiefly around the shattering recent events which constitute the main story line) add up at last to an account of his whole life, both among people and among ideas.

This is new, a way of getting into a novel more of Bellow's world and mind than ever before. But the book is also, inevitably, akin to all the others in the life-substance out of which it is made. And oddly enough, though it is the most ambitious in scope of Bellow's whole career, the novel it most resembles is his first, *Dangling Man*. For this one seems less a tale embodying an achieved insight than the author's own attempt to take stock, to get abreast of a life's confusions, in preparation for novels to come. Here too everything comes to us through the troubled mind of the protagonist, who achieves a reality much richer than that of the other characters. And Moses Elkanah Herzog, is he not Joseph again, though a Joseph whose first name, like his author's, is even more obviously Jewish and Biblical (his last name reminds us of "heart"), and who is twenty years older?

Like Joseph, Herzog is a student of history—a professor and writer of it this time, whose specialty is romanticism; a "throb-hearted" type; a man who, "bucking" the idea that "truth is true only as it brings down disgrace and dreariness on human beings . . . had characteristically, obstinately, defiantly, blindly, but without sufficient courage and intelligence, tried to be a *marvellous* Herzog who, perhaps clumsily, tried to live out marvellous qualities vaguely comprehended"; a man "unrealistic" in his expectations, his life-principle being, as he says, "I love little pussy,/ Her coat is so warm,/ And if I don't hurt her,/ She'll do me no harm," that is, be good and something (he taunts himself once with believing in God) will see that evil will pass you by.

But, as I have said, this is twenty years later and what a beating the man has taken. The opposition is not now a matter of a communist's snubs, a brother's affectionate contempt, tension with a loving young wife, *one* "affair" (short and without consequences), the drabness of Chicago—how idyllic seem the troubles of our youth! It is a horrible load of wounds and losses and shaming errors—two marriages failed and an embarrassing number of other women, amputation from dear children, incredible hatred and treason from people loved (his second wife and her lover, Herzog's intimate friend), sexual humiliation and crippling, the approach of age (he is losing his hair!), a career going bad. It is also—and here is that old Spirit of Alternatives—a lifetime's thought and learning become a wilderness full of destroying ideas: those of the current romanticism, for instance, in which man, disappointed in his dreams, turns to self-mockery and seeks the "inspired condition" in "a philosophy and literature of negation," or in sex, narcotics, crime; or else the ideas implied by our vast scientific and technological developments, which, even when they do good, devalue the tiny individual and make that earlier romanticism Herzog still honors, that preserver of "the most generous ideas of mankind," seem archaic.

But I said the book has a rough shape. Amid the troubles there have been all along hints and promises of something else; and at last Herzog's climactic agony, in which an impulse to kill his second wife and her lover ends, like most of the simple impulses of modern intellectuals, split up by the complicated truth, the lovers untouched and poor Herzog pushed deeper than before into the mud—this agony makes clear to him the woman's hatred and suddenly frees him from his obsession. There follows what can only be, though it is so tentative and, as it were, fevered, the stormy tale's deliberate conclusion. He goes back to his country place in the Berkshires, the abandoned battlefield of that second marriage and in need of repair, but permeated now by the summer's blooming and brightness. He is quivering within with the terribly rich accumulation of his life's thoughts and feelings; and yet, looking over the debris of his life, working in the yard, he feels peace come back to him, cheerfulness. He writes to Ramona (a woman who has "been around" and has pleasantly renewed his sexual joy, but who also timidly loves him and fills him with real tenderness): "Several interesting developments. I hesitate to make too many assertions yet, but at least I can admit what I never stopped asserting, or feeling. The light of truth is never far away, and no human being is too negligible or too corrupt to come to it." (An idea dear to Bellow—remember Augie's "axial lines" and Henderson's "perpetual forgiveness" even without "righteousness.") He writes to a fellow historian, rejecting once and for all the modern tendency to make an ideology out of suffering. Then, after a visit from his worried brother Will—Herzog, in his peculiar state, must fight tears at Will's quiet love for him, and at his own answering love— and while waiting for Ramona to come to dinner, he faces up to the problem of his peculiar "happiness":

> There are those who say this product of hearts is knowledge. . . . I couldn't say that, for sure. My face too blind, my mind too limited, my instincts too narrow. But this intensity, doesn't it mean anything? Is it an idiot joy that makes this animal, the most peculiar animal of all, exclaim something? And he thinks this reaction a sign, a proof of eternity? And he has it in his breast? But I have no arguments to make about it. "Thou movest me." "But what do you want, Herzog?" "But that's just it—not a solitary thing. I am pretty well satisfied to be, to be just as it is willed, and for as long as I may remain in occupancy."

And as the book ends, he ceases to write letters. He has no further messages for anyone.

This is very modest. It is not an idea. Herzog-Bellow's forty-seven turbulent years have chastened his proud hope of answering back the time's dispiriting ideologies with an ideology more clever. The religious might say he has found salvation—grace—in submission to the unfathomable will of God. Our author cannot quite say this. He is satisfied for the moment, with—bedrock, the given; that is, with the world's enduring beauty and the human heart's phoenix-like vitality, which, after all the storms, if life remains at all, renews itself in simple morning hope and joy. And that, I take it, is the point: to show how a man thus richly equipped to suffer and understand the problem of being human is driven past all illusory consolations, deeper than reason, to the original, the inexhaustible source of the energy by which we live.

There is an element in *Herzog* not yet mentioned, however, which seems to me to reveal the secret of its author's whole career, and of his obsessive recurrence to the great romantics. What this element reveals is that Bellow has been drawn to English romanticism because it gave expression to a faith he had acquired long before he read Wordsworth and Blake. A fine passage in Ignazio Silone's contribution to *The God That Failed* will suggest—and support—what I mean. He tells us that his latest faith in socialism, "in its essence," is "a refusal to admit the existence of destiny, an extension of the ethical impulse from the restricted individual and family sphere to the whole domain of human activity."

And he indicates what comes from, or at least goes with, that family-born impulse to shape one's life toward the good: "A need for brotherhood, an affirmation of the human person over all the economic and social mechanisms which oppress him . . . an intuition of man's dignity and a feeling of reverence for that which in man is always trying to outdistance itself." This, of course, is precisely Bellow's faith, though he is not political and does not speak of socialism, and its origin is precisely the same. All of Bellow's work is a stubborn declaration of allegiance, in the face of the pressures of grown-up twentieth-century cleverness, to his "restricted and individual family sphere"—that is, to the Jewish home in which his life began. Herzog speaks of "my (Jewish) mind" resisting the loss of "all considerations based on value." He suggests that it is education in moral principles of the "Jewish boy" that modern life is making obsolete. Writing indignantly to a Shapiro who has repeated "the cant and rant of pipsqueaks about Inauthenticity and Forlornness," he reminds him of his origins: "You are too intelligent for this. You inherited rich blood. Your father peddled apples." But plainest of all, there is the evidence of his thrilled memories of his Orthodox Jewish home in the Canadian ghetto, of his parents, and his cry, "Whom did I ever love as I loved them?"[2] What English romanticism says—at least at its deep human core—is what the Jewish mother and father feel in their bones and turn into the atmosphere their children breathe. (*The* Jewish mother and father? Very well: his kind, a kind happily not rare—it is also mine—and, as we are shown by Sholom Aleichem, the great living voice of central European Jews, it is the most characteristic.) In that home, Herzog-Bellow learned that feelings matter, that we should love and be good to each other, that the child is dear and precious—a *zisse neshumeleh* ("a sweet little soul"), as Herzog, only half mocking, remembers he was called—its pain a pity, its happiness a deserved blessing, its future full of golden promise. The ideas out of which all his novels come—the beliefs, now securely affirmed, now desperately struggled for—are those. This is why his characters are so full of feeling and of love—love of parents and children and brothers and friends, of women as objects of tenderness more than desire, and finally, of the self and its dearest hopes, a family-nourished love of the self which the adult Bellow refuses to yield to the belittling of modern psychology and modern culture. Indeed, is not his very style, that immediate expression of his originality, the style of—a boy on the block (that is, of the neighborhood), a boy who has read whole libraries, it's true, and knows all the big words, but who would be hurt to think himself cut off from his family, from the other guys on the block: in short, from that life of natural feeling which most of us tend—and even seek—to leave behind as we grow up?

Now it must be granted at once that the children of such loving Jewish homes are sometimes what is called "spoiled," that is, too soft and demanding and self-regarding to cope with harsh life. And not only has romanticism been so rebuked—and wisely rebuked—by stern adults like the elder Goethe, Irving Babbit, T. S. Eliot; this is the criticism which Bellow's irony is always directing at his own heroes. But what if that is true? If such critics are often right, isn't it also right that a life in which the soft, demanding, self-regarding child has been utterly silenced is a life hardly worth living, a life dehumanized? This, at any rate, is what Bellow's six novels have all been saying. And it is because he has had the talent and the nerve to bring us back, in his way, as the romantics did in theirs, to our heart's secret original home, to that time of "open" feeling, of love, and of faith in ourselves and in life, that Bellow is unique among our novelists. That is why he deserves what this reader has already confessed to feeling: gratitude.

A seventh Bellow novel, *Mr. Sammler's Planet,* appeared in 1970. And if his first six novels recall the attitudes of the great romantics, one way to get at what is new in *Mr. Sammler's Planet* might be to say that in it those attitudes seem, at first glance, to have been abandoned. The book seems to be, in large part, an attack on a generation of Americans which was trying to stay "alive" in Bellow's own sense of the word—to have a separate destiny, to be marvelous, just as his former heroes had done. One heard the complaint that the book was ungenerous and reactionary.

The fact is, however, Bellow did something far more interesting in *Mr. Sammler's Planet* than reverse himself. He had, it's true, moved from where he used to be; instead of the predictable repetition of old stances to which novelists incapable of growth tend to sink, he had sought, with unusual directness, to give expression to the new experience of a new time. But the changes in emphasis which this novel dramatized were changes required for Bellow to remain loyal, in the new time, to what had mattered most to him from the start. For though the rebellious young of the 60s were indeed loud in proclaiming his own view that each individual is precious and deserves a chance for rich fulfillments, it's an old story that a good cause may be in danger from its own champions. And what Bellow was now showing was that the current ways of asserting that belief were actually, for reasons that lay deep in the recent development of Western culture, ways of caricaturing it, vulgarizing it. To be sure, this is the work of a middle-aged man, and one whose protagonist-spokesman is even older, a man in his seventies. But it doesn't have to follow after all that it must therefore be less in touch with reality than the work of his youth. The distinction of *Mr. Sammler's Planet* is precisely that it is an embodiment, beautifully adequate to its subject, of the wisdom of Bellow's middle age.

To offer this new perspective, and to judge from it the new time, Bellow created a protagonist different from his others, as well as like them, in appropriate ways. Artur Sammler is a Polish Jew who was spoiled by well-to-do parents as a child, and who, as a young man, fell in love with English reasonableness and good manners (he was a friend of H. G. Wells)—in short, he was shaped, like earlier Bellow heroes, to expect good things of himself and others. But later there came a moment when he crawled naked and half blinded out of a mass grave of Nazi victims, leaving there the corpse of his wife. And soon after this he, in his turn, killed a German soldier he had disarmed and stripped—killed him deliberately, and with intense pleasure. For the rest of his life Sammler struggles against the message then delivered to him, "that reality was a terrible thing, and the final truth about mankind overwhelming and crushing."

It is a message renewed again and again, not only among the bloated corpses Sammler saw as an elderly journalist in the Sinai desert in 1967, but equally on New York's upper Broadway, where it seems "the implicit local orthodoxy." But he fights it. Mainly it is for him "a vulgar and cowardly conclusion, rejected . . . with all his heart." Now he is living in New York on the charity of a nephew who is a rich doctor, uncomfortable at what he sees around him, but hesitant to judge, increasingly fed up with "explanations"—to make "distinctions" is what he prefers—his favorite reading the work of Meister Eckhart, the medieval German mystic for whom the comfort of God requires that we abandon the false comfort offered us by His creatures. Yet others keep turning to Sammler as himself a source of mysterious comfort (even while his old-fashioned good manners make them smile): he remains hopelessly involved, through love as well as duty, with those same creatures. And the private vocation he has turned to in the leisure of old age is the search for "short views," a phrase of Sidney Smith's which, as Sammler uses it, generally means condensed conclusions about "some essence of experience," and which keeps recurring as the new hunger of his mind.

Sammler's, then, was the ripest intelligence Bellow had yet invented, a man educated not only by books, for he has learned at first hand the chief lessons of our time. And though the novel resembles *Herzog* in that its story comes to us entirely through its hero's idiosyncratic Jewish responses, and his wide-ranging memories and reflections, what makes it quite different is that it is actually just the sort of "condensation" a Mr. Sammler would have ordered. Actions, memories, reflections are not here an image of the turbulence of life, but always in league with each other and building forward, each of the six chapters clearly a unit in a theme's development. The story is, in fact, an account of a series of confrontations between the elderly humanist and a group of characters chosen to represent the Zeitgeist of the 60s. And these confrontations are given increasing urgency and point by a classic philosophic challenge that soon begins to haunt them all—that is, by Sammler's need, as the tale moves to its climax, to find some "word" for his dying nephew that might oppose the negation of death. The nephew, rich in part with Mafia abortion money, has been no angel. But Sammler recognizes in him a man "assigned" to feel, and especially to feel kinship—to reach out, please, help, as if the world were a family. And for this he loves him.

There is, first of all, to represent the new sexual morality, the dying man's daughter Angela, who has been set free by her beauty and her father's wealth for a "Roman" paganism of sexual behavior. *She* calls "perverse" not the "erotic business in Acapulco" that occurred when she and her fiancé played switch with some beach acquaintances, but his sudden jealousy afterward. Her brother Wallace is equally familiar—a "high I.Q. moron," who "finds out how to put things together . . . as he goes along," as in "action-painting," and whose one persistent motive seems to be to show his father that he can make it on his own, and that he can't—for his brilliant beginnings always end in failure that looks deliberately courted. Wallace's resemblance to Augie March, who also refused to let himself be pinned down or to risk, by accepting some limiting job or function, "a disappointed life," is symptomatic of Bellow's changed perspective. Augie, though he had his troubles, also had his author's sympathy. Wallace, unwilling to accept limits or models of being imposed by others, and yet incapable of respecting for long those chosen by himself, is clearly a failure and a waste.

Then there are two representatives of popular culture. One is the Columbia University student Feffer, who, for purposes of his own, cons Mr. Sammler into lecturing on Bloomsbury to a Columbia crowd gathered to hear about Sorel on violence, an affair that ends in a kind of explosion that became common during this period: a "thick-bearded, but possibly young" member of the New Left, offended by an irony quoted from Orwell, stops the lecture with shouts of "Hey! Old man! . . . That's a lot of shit!" and some remarks about Sammler's "dry balls." The second is Sammler's son-in-law Eisen, an Israeli avant-garde painter and sculptor. As Feffer turns chic ideas and liberal sentiments into ways of "making it," Eisen exploits the period's intimacy with terror. Not only does he paint living people as corpses, giving, by this gimmick of a death-oriented outrageousness, a hectic pseudo-potency to creative impotence. He also crushes skulls, when it seems reasonable to do so, without any crippling tremors of doubt or remorse. "You were a Partisan," he says, when the old man, in a scene I will sketch in a moment, protests in horror that he might have gained his end less bloodily. "You had a gun. So don't you know? . . . If in—in. No? If out—out. Yes? No? So answer." In Eisen, the traditional allegiances of both Jew and artist—to life, to man—have been abandoned. And he now goes after personal development and distinction—an American *"karyera"*—with the greedy single-mindedness of the ethically "liberated."

The book is strewn with Mr. Sammler's reflections on what these disheartening confrontations suggest—on the "individuality boom" that has resulted from the increase of freedom and the dread of "future-lessness"; on the drive to be "real" that has merely replaced traditional human models with "dime-store" models out of recent literature and Hollywood; on the resort to madness in order to demonstrate availability for "higher purposes," which purposes "do not necessarily appear"; on the "non-negotiable" demands for instant gratification made by people who, refusing to admit any limitations on the possible, are doomed to humiliating misery and dangerous rages. But the opening chapter's presentation of what is happening to Mr. Sammler's planet is completed by the introduction of two characters who, though they also represent the new age, are types of the human he can respect. First, there is a tall, gorgeously dressed black pickpocket. Having caught Sammler watching him in action, the pickpocket follows the frightened old man into his hotel lobby, presses him to a wall, and displays, in significant silence, his massive penis. Immediately after this warning, Sammler finds in his room a manuscript work on "The Future of the Moon," stolen for him by his half-mad daughter from an Indian scientist, Dr. V. Govinda Lal. Reading its first line, "How long will this earth remain the only home of man?" he closes the chapter with the inner cry, "How long? Oh Lord, you bet! Wasn't it the time—the very hour to go? . . . To blow this great blue, white, green planet, or to be blown from it."

The values represented by the black man—lawlessness, sexual potency, self-delight—may well have influenced mid-twentieth-century youth. But as the story proceeds, Sammler becomes aware that he is, in fact, like Sammler himself, an outsider and the new generation's victim. The pickpocket stole because "he took the slackness of the world for granted." Pumalike, *eine Natur* (Goethe's respectful phrase), he was mad, if at all, "with an idea of noblesse." Indeed, Feffer, hearing about him, is thrilled, as by a "sudden glory." But Feffer's response to the "glory" is to photograph the thief in action for magazine exploitation.

And when the black struggles with him for the camera and Sammler asks Eisen to help, that new-type Jewish artist coolly smashes the black's face with a bag of his crazy sculpture. It is the black who gets Sammler's passionate sympathy, the others his horrified rage.

As for Lal, Bellow has created in him a genuinely brilliant man of science, and, improbable though it may seem, the twenty-nine pages of philosophic dialogue which follow his meeting with Sammler are a moving and exciting fictional climax. (And yet why so improbable? For such men to meet, recognize each other's quality, and, winning over the normal inner and outer obstacles, share their deepest thought can be an experience as thrilling as love.) Lal, for whom nature, "more than an engineer, is an artist," is no mere opposite to Sammler; yet they differ on one point that relates to the novel's center. Lal is ready to call it quits on man's long struggle to make a home on this planet. For him space travel is not only the inevitable next step demanded by the human imagination. As an Indian, "super-sensitive to a surplus of humanity"—that is, already familiar with the future—he believes that refusal to make the voyages elsewhere which are growing possible would turn this crowded planet into a prison, and bring the human species, now "eating itself up," closer than ever to leaping into Kingdom Come. Moreover, amid the rigors of space and under the leadership of technicians endowed with their own kind of nobility, he believes that man may yet be disciplined into recovering lost virtues.

Sammler's response is no simple disagreement. In fact, much of what he says is an anguished attempt to understand what has caused "the shrinking scope for the great powers of nature in the individual, the abundant and generous powers." But he feels that there is "also an instinct against leaping into Kingdom Come. . . . The spirit knows that its continued growth is the real end of existence." And crowded and disappointing though it is, his own planet is still, for him, a home he cannot give up. Why not? His answer to this question—what he has to offer instead of that leap into space or Kingdom Come—constitutes the point of the book.

Mainly, of course, the answer is himself. But, as I have suggested, it is dramatized in his struggle to find some "word" which will comfort his nephew in the hour of his death. The struggle is real, its desperateness is genuinely evoked, especially in the mounting excitement that precedes the end: in that scene of blood when Eisen's killer-reasoning "sinks his heart," and then in his final confrontation in the hospital with Dr. Gruner's sexy daughter. Risking her rage, he tries to get Angela to put aside for once her own demands and grievances, to go to her father, say something, make some gesture, at least, that will show she is sorry her behavior, of which he has heard, has caused him pain.

But Angela, bold enough in other areas, naturally recoils from a scene so "hokey." ("You want an old-time deathbed scene . . . . But how could I—it goes against everything. You're talking to the wrong person. . . . What is there to say?") A few minutes later Sammler himself, standing alone beside his nephew's body, utters his "word" in the silent heartbroken prayer that ends the novel:

> Remember, God [Sammler prays], the soul of Elya Gruner, who, as willingly as possible and as well as he was able, and even in suffocation and even as death was coming, was eager, even childishly perhaps . . . to do what was required of him. At his best this man was much kinder than I at my very best have ever been or could ever be. He was aware that he must meet, and he did meet—through all the confusion and degraded clowning of this life through which we are now speeding—he did meet the terms of his contract. The terms which, in his inmost heart, every man knows. As I know mine. As all know. For that is the truth of it—that we all know, God, that we know, we know, we know.

Here, then, is the new emphasis to which Bellow has been led by the new age (and his own new age). The mere assertion of individuality, the "non-negotiable" demand for one's own way, the leaps to ecstasy or "significance" that bypass duties and commitments to others—such behavior debases the self it seeks to glorify. It is only by loyalty to the "human bond," to the "contract" implicit in our humanity, that we can safeguard our sense of the self's value.

Indeed, as Sammler becomes aware during a moment of horror, to find oneself with *no other* to turn to in a time of need is "death," is to be "not himself. . . . Someone between the human and non-human states, between content and void, meaning and not-meaning, between this world and no world. Flying, freed from gravitation, light with release and dread, doubting his destination, fearing there was nothing to receive him." For Sammler, a man who believes in God, even our sense of ultimate destinations and receptions depends on that "contract." The term implies a faith not merely in the fact of a "human bond," but also in our obligation to create it for each other. By looks, by signs, by words, we make this planet a home for each other, we make a web of relationships and meanings that reach even beyond the individual life and reduce even the terror of the unknown future.

But if Bellow has tried to body forth the idea of a "contract," he also makes clear that idea's terrible vulnerability. For Sammler, the young who cry "Shit!" to their elders do have a case. He is aware, for instance, that the old attitudes toward sex were not a success and that Angela's sexuality may well, as she cleverly observes, be the fulfillment of her father's repressed wishes. Even Eisen's killer-reasoning was once—or so it seemed—Sammler's own.

The truth is that Sammler's final "word" is no comfortable triumph. At best, it is a battle won in a war that will never end. Or more exactly, it is an assertion of faith, and faith is half the mere will that things be so and so, asserted against the undying possibility that they may not be. But—we don't know everything. To swallow current "explanations" as the whole truth is to submit needlessly to ignoble reduction. There is in life an inexhaustible wealth of possibilities, and therefore freedom. In that freedom intuitions of decency may be entitled to respect. (Bellow had already said something like this in *The Victim*. "Choose dignity," declared the sage Schlossberg. "Nobody knows enough to turn it down.") If nothing in culture is born out of unmixed conditions or causes, yet graces do emerge out of the mixture, ideas of human decency which, though they may be "compromised," may also be our chief safeguards against the brutes. To spit on such ideas in all relations because they have been alibis for evil in some may be itself a brute's way of justifying brutishness.

The novel has been called one-sided, its cast of characters not fully representative. There is some truth in this. We need other views of that time to place beside Bellow's. And yet the fact that there is more to say surely does not invalidate a work that attempts to describe a salient tendency. No novelist need be required to report everything. Moreover, since the intellectuals' consensus of the moment was all on the side of the "idealistic," demanding young, it was good to have around a man like Bellow, for whom, as for his Sammler, "the place of honor is outside." Who but the outsider in any age is likely to expose what its fashionable idealism conceals?

Once again, however, the study of a novel's meanings only partly accounts for its power. And the question of artistic power has a special interest with regard to this writer's work because he would seem to be laboring under a handicap. Saul Bellow is preeminently the novelist of man-in-culture, man swimming in an ocean of ideas in which he often feels near to being swamped ("There are times, states," thinks Sammler, "in which one lies under and feels the awful weight of cumulative consciousness. . . . Not at all funny"); and in art, as we are often told, ideas can be deadening. Yet the odd fact is that in Bellow's work the ideas are themselves a source of fictional vitality: they are part of the fun and the feeling. There are several reasons for this. One is that Bellow has a gift, reminiscent of Wordsworth, for evoking in his sentence rhythms, as well as in his words, the *experience* of thought, the drama of its emergence out of the life of the whole man. Another, related to the first, is that the experience of thought rises in his novels out of a thickly detailed physical world that both provokes it and helps give it expression. Then, even more important, Bellow is the kind of writer who knows, as Sammler puts it, "Once take a stand, draw a baseline, and contraries assail you. . . . All positions are mocked by their opposites." The ideas which underlie his characters and plots are, therefore, more likely to safeguard than to violate the mysteries of reality.

But there is a deeper reason for the emotional power of Bellow's thought, and for the uniquely intimate response he elicits from some of us. It is that he is concerned above all with *man*-in-culture, man swimming for his life among ideas, wincing at or delighting in them, and challenging them always to answer the naïve, irrepressible demands of the feeling heart. He carries amid the richest complexities of modern consciousness the claims and standards of our ordinary humanity. And from this concern *Mr. Sammler's Planet* is not a departure in the least. Far from contradicting the six earlier novels, it clearly joins them as a beautiful defense of that ordinary humanity against all the bogus idealism, as well as the frank savagery, that so often reject it as "corn."

Finally, to complete this survey of Bellow's novels, I add a word on his latest, *Humboldt's Gift* (1975).

The Humboldt of the title is the grandiloquently named poet Von Humboldt Fleisher, and the novel is based, as the news media have abundantly noted, on the contrast between the career of Bellow's friend Delmore Schwartz, the poet with the oddly fancy name, who started out so brilliantly in the thirties and then declined into creative impotence and paranoia and died a pauper in a cheap hotel, and that of Bellow himself, who achieved all the fame and money both had dreamed of. But the story's enjoyable gossip is not really its point. With the help of a good deal of comic invention, a meaningful arrangement of episodes, and the philosophic reflections that fill the friends' remembered talk and, even more, the remembering and ruminating mind of Charles Citrine (who tells their story), autobiography has become in this novel as much the embodiment of a theme as were the fantastic adventures of Henderson in Africa. Moreover, Bellow's *oeuvre* remains what it has been, a kind of model of living development, his novels both alike and different, like a human being getting older. In this novel too he has explored his permanent subject—the battle to stay "alive"— from the perspective of the latest stage of his life's journey.

Citrine is another version of the Bellow-hero, that is, a "throb-hearted," nobility-seeking type, whose spiritual quest is always being undermined by his behavior and mocked by "realistic" friends and enemies and his own ironical self-criticism. (He even has again a rich, much-loved tycoon of a brother, who scorns the inner life, though he feels for it a hidden hunger.) We meet Citrine working, in defiance of commercial good sense, on a study of boredom. And though this literary project begins by looking comically eccentric, its real meaning turns out to be just what we would expect of the Bellow-hero as writer—it is a study of the power of the time's fashionable ideas to take over our minds and estrange us from heartfelt intuitions and our true life. Moreover, Citrine's ambition as a writer also stamps him a Bellow-hero: it is "to go far, far beyond fellow intellectuals of my generation, who have lost the imaginative soul, and to tackle the main question about which nothing has been done . . . the death question."

But amid so much that is familiar, there are two things that are new. One is that the story is now about the protagonist's struggle with the ironies and distractions of a resounding American success, the swarm of parasites (some of them tempting women) who are after his money and his prestige making for much of the fun. So, we see him embroiled with a petty Chicago gangster who, after cheating him at cards, feels called on to educate the famous writer in real life: or being legally robbed by his ex-wife and her lawyers, with the help of a judge who shares their view that the big success ought to be made to pay up; or enticed away from his intellectual battle against death by the gorgeous sexual artist Renata, who wants to be Mrs. Citrine. (Renata, finding she can't get Citrine to stay with her in her world, runs off with a man whose occupation is comically allegorical—he is a high-powered undertaker who thrives on death—and since Bellow's characters often express, as well as enact, what they represent, she explains in her funny, richly knowing farewell letter what keeps them apart: "I live in nature. And I think that when you're dead you're dead.") The other novelty is that the Bellow hero is now pushing sixty. This means that the death-problem he is tackling is not merely death-in-life, but the death Renata bases her own views on, the kind which lands us in the grave. And for this problem, he seeks guidance from predecessors more extreme than the romantic poets—from the antimaterialist Rudolph Steiner and perhaps also Dostoevsky.

The trouble with American culture for Citrine is that "to accept the finality of death was part of the package," whereas "against all the assumptions of the Zeitgeist," his own sense of reality compels him to postulate "a core of the eternal in every human being." Further, he finds that "to assume, however queerly, the immortality of the soul" is necessary to enable us "to attempt the good without feeling the embarrassment of being unhistorical, illogical, masochistically passive, feebleminded." This sounds like Dostoevsky, whose Stepan Trofimovich says for his author at the end of *The Possessed*, "The infinite and the Eternal are as essential to man as the little planet on which he dwells," and whose Ivan Karamazov thinks that without a belief in immortality, "egoism even unto crime" becomes "inevitable" and "most rational." As for Steiner, Citrine's battle against the Zeitgeist is conducted mainly in meditations on Steiner's anthroposophy, which is, among other things, an account of the relationship of the souls of the dead to those of the living. Citrine admits that such notions seem like "lunacy," but his next thought is that "This is poetry . . . a great vision." One is reminded of Dahfu and his lions, also "absurd" and also a springboard to ways of thinking more in harmony with human needs than those of contemporary "educated society," which (Citrine tells us) "was something I had come to despise with all my heart." And though we may smile at Citrine's (or Steiner's) extravagances, there is nothing comic about the idea at their center—that we and the universe are somehow more than the sum of any parts our knowledge will ever be able to name, a more that the old concepts of "soul" and "God" helped us relate to, and that to deny this diminishes and cripples us.

As the real Bellow becomes in this novel the Bellow hero, so his old friend Schwartz also becomes an element in the permanent Bellow story. Like Dahfu, the poet is a champion of the imagination, and his role is "to drape the world in radiance." In the words of his last letter to Citrine, he was one who "intended to be a divine artist, a man of visionary states, enchantment, to prove the imagination was just as potent as machinery, to free and bless mankind." Though he ends by leaving Citrine a literal legacy, the gift referred to in the title is therefore first of all the gift of imagination, the power which, in one of Citrine's many accounts of it, can have "its own full and free connection with the universe—the universe as Goethe spoke of it . . . as the living garment of God." And the poet's terrible decline is seen as due to the fashionable culture Bellow has always opposed and now opposes with a new audacity because of the higher stakes—an immortal soul—he is fighting for. Humboldt loses his gift because "he was also out to be rich and famous," and because he thought the way to such success was the way of contemporary intellectual respectability. "Humboldt had become boring," Citrine reflects, "in the vesture of a superior person, in the style of high culture, with all his conforming abstractions. . . . A terrible breed, the educated nits, the mental bores of the highest caliber. . . . Poor Humboldt! What a mistake!" And more definitely, "Humboldt was overawed by rational orthodoxy, and because he was a poet this probably killed him."

Thus Citrine is obsessed with his dead friend because for all the paranoid revenge Humboldt took on him for his success (whence much of the novel's gruesome comedy), he sees the poet as a fallen warrior in his own cause, a cause he must go on serving for both of them. And he finds to his delight that Humboldt shared his view when he gets the farewell letter that constitutes the other, the literal gift referred to in the title. Written in a time of return, before death, of the poet's lucid best self, it contains, in fact, two important bequests. One is a film scenario which is based on Citrine and which tells how a writer's passion to publish a story of his great love results in the betrayal of that love and, while he achieves success, the loss of his talent. This scenario, in addition to its value as a warning, gives the novel its happy ending, for what it earns for Citrine (impoverished by his parasites) sets him free to go on with his spiritual researches. But it is the second bequest that moves Citrine most intensely—it is Humboldt's confirmation of the underlying idea of those researches in his final sentence: "Last of all, remember: We are not natural beings but supernatural beings." At the novel's end, that money, shared with Humboldt's old uncle, enables them to give the poet the proper burial his pauper's death had denied him, and as they leave the cemetery some early crocuses they notice announce the return of spring—with all that this suggests.

I confess that on a first reading of the novel I felt that my pleasure in the way Bellow writes—about anything—was seducing me to overlook the failure of Citrine's ideas to get dramatized in the story. There is the lively crowded comedy of the writer's struggle to escape from his enemies, to take comfort from friends, and, above all, to reach the sexual haven of Renata on their trip to Europe (where, in fact, he loses her and settles into old age)—and then there are his interrupting meditations on Humboldt and Steiner. But on a second reading—when I enjoyed the novel more, not less—the very irrelevance of Citrine's passionate reflections seemed to me their way of being relevant. For they have the dramatic character of a *recoil*, a recoil from the chaos and jungle warfare of his ordinary life into that world of thought (or "the spirit") which for "supernatural beings" is equally real and where "the True, the Good, and the Beautiful," as Citrine names them without irony, are not delusions of the naïve.

It no doubt remains true that for me the way Bellow writes redeems what I might complain of in others. But it does so because, in spite of his marvelous descriptive powers, he is after all not a conventional novelist whose chief aim is to get down accurately some chosen segment of the world. He is a writer whose specialty is wisdom, that is, intelligence and culture in the service of life—for more evidence of this, see his essays "Culture Now: Some Animadversions, Some Laughs," *Modern Occasions* (Winter 1971); "A World Too Much with Us," *Critical Inquiry* (Fall 1975); and "The Nobel Lecture," *American*

Scholar (Summer 1977). The result in his case is not only that his fiction keeps moving toward the comic extravagance of the illuminating cartoon, but that his own reflections are a chief source of his effects. More present to us than any character is the voice of Saul Bellow—in that remarkable style, which gets its quality precisely from the fact that he has turned himself loose to express his mind directly in all its flavorsome individuality, wit, poetry, and intellectual wealth, and, in particular, to enact his search for wisdom and to tell us what he finds.

What he mainly finds is that those "most generous ideas of mankind" are still relevant to the human condition. And, as these remarks have been suggesting, his work delights us in large part because in it those ideas are reborn in our own language and bring flashes of their old radiance into his twentieth-century version—our version—of man's sad and funny life.

Notes

Introduction

1. For a discussion of how, in the work of a seminal contemporary critic, this resistance to "professionalism" is related to teaching, see my essay review of Lionel Trilling's textbook *The Experience of Literature*, *College English*, November, 1967, pp. 160–68.

2. Here is Isaiah Berlin's distinction between intelligence and expertise in his fine introduction to Alexander Herzen's *My Past and Thoughts*: "He believed in reason, scientific methods, individual action, empirically discovered truths; but he tended to suspect that faith in general formulae, laws, prescriptions in human affairs was an attempt, sometimes catastrophic, always irrational, to escape from the uncertainty and unpredictable variety of life to the false security of our own symmetrical fantasies."

Goethe's *Wilhelm Meister's Apprenticeship*

1. I have used Thomas Carlyle's translation, which is accurate if a bit old-fashioned, except in several places where R. D. Boylan's is superior. Since editions differ, I am indicating the book and chapter from which quotations are made, rather than the page.

2. André Gide's debt to Goethe, which is also an affinity with him, will be touched on below. It is therefore worth mentioning here that this state of Wilhelm's is exactly the state dramatized by the labyrinth in Gide's *Theseus*, a place where seminarcotic vapors put the will to sleep, "induce a delicious intoxication, rich in flattering delusions, and provoke the mind, filled as this is with voluptuous mirages, to a certain pointless activity; 'pointless' . . . because it has merely an imaginary outcome, in visions and speculations without order, logic or substance" (Ch. 7). Both heroes, in short, face at the outset of their careers the trap of undisciplined self-indulgence.

3. Quoted by Thomas Mann in "Goethe and Tolstoy," *Essays of Three Decades* (New York, 1947), p. 159.

4. Boylan's translation, but with his "expose themselves to thoughtless or intentional danger" corrected.

5. In Bk. II, Ch. 8, Mignon moves Wilhelm deeply with a strange dance. She places a small carpet on the floor and four candles in each of its corners. In a pattern on the carpet, she places a number of eggs. Then, blindfolding herself, she dances to a violin, never leaving the carpet and never touching an egg. Her movements, "continuous as the motion of a clock," are "exact, precise and reserved, but vehement, and in situations where tenderness was to be displayed, more formal than attractive," yet Wilhelm saw with surprise "how remarkably the dance tended to unfold her character." All he had ever felt for her rose up in him. "He longed to take this forsaken child to his heart, to hold her in his embrace, and with the fulness of a father's love to awaken within her bosom all the joys of existence" (Boylan). Is not this dance the "dance" of classical art, where the

personal expresses itself through the formal rather than in defiance of it? And does not the last sentence quoted express Goethe's own desire to give existence to an art of such a kind?

6. Boylan's translation. Both he and Carlyle, however, call the aunt's nature "lovely," whereas Goethe says *liebevolle*, "loving."

7. Well may Gide have said that Goethe's was the one influence he had undergone. Are not all Gide's major themes to be found in this book: his criticism of Christian self-denial, as in *Strait Is the Gate*, and of self-indulgence, as in *The Immoralist*, and, finally, the rich compromise between them of *The Counterfeiters*? I have come to suspect, indeed, that this last novel represents a deliberate attempt to write a *Wilhelm Meister's Apprenticeship* for the twentieth century. In Gide's great novel too, the young hero seeks to learn how to live, and seeks amid interpretations of experience which perpetually vary in validity. Gide's novel too, in short, dramatizes its author's own struggle to understand his material, which is the course of life. But the German novel is the greater, both in quantity and quality.

Goethe's *Elective Affinities*

1. Letter to Charlotte von Stein, 25 June 1786, quoted in Ludwig Lewisohn, *Goethe: The Story of a Man* (New York, 1949), II, 307, Recollection of Benjamin Constant in Lewisohn, II, 96.

2. *Conversations of Goethe with Eckermann*, trans. John Oxenford (London, 1930), p. 305.

3. *Elective Affinities*, trans. Louise Bogan and Elizabeth Mayer (Chicago, 1963), Bk. I, Ch. 4. This is the best translation I have seen, though in this study I will make certain corrections in it. In the Bogan-Mayer translation, chapters are numbered consecutively rather than divided into two books of 18 chapters each, as Goethe intended. I restore Goethe's arrangement for more convenient location of sources.

4. *Elective Affinities*, Bk. II, Ch. 15. Bogan and Mayer, for some reason, omit the important word "striving," though Goethe here wrote *"aber immer nach seiner Sinnesweise hoffend und strebend."* In resorting to the original German, I have been helped throughout by my colleage Professor Lynn Dhority, German Department, University of Massachusetts—Boston.

5. In a letter to J. S. Zauper, 7 December 1821.

6. Heinrich Henel.

7. Thomas Mann, "Fantasy on Goethe," in *Last Essays* (New York, 1959), p. 128.

Dostoevsky's *The Brothers Karamazov*

1. F. M. Dostoevsky, *The Brothers Karamazov*, trans. Contance Garnett, rev. ed., ed. Ralph E. Matlaw (New York: Norton, 1976), pp. 759–60. All quotations from the novel are from this edition, but since such quotations are numerous and are easily located, I will hereafter give the page numbers only of quotations from the letters and *Notebooks*, and give them without footnotes, in the text.

2. Nikolai Gogol, "The Overcoat," in *The Diary of a Madman and Other Stories*, trans. Andrew R. MacAndrew (New York: New American Library, 1960), p. 70.

3. Joseph Frank in his *Dostoevsky: The Seeds of Revolt 1821–1849* (Princeton: Princeton University Press, 1976), p. 86, tells us in a footnote added as his book went to press that new material just then brought to light suggests that the father was not murdered at

all, though Dostoevsky's belief that he was remains an important element in his life story. I take this opportunity to add that I am indebted to Professor Frank's book, which we are told is the first volume of four, for its masterly recreation of the world of ideas in which Dostoevsky came to maturity, though, of course, Professor Frank is not responsible for my reading of this novel.

4. Marc Slonim, in *Three Loves of Dostoevsky* (New York: Rinehart, 1955), pp. 105–6, tells us that Dostoevsky was said to have confessed to having had sexual relations with a little girl, but comments finally (p. 268) that we will probably never know whether the report is true. He adds, reasonably enough, "But that a sexual fantasy of this sort dwelt within him . . . appears undeniable."

5. Leonid Grossman, *Dostoevsky*, trans. Mary Mackler (New York: Bobbs-Merrill, 1975), p. 73. Also Frank, p. 296.

6. *The Best Short Stories of Dostoevsky*, trans. David Magarshack (New York: Random House, Modern Library, n.d.), p. 121.

7. Quoted in Konstantin Mochulsky, *Dostoevsky: His Life and Work*, trans. Michael A. Minihan (Princeton: Princeton University Press, 1967), p. 256.

8. A woman was attracted into a butcher shop by a window sign advertising steak at two dollars a pound, but was told by the proprietor when she ordered some that, unfortunately, he was out of steak at the present time. Later, she complained to her own butcher that his steak prices were much higher than his competitor's. He answered, "I would also charge two dollars a pound for steak—if I was out of it."

9. Shortly after his release from prison in 1854, Dostoevsky wrote to a friend: "If anyone were to prove to me that Christ is outside the truth, and if it were *actually* to turn out that truth is outside of Christ, I would want to remain with Christ rather than with the truth." But what that "if" suggests emerged in a letter to his brother written at about the same time: "I am a child of the age, a child of unbelief and doubt to this very day and (this I know) until the coffin lid comes down on me. What fearful torments this thirst to believe has cost me, and is still costing me." Slonim, pp. 44–45.

10. I said Dostoevsky's answer to Ivan's negativeness is Christian in being the kind of insight enacted and expressed by Christ. But in spite of Dostoevsky, it was originally— and has remained—equally Jewish. Here are some sayings from the Talmud, the great accumulation of rabbinical commentaries on the Oral Law of the Jewish people (as distinct from the Scriptures) set down between the first and sixth centuries A.D., sayings that foreshadow those of Father Zosima.

He who devotes himself to the mere study of religion without engaging in works of mercy is like one who has no God.

Under the wings of the Seraphim are stretched the arms of divine mercy, ever ready to receive the sinner.

The mercy we show to others, Heaven will show to us.

Man sees the mote in his neighbor's eye, but knows not the beam in his own.

God alone can judge.

Whosoever does not persecute them that persecute him, whosoever takes an offense in silence, he who does good because of love, he who is cheerful under his suffering— they are the friends of God, and of them the Scripture says, "They shall shine forth as does the sun at noonday."

Even the most righteous shall not attain so high a place as the truly repentant.

11. The child-torture which obsessed Lise comes from a story she has read about Jews who steal and kill Christian children at Easter. For me it is an especially painful instance of Dostoevsky's anti-Semitism that when she asks Alyosha if the story is true, this wise youth, instead of rejecting the murderous, medieval slander with disgust, actually replies, "I don't know."

Thomas Mann's *The Holy Sinner*

1. It is pleasant, long after writing that, to find in Hans Bürgin and Hans-Otto Mayer, *Thomas Mann: A Chronicle of His Life*, trans. Eugene Dobson (College: University of Alabama Press, 1969), p. 250, the following remark by Mann: "I feel a bit bored when criticism defines my work absolutely and completely through the concept of irony. . . . I am always pleased when one sees in me less an ironic writer than a humorous one." Of course, this was already suggested in the letter from Mann I quote at the end of the essay.

2. All my quotations from the novel are from the translation of Mrs. H. T. Lowe-Porter.

3. There is a meaning in this that is pertinent to Mann's own career. He seems to have copied the first sentence of this quotation from his foreword to the one-volume edition of *Joseph and His Brothers* (New York: Knopf, 1948), p. xiii, where he thus defended himself from the charge that his language, all mixed with foreign elements, was no longer German. "Really?" the present novel ironically comments. "Behold, then, how much further I dare go in the same direction. We shall see who is master, language or the human mind."

4. That it was Mann who made Gregor's parents twins is true according to my present knowledge, at least. Of course, it doesn't matter where the detail comes from—its *meaning* is now *Mann's*.

5. At this point in the argument, certain intelligent readers of my essay have recoiled—as if the audacity were my own and not Mann's. Let me, therefore, add a bit more evidence that Mann intends us to see such a parallel. First, when the abbot (of the cloister Agonia Dei) learns from the tablet that the baby he has found is "brother and nephew and niece of its own parents," he reflects: "God had made our sin His own agony, sin and cross, they were one in Him, and above all He was the God of sinners. He therefore had consigned this stateless little scion to His stronghold of God's Passion as a state and status." Is it to mean nothing to us that the sin of Gregor's parents *too* becomes his agony, and that "God's Passion" becomes Gregor's "state and status"?

Second, when Gregor, no more inclined to shirk his coming agony than Christ had been, runs after the fisherman who was about to leave him behind, he too staggers under the instruments needful for that agony—a leg-iron to chain him and a ladder to raise him up. "Carry it," cries the pitying fisherman's wife of the ladder "as the Lord Christ His Cross."

Lastly, here is something to put beside the Duchess's ambiguous prayer. It is a poem uttered by Gregor shortly after his penance has ended and his glory begun.

> Shall I find my life's black story
> Turn to lustre in Thy glory?
> With what wonder do I see,
> Lord, Thy heavenly alchemy
> Clear the flesh's shame and pain
> Back to purity again,
> To the spouse and son of sinning
> Highly from the Highest winning
> Leave for earthly need where'er
> To open Paradise's door.

Since Christ, as a Son of fallen humanity, is necessarily a "son of sinning," and since Mary is the spouse of her own Son (Christ and God being One), and, indeed, in spite of the Virgin Birth which guarantees her personal purity, is human and a daughter of Eve, how can we fail to grant the double application of all the rest of this verse?

But the clincher is in Mann's own statement in his April 29, 1952 letter quoted in my Introduction: "All mythology teems with marital unions of brothers and sisters, sons and mothers. And such minglings extend from the Near East down to the Christian mystery of the Mother of God. Not for nothing does Sybilla [the sinner's mother-wife, addressing herself to Mary] pray: 'Thou of the Highest child, mother and bride.' "

Hawthorne's *The Blithedale Romance*

1. Henry James, *Hawthorne* (1879; rpt. in *The Shock of Recognition,* ed. Edmund Wilson, New York: Farrar, Straus and Cudahy, 1949), p. 527.

2. Frederick C. Crews, *The Sins of the Fathers* (Oxford: Oxford University Press, 1966), pp. 193 et seq.

3. Though I have said that Goethe, in *Wilhelm Meister's Apprenticeship,* does see life as "a problem to be solved," it belongs among these "wisdom-novels" because his "solution" requires us to treat all our ideas as provisional, as "working hypotheses."

4. *The Scarlet Letter* (1850; rpt. New York: Norton, 1961), p. 31.

5. Mark Van Doren, *Nathaniel Hawthorne* (New York: Viking, 1949), pp. 189–91.

6. All quotations from *The Blithedale Romance* are from Volume III of the Ohio State University *Centenary Edition,* ed. William Charvat et al. I cite the chapter as well as the page for the sake of those who will read it in other editions. Ch. II, 10–11.

7. A word may be in order about the familiar complaint that Hollingsworth is a weakness in the fiction. Granted that the type he represents is baldly stated as a given too long before it has been dramatized. But in my opinion, this spoils things only at first. The defect is at last quite sufficiently made up for, not only by his becoming a genuine actor in the drama, but by the subtle truth with which his type is often directly described. Truth—mere truth—also has a certain dramatic force.

8. "But his relation to it [the Puritan conscience] was only, as one might say, intellectual. . . . He played with it and used it as a pigment." *The Shock of Recognition,* p. 471.

9. D. H. Lawrence, who "saw through" with the power of genius, seems to be responsible for the tradition which has become the cliché. He wrote: "*Zenobia:* a dark, proudly voluptuous clever woman with a tropical flower in her hair. Said to be sketched from Margaret Fuller, in whom Hawthorne saw some 'evil nature.' Nathaniel was more aware of Zenobia's voluptuousness than of her 'mind.' " *Studies in Classic American Literature* (1922; rpt. in *The Shock of Recognition),* p. 1007.

10. *The Scarlet Letter,* p. 186.

11. " 'What is he?' murmurs one gray shadow of my forefathers to the other. 'A writer of story-books! What kind of a business in life,—what mode of glorifying God, or being serviceable to mankind in his day and generation—may that be? Why the degenerate fellow might as well have been a fiddler!' " *The Scarlet Letter,* p. 12.

12. "The old Kröger family gradually declined, and some people quite rightly considered Tonio Kröger's own existence [as an artist] . . . as one of the signs of decay." With those disapproving people he often agreed. He led a life, inner and outer, "which at bottom he, Tonio Kröger, despised. . . . 'As though I had a wagonful of traveling gypsies for my ancestors!' " Thomas Mann, *Stories of Three Decades,* trans. H. T. Lowe-Porter (New York: Knopf, 1936), pp. 98–99.

13. "Obviously infatuated with her [Zenobia], he is not the man to submit to such a feeling. By what is plainly a psychological detour—analysts would see in it an example of protective displacement—he persuades himself that his real attachment is to Zenobia's half-sister [Priscilla]." Philip Rahv, *Image and Idea* (New York: New Directions, 1957), pp. 44–45. And even more high-handed is this from a later critic: "One suspects, really, that he has loved Zenobia. This may be supposed not merely because of the obvious fascination her personality has exercised upon him—he has, after all, also been interested in his other two friends, Hollingsworth and Priscilla. But Zenobia is plainly one of Hawthorne's

magnetic ladies of experience." Millicent Bell, *Hawthorne's View of the Artist* (New York: SUNY Press, 1962), p. 159. Ms. Bell and I agree that the novel gives Hawthorne's view of the artist. But she seems content to note only the artist's defects—i.e., one aspect of the theme—rather than to interpret the novel and judge its artist as wholes.

14. "If anything is capable of making a poet of a literary man, it is my *bourgeois* love of the human, the living and usual. It is the source of all warmth, goodness, and humour; I even almost think it is itself that love of which it stands written that one may speak with the tongues of men and of angels and yet having it not is as sounding brass and tinkling cymbals." Mann, p. 132.

George Eliot's *Daniel Deronda*

1. F. R. Leavis, *The Great Tradition* (1948; rpt. New York: Doubleday, 1956). The quotations from this book are all from pp. 105–8 and 304, the latter from the Henry James essay "*Daniel Deronda*: A Conversation," which Leavis reprints in an appendix.

2. *The George Eliot Letters*, ed. Gordon Haight (New Haven: Yale University Press, 1954), VI, 208, letter dated 2 October 1876.

3. *Letters*, V, 216, letter dated 25 January 1876.

4. George Eliot, *Daniel Deronda* (Harmondsworth, England: Penguin, 1967) is the edition from which all quotations are made.

5. *Letters*, V, 312, letter dated 25 November 1872.

6. I share the opinion of James and Leavis that Deronda's trick of gripping his lapels at moments of crisis reveals, not Deronda, but the author's fear that he is not sufficiently visible. But James puts the objection into the mouth of Pulcheria, who considers the whole novel a bore—and couldn't even get through Eliot's greatest novel *Middlemarch*, of which his judicious critic Constantius has "an immense opinion." Isn't this a hint that such flaws matter a lot or a little according to one's sense of the whole?

7. He puts Mirah under the care of the mother and two sisters of his college friend Hans Meyrick. I mention them here to get in, if only in a footnote, my view that all these Meyricks are among the pleasures of the novel. If they are Dickensian (as Leavis asserts in disapproval), they are so with the important difference that they are not merely sweet and lovable; they have sharp and witty minds. Hans's long letter to Deronda in Genoa, informing him of events back home, is a delight.

8. That it depends on this seems worth emphasizing in view of an interesting footnote in a recent essay on Eliot by Steven Marcus ("Literature and Social Theory," in his *Representations: Essays on Literature and Society* [New York: Random House, 1975], p. 212) that offers "one more demonstration in detail [he means by way of a detail] of why the plot [of *Daniel Deronda*] does not . . . work." The detail, noted for the first time, we are told, by a graduate student of the author's, is that "given the conventions of medical practice at the time," for Deronda to remain ignorant of his Jewishness his "circumcised penis must be invisible or nonexistent." This is a clever observation by that graduate student, but the cleverness is very much like that of the "village atheist" which used to pounce on factual discrepancies in the Bible. It shows an alertness to what doesn't matter that often goes along with obtuseness to what does. If generations of readers overlooked that detail—or that way of explaining the novel's silence about it—it is surely because they had good reason to be looking elsewhere. Psychological and moral truth can't be tested by consulting history books, medical or other kinds. What this plot rests on is the recognizable reality of characters and relationships, the felt truth we will now examine. If our experience of life confirms all that, it's easy enough to accept the story's necessary assumption that, given the barest possibility of another explanation,

Deronda's rooted preconceptions—for instance, that he was Sir Hugo's son—would prevent him from seeing or thinking what was "obvious." We are all of us blind in the same way.

9. Since I am quoting in part because of the interest of all this as historical foresight, I might grant that each of these dreams—of America and Israel—came into existence as realities, with all of reality's difficulties and compromises. But that natural complication invalidates neither the dream nor the reality and surely leaves the essential accuracy of Eliot's foresight untouched.

The Novels of William Hale White

1. W. H. White, "Black Notebook," an unpublished journal once in the possession of the late Mrs. D. V. White.

2. Hale White preferred to write "Ethic" without the "s." The second Spinoza work is also known as *Correction of the Understanding*. Joseph Ratner, ed., *The Philosophy of Spinoza* (New York: Random House, Modern Library, 1922), p. vii.

3. William Dean Howells, "The Editor's Study," *Harper's New Monthly Magazine* LXXII (February 1886), p. 485. Arnold: In a letter of 24 June 1913, formerly in the possession of Mrs. D. V. White, John W. Gulland, member of Parliament, wrote to Mrs. White: "My colleague here, William Jones, the Welsh Whip, used to be a teacher in Wales and Matthew Arnold was his Inspector. They had talks on literature and Arnold always 'enthused' over Mark Rutherford and told Jones on no account ever to miss anything that Mark Rutherford ever wrote." Swinburne: On 22 September 1909, W. T. Watts-Dunton wrote to Hale White of "your 'Mark Rutherford' books which both Swinburne and I read with profound admiration." (W. H. White, *Letters to Three Friends*, ed. Dorothy V. White [London: Oxford University Press, 1924], p. 362 n.) Conrad: In a letter of 3 September 1904, quoted in G. Jean-Aubry, ed., *Joseph Conrad: Life and Letters* (London, 1927), I, p. 335. Crane: See John Berryman, *Stephen Crane* (New York: William Sloan Associates, 1950), p. 248.

4. Gosse was reviewing *Pages and More Pages from a Journal* in the *Morning Post*, London, 14 November 1910.

5. H. W. Massingham in his "Memorial Introduction" to *The Autobiography of Mark Rutherford*, 3d ed. (London, 1923), p. vii; A. Bennett, in the *New Statesman* XXII (13 October 1923), supplement, p. viii; *The Letters of D. H. Lawrence*, ed. Aldous Huxley (New York: Viking, 1932), p. 83.

6. J. M. Murry, in *Daily News and Leader*, London, 8 October 1915; *To the Unknown God: Essays Toward a Religion* (London: Jonathan Cape, 1924), pp. 260–62.

7. *The Journals of André Gide*, trans. Justin O'Brien, 4 vols. (New York: Knopf, 1947–51), II, 101.

8. Ibid., III, 337–38.

9. Ibid.

10. Unpublished letter to Jack Hale-White, dated 8 August 1889, copy once in the possession of Dr. R. Hale-White.

11. W. H. White, *The Revolution in Tanner's Lane* (New York: Dodd, Mead, 1899), ch. 14.

12. W. H. White, *Pages from a Journal*, 2d ed. (London, 1910), p. 108.

13. *Ethic of Benedict Spinoza*, trans. W. H. White and Amelia H. Stirling, 4th ed. (London, 1910), preface, p. v.

14. Unpublished letter to Sophie Partridge, 3 September 1904, copy once in the possession of Mrs. D. V. White.

15. First quote: unpublished letter to his father, 3 May 1853, copy once in the possession of Dr. R. Hale-White; second quote: W. H. White, *Clara Hopgood* (New York: George H. Doran, undated), ch. 19.

16. *The Autobiography*, ch. 2.

17. Quoted by Mrs. D. V. White in *The Groombridge Diary* (London: Oxford University Press, 1924), p. 176.

18. *The Autobiography*, ch. 1.

19. First quote: W. H. White, *The Early Life of Mark Rutherford by Himself* (London: Oxford University Press, 1913), pp. 30–31; second quote: *The Revolution*, ch. 11.

20. Unpublished letter to Jack Hale-White, dated 29 August 1893, copy once in the possession of the late Dr. R. Hale-White.

21. *Pages*, p. 191. In a perceptive criticism of *The Autobiography* in *The Groombridge Diary* (p. 66), Mrs. D. V. White says: "I noticed in this chapter (V) a good illustration of his favourite sudden transition from the 'particular' to the 'general,' the small to the great. These transitions produce a marked effect upon his style, which is very orderly, and yet full of strange surprises, every sort of climax, cadence and attack. Here, sandwiched in between an apparently trivial story about Mr. and Mrs. Hexton, and an apparently bald description of Mr. Hexton's way of life, is this sentence: 'I do not believe there was a single point in Mr. Hexton's character in which he touched the universal.' . . . *Immediately before*: ' . . . a plate fell down and was broken; everything was in confusion; I was ashamed and degraded.' *Immediately after*: 'If he had kept bees. . . . ' "

22. W. H. White, *Last Pages from a Journal*, ed. Dorothy V. White (London: Oxford University Press, 1915), pp. 43–44.

23. *Clara Hopgood*, ch. 18; *The Revolution*, ch. 3; W. H. White, ed., *Selections from Dr. Johnson's "Rambler"* (London: Oxford University Press, 1907), p. xviii; *Clara Hopgood*, ch. 28; W. H. White, "Principles," *Mark Rutherford's Deliverance*, 11th ed. (London, undated); W. H. White, introduction to T. Carlyle, *The Life of Sterling*, World's Classics edition (London: Oxford University Press, 1907), p. xx.

24. *Last Pages*, p. 297.

25. André Gide, *Fruits of the Earth*, trans. Dorothy Bussy (New York: Knopf, 1949), p. 222.

26. *Pages*, p. 76.

27. "Principles," *Deliverance*.

28. André Gide, *The Counterfeiters*, trans. Dorothy Bussy (New York: Knopf, 1927), p. 130.

29. André Gide, *Two Legends: Œdipus and Theseus*, trans. John Russell (New York: Knopf, 1950), pp. 85–86.

30. E. M. Forster, *Aspects of the Novel* (New York: Harcourt, Brace, 1927), p. 206.

31. T. S. Eliot, "The Function of Criticism," *Selected Essays*, 2d ed. (London, 1946), p. 27.

The Novels of Saul Bellow

1. Plate number 9 of the series of captioned drawings by Blake called "The Gates of Paradise" shows a man starting to climb a ladder to the distant moon. The caption is, "I want! I want!" The poem that introduces the drawings begins, "Mutual Forgiveness of each Vice/ Such are the Gates of Paradise." For that matter, in his introduction to "Jerusalem" Blake writes, "The Spirit of Jesus is continual forgiveness: he who waits to be righteous before he enters into the Saviour's kingdom . . . will never enter there."

2. Something I came across since finishing this study seems worth adding here as a hint from Bellow that he regards the whole novel as precisely a "Jewish" enterprise.

Herzog says once that in writing all those letters he is going "after reality with language," and this in order "to force Madeleine and Gersbach to have a *Conscience* . . . to keep tight the tensions without which human beings can no longer be called human . . . to prevent their escape. I want them in human form, and so I conjure up a whole environment and catch them in the middle." And in his preface to the Dell collection of *Great Jewish Short Stories*, Bellow quotes the dying Hamlet's request to Horatio ("Tell my story") and adds: "In defeat, a story contains the hope of vindication, of justice. The storyteller is able to make others accept his version of things. And in the stories of the Jewish tradition, the world, and even the universe, have a human meaning. Indeed, the Jewish imagination has sometimes been found guilty of overhumanizing everything, of making too much of a case for us, for mankind, and of investing externals with too many meanings."

Index

Persons and Works Cited